# The [illegible]
# of Education

**Also by Geraint Johnes**

ECONOMICS FOR MANAGERS
WAGE FLEXIBILITY AND UNEMPLOYMENT DYNAMICS IN REGIONAL LABOR MARKETS (*with T. J. Hyclak*)

# The Economics of Education

Geraint Johnes

© Geraint Johnes 1993

All rights reserved. No reproduction, copy or transmission of this publication may be made without written permission.

No paragraph of this publication may be reproduced, copied or transmitted save with written permission or in accordance with the provisions of the Copyright, Designs and Patents Act 1988, or under the terms of any licence permitting limited copying issued by the Copyright Licensing Agency, 90 Tottenham Court Road, London W1P 9HE.

Any person who does any unauthorised act in relation to this publication may be liable to criminal prosecution and civil claims for damages.

First published 1993 by
THE MACMILLAN PRESS LTD
Houndmills, Basingstoke, Hampshire RG21 2XS
and London
Companies and representatives
throughout the world

ISBN 0–333–56835–4 hardcover
ISBN 0–333–56836–2 paperback

A catalogue record for this book is available
from the British Library.

Copy-edited and typeset by Povey–Edmondson
Okehampton and Rochdale, England

Printed in Hong Kong

*To Becky and Tom*

# Contents

# List of Figures and Tables

## Figures



## Tables

# Preface

In the beginning, students of economics learn the basic premise upon which the subject is founded: our wants are greater than our means. Economics tells the story of how we try to make the best of an imperfect world. Likewise, although we shall never become omniscient, we use education as a means of improving our imperfect knowledge. Given our finite resources, we cannot reach nirvana.

Like the provision of other goods, the supply of educational services involves an opportunity cost. There are therefore limits to the availability of education. Choices have to be made: individuals choose how much education to consume; by voting for different political parties, they choose what proportion of education should be provided through the public purse; they choose whether or not to become educators; and the suppliers of educational services make choices about how their output should be produced. The economics of education is about how all these decisions are reached.

It is often argued that the economics of education is rooted in the theory of human capital. That is where this book begins. The demand for education is derived from the benefits of an augmented human capital stock. Education is not a pure private good, however; its provision is (within limits) non-rival, so that scale economies can be exploited if it is provided by a club or as a public good. Public choice theory is therefore pertinent as we study the supply of education, and this forms the next part of the book. The provision of educational services also raises questions about the evaluation of costs and measurement of performance: these are considered in some detail. Finally, we consider the labour market for educators. Teachers form a large group of workers whose training period is unusually long; it is no surprise then to find that the market for educators often operates very imperfectly.

It is recommended that the reader should be familiar with the content of typical courses in intermediate microeconomics, basic statistics and calculus. The book is based upon a final-year undergraduate course taught at Lancaster, but in parts it will be useful also to intermediate-level undergraduates and to non-specialist postgraduates. Many of the tools of theoretical analysis introduced in the book are used in all branches of economics, and I would therefore expect the sections on overlapping generations, principal–agent problems and auction models to be useful to students on a wide variety of courses.

Finally, I have a word of encouragement for students of education economics who use this book. You are studying an exciting and important topic. It is a field where much remains to be discovered. I hope you will find that this book communicates well what is already known about the economics of education, and that it makes you inquisitive about the things that we do not know. If you have any comments or suggestions, get in touch: I'm only a letter, fax or phone call away.

*Geraint Johnes*

# Acknowledgements

The list of people whose efforts have, in one way or another, helped make this book possible is close to endless. I shall endeavour to acknowledge only some of the most important here. First, two of the economists who educated me deserve special mention. The first is John Hudson, without whose guidance I would never have attempted to become an economist. The second is Jim Taylor, who introduced me to the economics of education. A third academic economist also deserves mention here; although he may have no recollection of the incident, about three years ago Tony Culyer and I were talking about the general growth of interest in the economics of education. That was the spark that lit the fuse which got this book off the ground. My colleagues at Lancaster University have been a constant source of encouragement throughout my time here. In any league table designed to judge the best bunch of people to work with, they would come joint top. With them would be our students. The care and attention to detail given by Stephen Rutt and his team at the publishers should also be acknowledged here; without them the book would be less well written and less well read.

It is usual for authors to thank their spouses and offspring at this stage, often just for keeping out of their way while the book is being written! I am too fortunate for that. My wife, Jill, has helped, and not only by being the perfect partner: she also happens to be a first-rate education economist. As such she read the whole book at draft stage; her incisive comments have substantially improved the final product. As for our children, may they always be as well behaved as they were while this book was being written! Perhaps the fact that I am dedicating this book to them will help.

The author and publishers wish to thank the following for permission to reproduce copyright material: Richard Freeman and the Academic Press (Figure 3.1); the *Journal of Human Resources* (Table 3.3); Pergamon Press (Tables 3.4 and 3.5); Elsevier Science Publishers BV (Tables 8.1 and 11.1); Kluwer Academic Publishers

(Tables 8.2, 10.1 and 10.2); Open Books (Table 9.1); Oxford University Press (Table 9.3). Every effort has been made to contact all the copyright-holders, but if any have been inadvertently overlooked the necessary arrangement will be made at the first opportunity.

*Geraint Johnes*

# 1 Introduction

The birth of the economics of education is said to have occurred on 28 December 1960 in St Louis (Blaug, 1976). There Theodore Schultz (1961) delivered his lecture to the American Economic Association on the topic of 'investment in human capital'. As is usual, the baby could be felt kicking for a little while before its true birth: in the UK, work by Vaizey (1958) and Wiseman (1959) are early landmarks. So the subject is a relatively new one.

That economists should have waited so long to enter this field is surprising in view of the massive amount of resources devoted to education: education accounts for as much public sector spending in the UK as does either defence or the National Health Service (NHS); some 18 per cent of the population is currently in full-time education; and around 8 per cent of all employees work in the education industry. But the young vintage of the research means that it is an area of economics which is fresh and vibrant. Important new insights are frequent: many questions remain unresolved and these are the subject of intense and exciting debate. Doubtless many other questions of importance have yet to be asked.

Before proceeding further, it is useful to define some concepts. Economics is the study of choice. Education is the augmentation of the stock of skills, knowledge and understanding possessed either by individuals or by society as a whole. The economics of education therefore concerns the manner in which choices affecting this stock are made, both by individuals who demand education and by the teachers and institutions which supply it.

Education is often regarded as a basic human right. Some people go further and argue that education should therefore be freely available to all, and that economic considerations should not enter debates about education. If that argument were logically sound, there would be no need for this book. However, even basic human rights use up scarce resources. The production of education (or health services or food) involves sacrificing the production of something else. Choices have to be made, and so an opportunity cost (or a price) attaches to the provision of education. Society must determine how much education it wants to consume, given the sacrifice of other goods which that implies. Economics matters.

Much early work in the field of the economics of education has followed the lead of Schultz in emphasising the role of education as an investment in the future. Since education and training might be expected to increase an individual's productivity in the workplace, it should also serve to raise her expected stream of future wage income. The questions then arise: does education offer better returns than other forms of investment? Do some kinds of education yield better returns than others? These questions have led to the development of a substantial literature on the rates of return to schooling.

The information yielded by these studies is important, particularly since the rate of return to education is likely in large part to determine the demand for educational services. If supply is to respond to demand fluctuations, then the institutions responsible for planning the provision of educational services must bear in mind the information provided by rates of return analyses. The supply of tuition in fields of study currently offering a high rate of return should be increased if the system is to work efficiently.

Efficiency is only one goal, however. Considerations of equity are also of importance when considering education. Education generally serves to improve one's lot; if only the rich had access to education (perhaps because of imperfect capital markets), then income inequalities would be exacerbated. Partly because of this, economists virtually unanimously advocate some degree of state finance of education, although it should be noted that state *control* of the education system is another matter altogether. It often happens that efficiency and equity conflict one with the other. Striking the right balance between these twin goals is difficult, not least because there is in general no consensus about the weights which should be attached to each goal. The theory of social choice helps guide us through this minefield, but as any student of social choice knows, it is not always possible sensibly to aggregate preferences across all economic agents to derive a socially optimal policy.

In the main, educational institutions are not for-profit organisations. Often these are owned and controlled by the state. Like any other productive organisation, these institutions must make economic decisions and must respond to economic events which are imposed upon them. Their objective function may not be profit, but they still must make choices in an economic manner. For instance, their objective may be to minimise costs subject to a minimum standard of provision. The theory of the firm, and more generally the literature of industrial economics, is of relevance in this context. In studying the economics of education, therefore, we must investigate the structure of the education industry, the objectives of educational institutions, and the factors which determine their costs and their performance.

Twenty years ago, the economics of education could fairly have been regarded as a minor topic within labour economics. This is no longer the case. As we have seen above, elements of labour economics remain, but now are combined with ideas borrowed from public finance, welfare economics, industrial economics and other specialist areas. The economics of education is coming of age as a distinct subdiscipline. At the same time, widespread reforms of education systems give the economic analysis of educational matters new significance. It is an exciting time to study these issues.

The structure of this book is as follows: the demand for education is the focus of the next three chapters. Chapters 2 and 3 concern the theory of human capital and the calculation of rates of return. These determine the demand for post-compulsory education. In Chapter 4 we study the manner in which labour market signals are passed down through the education system so that entrants to post-compulsory education and training courses can make rational choices. The next few chapters concentrate on the supply side of the market. Chapter 5 concerns the issues of ownership and control: should education be privatised? Chapter 6 studies the costs of provision, and the following chapter investigates innovative forms of finance in the education sector. In Chapter 8, the special role of universities in producing new knowledge (research) as well as disseminating existing knowledge (teaching) will be investigated. The next two chapters concern the problems attached to measuring the performance of (or value added by) educational institutions. In Chapter 11, the labour market for educators is studied. We end with a short concluding chapter which ties together the various threads and which suggests areas in which the study of the economics of education is developing.

# 2 Human Capital

## Introduction

Economic agents are utility maximisers. Every time we make a choice we select the alternative which yields the greatest utility, subject to the resources available. Sometimes the utility which we derive is enjoyed in the short run (like a take-away meal); sometimes it is enjoyed over a longer period (like household durable goods). In all cases, though, the decision is made on the basis of the discounted stream of expected utility over the period from the present up to the time horizon.

Education exists because it provides utility. If it did not, there would be no demand for it. Likewise, the student of education economics studies this subject because to do so gives her utility. Ideally, some of that utility is enjoyed in the short run: it is a pleasure to learn about the world. This may be described as the consumption element of education. Many courses, however, are worth more to the student than instant gratification; they equip her with knowledge and skills which will enhance her productivity at work for years to come. Since productivity in large part determines remuneration, education now can increase earnings later. In this sense, education may be regarded as an investment by the student in herself. This is the investment element of education.

Since both the consumption element and the investment element of education provide utility (now or later), they both contribute to the discounted stream of utility enjoyed by the economic agent. In this respect, education is little different from any other durable good.

In a number of other respects, however, education is unusual. First, the return to the investment element of education can easily be measured. Abstracting from the consumption element, we would expect that, other things being equal, the discounted present value of the lifetime earnings of a highly educated person would exceed those of a less educated person. This earnings differential provides a measure of the return to the gap between their education attainments. Second, the costs of education are borne over a long time. We cannot shop for a qualification in the same way as we shop for a car: the acquisition of qualifications necessitates an expenditure of time as well as of money. Third, the benefits of an education are especially durable. While most goods depreciate in value over time, knowledge and skills tend not to do so as long as they are regularly exercised.

These three characteristics of education have one feature in common: the role of time. In contrast with most other goods, the market for education cannot usefully be described by a static model in which only today's utility and costs matter. A longer view has to be taken. The discounted stream of future costs and benefits must be considered, just as a businessman must consider net present values when making an investment in a new piece of capital. This insight, due to Gary Becker (1964), led to the development of the theory of human capital. An investment in education is tantamount to an investment in a machine which can be fitted on to the human body and which improves one's performance in the workplace; the future returns to such a machine – or to the educated individual – are expected to exceed the outlay of time and money involved in its purchase.

The theory of human capital has greatly improved our understanding of the role played by education in the economy. In the remainder of this chapter, these improvements will be considered in greater depth.

# The Basic Model

Consider an individual. Let $C_i$ denote the cost of the marginal unit of education and training in period $i$, $R_i$ the return to that training in the $i$th period, and $r$ the interest rate. Suppose that education lasts $t$ years and that the individual expects subsequently to work until year $T$. The base period, where $i=0$, is defined as the period in which education and training commences. Then the individual will invest in human capital up to the point at which, for the marginal unit of education,

$$\int_0^t C_i e^{-ri}\, di = \int_t^T R_i e^{-ri}\, di \tag{2.1}$$

This relatively simple model of educational investment has a number of implications.

1. The greater the gap between $T$ and $t$, the greater the returns to education will be, other things being equal. This is so simply because the returns accrue over a longer period. The time horizon, $T$, is fixed by statutory retirement age or by death, but the worker's age when beginning education (that is, when $i=0$) is a choice variable. It follows that the returns are greatest when the investment in education is made early in life. This is one reason why, in general, we go to school when we are young and go to work when we are older.
2. The lower the sacrifice, $C$, involved in investing in human capital, the greater will be the investment. Older workers, who frequently enjoy relatively high levels of remuneration owing to their experience and seniority; generally invest little in education, since the sacrifice of time (and so also of wages) would generally exceed the benefits.
3. The greater the returns to education, $R$, the more investment will there be, other things remaining equal. Thus those individuals with a capacity to learn new material quickly and thoroughly tend to invest more in education than do others, since the returns are expected to be greater. Moreover, if the earnings differential between 'educated' and 'uneducated' groups of workers increases, we would expect the demand for education to increase.
4. The higher the rate of interest, $r$, the lower will be the demand for education, other things being equal. This is because the postponement of earnings potential implied by full-time education more severely reduces the net present value of future earnings when interest rates are relatively high.
5. Investment in education will occur so long as the marginal (discounted) benefits exceed or equal the marginal (discounted) costs. The net present value of the total benefits must therefore exceed that of the total costs. Put another way, there must be a

positive rate of return to education. Otherwise, education would not exist.

## Dynamic Optimisation

While it is a useful starting point, the model described in the last section is restrictive in that it assumes that education and work are mutually exclusive within any one time period. A more general model should allow part-time education and training to occur simultaneously with part-time work. The individual should then be able to decide how much of her non-leisure time is devoted to each activity. Such a model has been developed by Ben-Porath (1967). Various extensions have been proposed by Haley (1973), Heckman (1976) and Rosen (1976). Here, we shall consider a particularly simple variant of the dynamic optimisation model.

Let the individual's stock of human capital in the $i$th time period be denoted by $K_i$. Let her hourly earnings depend on human capital stock; more specifically, it is convenient to let hourly earnings equal $K_i$. Let $w_i$ denote the proportion of non-leisure time in the $i$th period spent at work. Hence

$$\int_0^T w_i K_i e^{-ri} \, di \tag{2.2}$$

denotes the net present value of lifetime earnings. For simplicity in the sequel we shall assume a zero rate of interest.

Clearly the rate of growth of the stock of human capital must equal gross investment in human capital net of any erosion of skills due to the passage of time. The time spent acquiring human capital in the $i$th period may be measured by $(1-w_i)$. Diminishing returns to human capital investment suggest, however, that as the worker ages, the time sacrifice required in order to gain a given amount of additional human capital increases. We may therefore suppose that the rate of growth of human capital stock is given by

$$\dot{K} = 1 - iw_i - \delta K_i \tag{2.3}$$

where $\delta$ represents the depreciation rate, and where a dot above a variable represents the time rate of change.

The problem faced by the individual is to maximise the net present value of expected lifetime earnings (2.2), subject to the human capital accumulation rule which she faces – namely (2.3) – and subject to the constraint that human capital stock cannot be negative. It will be convenient at a later stage also to impose the terminal condition that capital stock at the end of the time horizon is given. Hence

$$K_T = \bar{K}_T \tag{2.4}$$

The problem set by equations (2.2)–(2.4) is solved by appeal to Pontryagin's maximum principle (see, for example, Pontryagin *et al.*, 1962; Dixit, 1990); readers unfamiliar with this technique may wish to skip directly to equation (2.12).

The Hamiltonian function is given by

$$H = w_i K_i - \pi_i(\dot{K} - 1 + iw_i + \delta K_i) \tag{2.5}$$

Here $\pi_i$ represents a Lagrange multiplier which is differentiable over time. The optimal conditions may straightforwardly be derived as

$$\partial H/\partial w_i = K_i - i\pi_i = 0 \tag{2.6}$$

$$\partial H/\partial K_i = w_i - \pi_i \delta = -\dot{\pi}_i \tag{2.7}$$

$$\partial H/\partial \pi_i = \dot{K}_i - 1 + iw_i + \delta \tag{2.8}$$

These conditions provide us with three equations in three unknowns. Straightforward manipulation of (2.5), (2.6) and (2.7) implies

$$\dot{K}_i = 1/2 + K_i(1/2i - \delta) \tag{2.9}$$

This equation is a first order differential equation in human capital, $K_i$. Routine solution of this equation, using the terminal condition on $K_i$ in order to identify the constant of integration, gives an expression in which $K_i$ depends only on time, $i$, and the parameters of the model. The solution is

$$K_i = \bar{K}_T + i/2\,(1 + lni/2 + i\delta) - T/2(1 + lnT/2 + T\delta) \tag{2.10}$$

It is straightforward to show, from equations (2.6)–(2.8), that

$$w_i = (1 - K_i/i)/2i \tag{2.11}$$

In order to establish the pattern of per period earnings over the life cycle, it is necessary to multiply potential earnings, $w_i$, by the proportion of non-leisure time spent at work, $K_i$. This yields the earnings function

$$E_i = w_i K_i = (1 - K_i/i)K_i/2i \tag{2.12}$$

It is clear from this earnings function that as the worker's age, $i$, increases, earnings, $E_i = w_i K_i$, initially rise. In general, earnings will peak at a point short of the time horizon, and will thereafter fall for the remainder of the individual's working life. This is a powerful result which has generated a great deal of interest, not least because it accords with empirical observation in many countries.

The workings of the above model can be illustrated by way of a simple numerical example. Suppose that $T=100$, $\delta=0.01$ and $K_T=10$. By substituting these values into equation (2.10), we can find the path of human capital accumulation over the worker's life cycle. Human capital stock rises steadily over the worker's life, tending towards the final value of 10 units (which is imposed by assumption). Substituting the time path of $K_i$ into equation (2.11) yields the time path for the proportion of non-leisure time devoted by the worker to work (as opposed to education and training). Finally, we can derive the worker's age–earnings profile by solving equation (2.12). In this example the worker's earnings rise initially as she grows older. Earnings eventually peak, and subsequently decline (see Figure 2.1).

Although the mathematics used to solve this model rely on recently developed and rather sophisticated techniques, the intuition is straightforward, and the economic basis of the model is easy to understand. As the worker ages, she invests in human capital in order to enhance her future earnings capability. The more she knows, the more she can earn (given the proportion of her time spent at work). However, it is also the case that the more she knows, the more she forgets (or the more her knowledge becomes obsolete). Early in life, the worker devotes much time to human capital investment, since the returns are there to be gained over a long

**FIGURE 2.1**
**The Age–Earnings Profile**

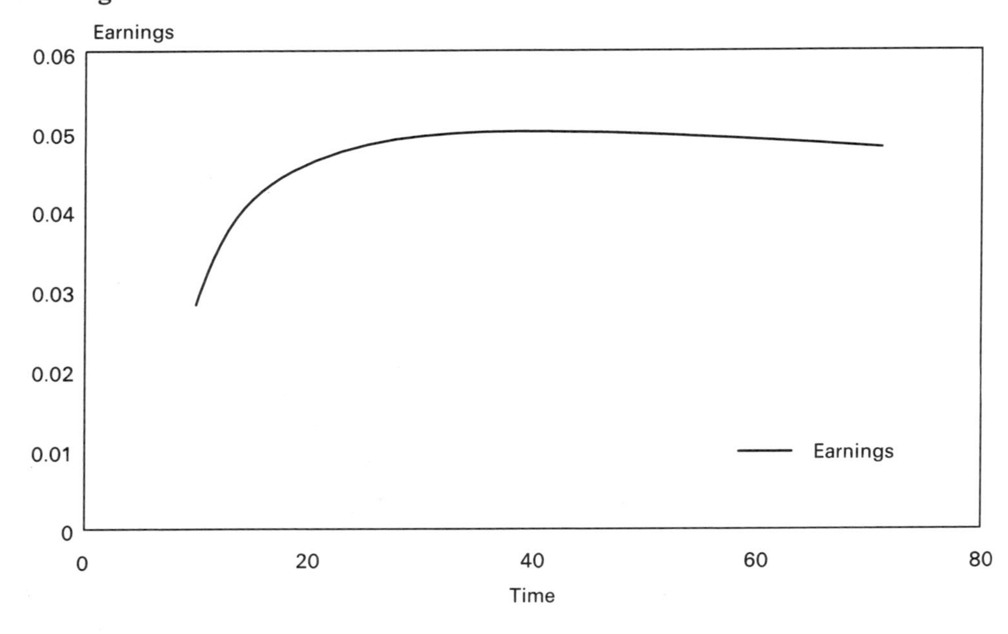

period into the future. In middle life, she will reap the reward of this investment in the form of high earnings. Before the end of her time horizon, however, her earnings will start to fall. This is so for two reasons. First, her stock of human capital is high and therefore depreciates rapidly. Second, in order to compensate for this loss of human capital, she must devote additional time to training, thus leading to a decline in earnings as retirement approaches.

This model has a number of considerable advantages over the simpler model of the last section. First, the model is truly dynamic in that the worker identifies a time-path for $w$ which passes from the present right up to the time horizon. This contrasts with the simple model which seeks only to answer the question of whether or not to undertake a specific investment at the beginning of the time horizon. Second, earnings are endogenised, so that the impact of schooling on future remuneration is not, as in the simple model, depicted in an *ad hoc* manner. Third, the structure of this model enables us to identify the pattern according to which earnings are likely to vary over the worker's life cycle. We shall turn to an empirical investigation of this at a later stage in this chapter.

## State Provision of Education

Hitherto we have assumed that the full costs of all human capital accumulation are borne by the worker. In this section it will be demonstrated that there are likely to be cases where this is not so. Firms often find it in their interest to finance some or all of a worker's training. Moreover, formal full-time education at schools and colleges is largely financed by government. If education exists primarily to improve the worker's own labour market prospects, it is necessary to investigate why the authorities and private firms intervene in order to support education.

Were all markets perfect, there would be no need for state intervention in education. The perfect market assumption is, however, a strong one. It assumes, *inter alia*, that there are no externalities, that consumption is rival, and that all economic agents are perfectly informed. Moreover, it assumes the perfect operation of capital markets, so that parents unable to provide collateral security for loans financing their children's education could nonetheless secure funding. These assumptions are all wholly inappropriate in the context of education.

The externalities involved in education are similar to those involved in owning a facsimile machine. If no one else owned a fax, there would be little point in you buying one. As more and more people purchase faxes, their usefulness to those already owning one is augmented. This is a clear case of an external effect which the market cannot fully take into account. The case of education is similar. There would be little point in your learning to read and write if no one else could do the same. You benefit when others learn, because the education offered to others improves your own ability to communicate with them. Few people would dispute that basic literacy and numeracy skills are an essential lubricant for the operation of an advanced economy. At a more advanced and specialised level, there are external effects associated with the training of specialists (whose productivity increases with proximity to others working in the same field), but in these latter cases the externalities are probably not so great.

The requirement that consumption should be rival in a perfect market implies that consumption of education services by one individual precludes their consumption by another. This requirement is not met in the case of education. Teachers generally teach classes of more than one pupil; one pupil's attendance at the teacher's lesson does not prevent others from being there at the same time. Libraries ensure that more than one pupil can read from the same book. This does not mean that there must inevitably be slack in the system. Given fixed capital in the short run – for example, the given size of classrooms – and given the time a teacher must devote to each pupil on a one-to-one basis, there must be capacity constraints. But nevertheless, the essentially non-rival nature of education means that individual demand curves need to be summed vertically in order to calculate market demand (not horizontally as is the case with private goods). When this is the case, the problems of determining optimal provision, familiar from the theory of public goods, arise. Some would be prepared to pay the 'market' price (as do parents whose children attend private sector schools), but others would not.

The assumption of perfect knowledge is also deeply flawed in the case of education. Inevitably we do not know whether we can do something until we try it. To establish whether or not you have the ability to become a nuclear scientist, you must undergo the training involved. That involves an investment of time and money which is subject to risk. If you fail, your investment has been wasted. There is no way of perfectly predicting the outcome. Consequently decisions made about education are generally made in a world of uncertainty. The government cannot reduce this uncertainty but, if parents are risk averse, a government subsidy to education may offset the tendency for parents to underprovide education for their offspring.

The arguments in favour of state provision of education therefore rely on the widespread belief that the market for educational services fails when left to its own devices. The form that state intervention should take is not so easy to prescribe, however. Some observers (see, for example, Blaug, 1970) have argued for the state to set minimum standards and give financial support to poorer families, but otherwise to allow education to be privately provided. This would enable the market for educational services to be liberated from government control. The efficient operation of such a market would, however, necessitate the existence of surplus capacity in the system: parents can only exercise free choice of school for their children when the schools have vacancies available. Other commentators (such as Levin, 1980) argue that the benefits of a less regulated system of education will be more than offset by the loss of some important externalities; these include the social cohesion fostered by schools with a well-defined and inviolable geographical catchment area. Clearly the opposing views cannot be reconciled by appeal to economic theory alone, since social and political issues influence the commentators' preferences. It is nonetheless important to note that on both sides of the debate there is agreement that the government should finance the education of (at least some of) our children.

## General and Specific Human Capital

Let us turn now to consider the reasons why firms should finance part of the training of their workforce. In order to do this it is necessary to divide the human capital stock into two distinct components. The first component is general human capital, and the second is specific human capital. General human capital is defined as skill and knowledge which enhances the worker's productivity, regardless of where she is employed. A worker with a relatively large stock of general human capital would therefore appeal to a relatively large number of potential employers, other things being equal. Specific human capital, on the other hand, refers to skills which can productively be used only by the worker's current employer. Thus a worker possessing much specific human capital can be very valuable to her own firm, but would not be especially attractive to other employers.

Examples of general human capital include literacy, numeracy and the other fruits of formal education. Examples of specific human capital include familiarity with filing systems, networks of contacts within the firm and the organisation of the firm's management structure. In cases where the firm is a monopsonist in the labour market, specific human capital may be more broadly defined. For instance, in the UK, the markets for railwaymen, doctors, dentists and teachers are each dominated by a single employer. Any training which these workers receive which enhances their productivity will therefore augment their stock of specific human capital, since the benefits of the training are not easily transportable to another employer.

Now consider a worker who possesses some general human capital but no specific human capital. Assume that the labour market works perfectly. The worker's productivity is enhanced in all firms by her stock of human capital. Since, in a competitive labour market, the wage is equal to the value of the marginal product, the worker benefits from her stock of human capital. The general human capital which she possesses enables her to earn a higher wage than would otherwise be possible. She is free to move without penalty to another employer at any time, because her skills are portable. Her firm will not, therefore, contribute to her investment in general human capital for fear of losing her. In general, firms will pay for this type of training only if they can arrange contracts with their employees which compel those who quit to reimburse training costs incurred by the firm. (Contracts in the armed forces may be viewed as an example of such an arrangement.) Such exceptions apart, firms will not finance investment in general human capital.

Let us now turn to a worker who seeks to augment her stock of specific human capital. The increase in her productivity which results from the investment can only be realised within the firm where she is currently employed. As a result of the investment she will be more productive in that firm than she could be elsewhere. In consequence, her employer can raise her wage above levels which she would be offered by other firms. In general, though, her pay will not rise by as much as her marginal product. This is because the firm can exploit the fact that the worker would not be so productive (and so would not earn as much) if employed in another company. Both the worker and the firm therefore earn rents from specific training, and the costs of such training are shared between employer and employee.

The central ideas discussed above can be expressed succinctly in a formal model. Consider a representative firm in a competitive labour market. The firm hires labour because of the human capital services, $K$, offered by that labour. Human capital consists of general human capital, $G$, and specific human capital, $S$. The relationship between total human capital stock and its constituent parts is given by

$$K = G^{\alpha} S^{1-\alpha} \tag{2.13}$$

where $\alpha$ represents the relative importance of general skills. It is convenient to assume that specific human capital is a fixed proportion of the total stock of human capital, so that

$$S = (1 - \alpha)K \tag{2.14}$$

The firm's production function follows the usual concavity rules. More specifically,

$$Y = K^{\beta} \tag{2.15}$$

Profits are defined as total revenue minus total costs. Since specific human capital is not portable across firms, the firm need not reward it. Consequently the only cost borne by the firm is the remuneration paid to general human capital. The wage paid per unit of general human capital is denoted by $w$. For simplicity, we assume that product market prices, $P$, are given and have unit value. Hence the profit function may be written as

$$\pi = PY - wG = K^{\beta} - wK(1 - \alpha)^{-(1-\alpha)/\alpha} \tag{2.16}$$

We now proceed to solve the model. Following convention, we assume that the firm is a profit maximiser. The first order condition for maximising profits is obtained by differentiating equation (2.16) with respect to $K$ and setting the result equal to zero. This yields the optimal wage

$$w = \frac{\partial Y}{\partial K}(1-\alpha)^{(1-\alpha)/\alpha} \tag{2.17}$$

Equation (2.17) is the key. It describes the relationship between the wage and the marginal product of labour in a model where labour services consist of specific as well as general human capital.

In order to interpret equation (2.17), it is useful to concentrate on two extreme cases. First of all, consider the case where the weight attached to specific human capital is very low. In this instance $\alpha \rightarrow 1$, and so little specific human capital is employed. Labour possesses skills which are perfectly portable across firms. This means that labour is mobile, so that the wages paid by our firm will be subject to the disciplines of the market. In this case equation (2.17) reduces to the following rule

$$\text{As } \alpha \rightarrow 1 \quad \text{So } w \rightarrow \partial Y/\partial K \tag{2.18}$$

In other words, where specific skills are absent, labour is paid its marginal product. This accords with the simple theory of wage setting in a perfect labour market, and should be a very familiar result.

Consider now the opposite extreme. Suppose that the firm attaches little weight to general human capital but affords great importance to specific skills. In this instance $\alpha \rightarrow 0$, so that little general human capital is employed. The skills possessed by labour are not, in this case, portable across firms. Consequently labour is immobile, and the workforce of our firm is unlikely to be able to secure employment elsewhere even though it is productive in its present occupation. The firm is thus insulated from outside market forces. Hence, equation (2.17) reduces to the rule that

$$\text{As } \alpha \rightarrow 0 \quad \text{So } w \rightarrow 0 \tag{2.19}$$

Intermediate cases are also interesting. If $\alpha$ takes a value between zero and one, the wage will be positive but will lie below the marginal product. So, other things being equal, labour will receive its marginal product only in cases where human capital is entirely of the general type.

Since the firm benefits from specific training, any cost attached to such training must be borne by the firm. (Note, however, that such costs have not been incorporated into the above model; if they were, the firm's desire to protect its investment would induce it partially to reward specific skills.) The returns to general training accrue to the individual in the form of higher wages, and so in this case it is the individual who must incur the training costs.

The distinction between general and specific human capital helps explain many stylised facts. Apprentices are typically paid low wages during their training period, and so incur the costs of their general training. Students forego earnings during the years in which they engage full-time in acquiring general human capital. Training courses in which workers learn about the management structure of their firm contain a large component of specific training, and are usually provided at the firm's expense.

Hitherto we have concentrated on providing an outline of the theory of human capital, together with some useful extensions. In the next section, some of the arguments proposed by critics of the theory are evaluated.

## Signalling and Screening

While the theory of human capital has been very influential in both education and labour economics, it has been criticised on a number of counts. Most of the criticism aimed at the model has focused on the issue of whether education truly enhances productivity, or whether it merely acts as a means whereby unusually productive individuals may be identified.

Human beings are not all born with abilities which the market considers equal. Highly intelligent individuals (as measured by IQ tests) are likely to be productive and to command high salaries in the jobs market; they are likely also to invest in much education. It is not necessarily the education that raises their earnings, therefore, since their remuneration may be a function of their innate ability. Employers may nevertheless use educational attainment as a proxy for the likely productivity of prospective employees.

Two models may be distinguished. In the first, employers use educational attainment as a means of identifying the workers who are potentially the most productive (see Spence, 1973). This enables those workers to be paid more than other workers who are employed to perform (albeit less productively) the same tasks. Rather than pay everyone the same wage (based on marginal productivity averaged across all workers), the firm pays each worker an amount which varies positively with her educational attainment and which therefore approximates her own marginal product. Output and remuneration aggregated across all workers remains unchanged, but individual workers can benefit by investing in education, since their wages would rise as a result. The opportunity to benefit in this way from education is exploited only by those workers with most innate ability, since for them educational qualifications are relatively easy to acquire (and are thus relatively cheap in terms of the opportunity cost of time spent studying). In this model, education serves as a signal to employers of the likely productivity of employees. It is therefore called the *signalling* model.

The second model is a little more sophisticated (see Arrow, 1973). We now introduce the possibility that firms employ labour to perform more than one type of task. Assume that the performance of some tasks requires more ability on the part of the worker than does the performance of other tasks. It would be inefficient, therefore, for the firm to employ talented workers in the less demanding jobs while less able workers are employed in the more challenging occupations. Some measure of the likely productivity of workers is likely to be useful to firms in assigning tasks between workers. Educational attainment can be a useful proxy for expected productivity, and so is likely to be used by firms as a means of sorting (or screening) workers into different posts. This is the *screening* model.

The signalling model is clearly a special case of the screening model (the case where there is only one task). Nevertheless, the two models have different implications for the role of education. Assume for the moment that education has no role to play in the augmentation of human capital stock. The signalling model would then imply that education serves no socially useful purpose; it raises the earnings of the educated, reduces those of the uneducated, and leaves output unaffected. The screening model, on the other hand, implies that education has a role to play in enhancing efficiency because, with educational attainment as a screen, workers can be more efficiently allocated amongst jobs than otherwise would be possible. Therefore output rises. It is not at all clear, though, that education is the cheapest available screen, and so many critics of human capital theory would argue that society should seek a cheaper alternative.

The above assumes that the consumption element of education is absent and that education cannot augment productivity. Such assumptions are, of course, extreme. The signalling and screening models therefore need to be confronted with the empirical facts in order to assess their validity. On balance, the weight of evidence suggests that signalling and screening account for only a small part of the differential between the earnings of relatively educated and less educated individuals. The tests which have been designed to assess the validity of the sorting hypothesis are not, in general, terribly robust, however. The remainder of this section is devoted to a consideration of the evidence.

Layard and Psacharopoulos (1974) test for the presence of sorting effects in three ways. First, they examine the wages earned by university drop-outs and find that they are high relative to otherwise similar workers who received no higher education at all. They infer from this that it is not the possession of a degree but the training received in preparing for that degree which enhances earnings. This runs counter to the sorting models which postulate that qualifications are a proxy for productivity. It should be noted, however, that this is a weak test of the hypothesis, since – as the authors of the study point out – it may well be the case that employers use attendance at institutions of higher education as a screen, rather than possession of a degree.

The second test used by Layard and Psacharopoulos considers the manner in which the wage differential between the highly educated and less educated groups varies over the life cycle. If the sorting hypothesis accurately depicts the behaviour of employers, we would expect that the premium paid to graduates should not rise with respect to experience. This is because that premium is a reward to time-invariant characteristics possessed by the worker. In practice, though, the wage gap between highly educated workers and others does rise with tenure. This appears to violate the sorting hypothesis. It may, however, be explained by differential training; if the propensity of more highly educated workers to undergo training is higher than that of their less educated counterparts, we would indeed expect their wages to rise faster.

The third test is simpler, and derives from a revealed preference approach to education. If the main purpose of education is to provide a screening mechanism, it is highly unlikely that the system would have survived several centuries in the face of cheaper alternatives. This probably contains an element of truth, but cannot stand alone as a convincing argument; what if all previous generations argued the same way?

Some further evidence on the sorting hypothesis is provided in studies by Horowitz and Sherman (1980) and Huffman (1981). These test for the impact of education on productivity directly, and make no reference to wages. The former study investigates the productivity of blue-collar workers in the US Navy during the early 1970s, while the latter considers agricultural workers in the southern USA in 1964. In the former study, differences in the quality of ship maintenance (across ships) are explained as a function of the education received by the workforce since they joined the Navy. The latter study concentrates on self-employed workers; the sorting model cannot apply in this case because there is no need to use qualifications to proxy one's own (presumably known) innate ability. In both studies it is demonstrated that education raises productivity; since sorting is not a feasible explanation in either case, the productivity gap must be due to human capital accumulation.

In the UK, Williams and Gordon (1981) have studied responses to a survey which asked a group of 15-year olds about their expected lifetime earnings. They found that the expected earnings of those intending to pursue degree courses were higher than the expected earnings of those who did not intend to proceed to higher education. However, some 30 per cent of the differential could be explained by innate ability, social and psychological variables. This implies that the proportion of the earnings differential enjoyed by graduates which can be attributed to acquired human capital advantages – the so-called 'alpha factor' – is about 70 per cent. The authors also estimated the alpha factor associated with post-compulsory secondary education (that is, from the ages of 16 to 18), and this amounted to about 60 per cent. These estimates are both in line with the US evidence presented by Psacharopoulos (1975); he reports alpha factors of between 65 and 97 per cent for higher education, and between 40 and 88 per cent for secondary education.

The above suggests that sorting may well account for some of the observed gap between the earnings of highly educated workers and others. It does not, however, account for the whole of the gap; indeed, the evidence suggests that sorting is responsible for somewhat less than half of the gap.

## Empirical Studies

In the foregoing sections we have considered the theory of human capital. This provides a considerable insight into decisions made by individuals concerning their investments in education and training. In particular, we have seen that the theory predicts that workers will tend to invest most heavily in education when they are young. We have also seen that (partly owing to the pattern of educational investment over the life cycle) workers' earnings first rise and then later fall as they get older. The distinction between general and specific human capital has been drawn, and the implications of each for patterns of remuneration for work have been investigated. The predictions of theory have been seen to tally well with the stylised facts.

In the present section we confront the human capital model more directly with empirical evidence. We would expect empirical investigation to confirm the following predictions of the theory:

(a) earnings are positively related to educational attainment;
(b) earnings initially rise but later fall as the worker ages;
(c) the rate of return to marginal units of education falls as educational attainment rises.

In order to investigate the extent to which these hypotheses hold true, it is convenient to estimate empirical earnings functions. To do so, the econometric technique of regression analysis is used. The results which are reported below are derived from data which refer to a number of different countries and time periods. In all cases the method of least squares regression has been used in order to estimate the parameters of the equation:

$$lnw = \alpha + \beta S + \gamma X + \delta X^2 + \varepsilon Z \qquad (2.20)$$

Here, $w$ represents earnings, $S$ is a vector of variables which indicates the worker's educational attainment, $X$ measures years of post-school labour market experience, and $Z$ is a rag-bag of miscellaneous variables. The quadratic term in experience is designed to capture the non-linearity of the age–earnings profile. It is therefore hypothesised that $\beta$ and $\gamma$ exceed zero, while $\delta$ is negative. This general class of specifications of the human capital earnings function derives from the work of Mincer (1974); such equations are therefore frequently referred to as Mincerian earnings functions. More recent studies (for example, Murphy and Welch, 1990) have preferred a somewhat more sophisticated model in which cubic and quartic terms in experience are also included; this too enables the estimated age–earnings profile to peak before the end of the representative individual's working life.

The results obtained in several recent studies using the Mincerian model are reported in Table 2.1. In each case the dependent variable is the natural logarithm of annual earnings. It is easily seen that the results obtained in these studies are remarkably similar, even though they refer to different countries and time periods, and even concentrate on different skill groups. In all instances, extra years of schooling serve to raise earnings. It should be stressed that the return to schooling implied in these estimates may include signalling and screening effects as well as a genuine improvement in productivity due to education. Years of work experience also influence earnings in the manner that theory predicts: first, earnings rise as the worker gains in experience, but eventually they reach a peak and subsequently fall. That this is so is confirmed by the positive sign on experience and the negative coefficient on experience squared. The point at which earnings peak can be found by differentiating the earnings function with respect to experience and setting the result to zero. This indicates that the level of experience at which earnings peak, $X^*$, is

$$X^* = \gamma/2\delta \tag{2.21}$$

Solving for $X^*$ in the case of the four studies reported in Table 2.1 gives estimates ranging from 11 to 32 years. This may seem a wide spread, but note that all four estimates yield a turning point well within the working life of most workers. The inverted U shape of the age–earnings profile therefore seems to be a remarkably robust phenomenon across countries and time periods.

**TABLE 2.1**
**Mincerian Earnings Functions for Three Countries**

| | GB 1981 | UK 1979–84 | USA 1966 | Canada 1973 |
|---|---|---|---|---|
| Constant | 8.700 | 0.236 | 3.670 | 5.180 |
| | | (3.19) | (15.89) | |
| Years of schooling | | 0.012 | 0.122 | 0.036 |
| | | (2.38) | (7.63) | (15.06) |
| Years worked | 0.045 | 0.028 | 0.063 | 0.034 |
| | | (15.84) | (3.94) | (18.60) |
| Square of years worked | −0.001 | −0.001 | −0.003 | −0.001 |
| | | (19.56) | (1.50) | (16.85) |
| *Highest qualification*: | | | | |
| BSc | 0.140 | | | |
| MSc or postgraduate diploma | 0.196 | | | |
| PhD | 0.323 | | | |

Note: Dependent variable is the natural logarithm of annual earnings in local currency. Figures in parentheses are *t* ratios; the estimated coefficients in column 1 are all significant at 1 per cent. Definitions of variables differ slightly across studies. In all cases numerous controls not reported here were included as independent variables; these include interaction terms which render difficult the interpretation of the coefficient on years of schooling.

Sources: Column 1: Wilson (1987), Table 4, column 10. Male professional engineers only. Column 2: Blanchflower and Oswald (1989), Table 6, column 1. Male manual workers only. Column 3: Lang and Ruud (1986), Table 1, column 1. Column 4: Meng (1987), Table 2, column 1.

Of particular interest amongst the results of Table 2.1 are those of the first column. In this case, schooling does not appear as a continuous variable measuring number of years of full-time education. Instead, binary variables are used to identify workers with particular qualifications over and above the minimum requirements for entry into the engineering profession. From the estimated coefficients we can calculate that those with a BSc degree earn some 15 per cent more than do those with only the minimum required qualifications. The corresponding premium for those with an MSc or postgraduate diploma is 22 per cent, and that for engineers possessing a PhD is some 38 per cent. These figures confirm that additional investments in education serve to supplement susequent income.

For the USA, a more detailed set of estimates of the returns to educational investments is available. Murphy and Welch (1989) provide a time series of the wage premia which attach to various levels of education. This is reproduced in Table 2.2. A quick look at this table indicates that the returns to education have markedly increased over recent decades, and especially since the mid-1970s. Over this period, access to post-compulsory education in the USA has been widening, so that those enduring extremes of economic disadvantage now form a relatively large proportion of those who have received little formal schooling. It is, however, difficult to reach meaningful conclusions from these data if they are viewed in a vacuum, with no reference to the costs of education. A more comprehensive approach to the study of the returns to education forms the basis of the next chapter.

The above studies lend a considerable measure of support for the theory of human capital. The measures of the returns to various levels of educational attainment are consistent with the theory, as are the estimated age–earnings profiles. In the next chapter we shall return to the estimation of human capital earnings functions in order to study the rates of return to education in greater detail.

**TABLE 2.2**
**Returns to Education, USA, 1963–86**

| Years | High school | Some college | College | Graduate school |
|---|---|---|---|---|
| 1963–80 | 10.7 | 16.7 | 31.4 | 13.6 |
| 1969–74 | 9.5 | 17.1 | 34.2 | 14.2 |
| 1975–80 | 11.0 | 12.6 | 33.8 | 16.9 |
| 1981–6 | 14.2 | 14.8 | 37.6 | 17.7 |

Note: The returns in this table represent the percentage by which the average wage for the chosen schooling group exceeds that of the next lowest schooling group.

Source: Murphy and Welch (1989).

# Conclusion

In this chapter we have reviewed the theory of human capital. While education may offer certain consumption benefits, the demand for education is, in this model, a derived demand. It derives from the potential future earnings premia which may result from the successful completion of a course. Thus education and training are regarded as investments in human capital, and an individual will invest in herself so long as the expected net present value of the returns exceed the costs of the investment.

The number of empirical studies which use the Mincerian human capital earnings function is, by now, vast. These generally lend considerable support to the model. Some have been studied in the foregoing pages. Others enable a more detailed study of rates of return, and these will form the subject of the next chapter.

# 3 Rates of Return

## Introduction

In the last chapter the theory of human capital was introduced and used in order to explain some stylised facts about the labour market. In the present chapter we focus more closely on the empirical application of human capital analysis. In particular, we concentrate on the estimation of rates of return. In so doing, we shall see that the market for education does not always work as smoothly as it ideally should. This market failure has important policy implications, and it may sometimes be the result of government interference. Elsewhere the source of imperfection may lie in the private sector, and government interference may be warranted as a means of improving the operation of a market which, left to its own devices, would remain flawed.

The analysis of rates of return can highlight problems of resource allocation in the education sector. In particular, a careful study of rates of return can divulge whether too little or too much investment in education is taking place. At a finer level of disaggregation, rates of return can identify situations where the government should divert funds from one area within the education industry to another (say, from the universities to the primary schools). More detailed analyses still can suggest changes in subject balance which might be economically efficient. For instance, there may be a case for diverting resources earmarked for vocational subjects in higher education away from areas where tuition is relatively costly (such as engineering) to other fields where tuition is cheaper (such as management). These are all empirical issues which will be addressed later in this chapter.

# Calculating Rates of Return

Several methods exist which may be used to calculate the rates of return to educational investment (Psacharopoulos, 1981). In this section we concentrate on the two most important methods. These are the algebraic method and the earnings function method.

The algebraic method derives from the precise algebraic definition of the rate of return. Suppose that we are interested in calculating the rate of return associated with an investment in education at level $x$. The training period involved starts now and lasts for $c$ years, and the individual is expected to retire from the labour force $n$ years from now. For instance, $x$ may equal 1 for primary education, 2 for secondary education and 3 for tertiary education. Then the rate of return is the value of $r$ which satisfies the following equation

$$\sum_{t=c}^{n}(Y_x - Y_{x-1})_t(1+r)^{-t} = \sum_{t=0}^{c-1} Z_t(1+r)^{-t} \tag{3.1}$$

where $Y_x$ denotes the income of an individual who has attained the $x$th level of education, and $Z$ is the cost of education. The subscript $t$ denotes the year referred to by the variable to which it is attached. This is a high power equation and, since iterative methods must be invoked, its solution is best left to a computer. It is important at this stage to distinguish between the private rate of return and the social rate of return. The private rate of return is the annual value of the (discounted lifetime) gains due to an individual's education expressed as a percentage of the (discounted) cost *to the individual* of acquiring that education. In this case the cost of education, $Z$, typically consists only of forgone earnings, so that $Z = Y_{x-1}$ for all $t$. The social rate of return differs from the private rate of return in that it takes account not only of the private costs borne by the individual, but also of the amount which the rest of society pays (usually through taxes) in order that the individual can receive educational services. The cost of education now includes not only forgone earnings but also the tuition fee (since this is usually paid for by government) plus an allowance for the externalities associated with education. So in calculating the social rate of return the value of $Z$ used normally exceeds that used in calculating the private rate of return. For this reason estimates of the social rate of return to education are usually lower than those of the private rates of return.

The algebraic method is clearly expensive in terms of data requirements. Full age–earnings profiles are needed separately for each level of educational attainment. Although such detailed data are available, sporadically at least, for many countries, they are rarely collated in a form suitable for analysis. So the researcher must extract the relevant information from the magnetic tapes which contain the survey material directly (a tedious process). Since sample surveys often afford only small numbers of observations for many of the levels of educational attainment, and since individuals often experience erratic earnings profiles, the calculation of attainment-specific age–earnings profiles requires that observed profiles be smoothed out using a standard statistical procedure. All this makes the algebraic method rather cumbersome.

An alternative is to use the second method of calculating rates of return. This is the earnings function approach, and it relies on the assumptions of human capital theory in order to provide accurate estimates of the rate of return. Consider the simple Mincerian earnings function

$$ln\ Y = a + bS + cX + dX^2 \tag{3.2}$$

where $Y$ represents earnings, $S$ is years of schooling, and $X$ is years of work experience. Equation (3.2) can be estimated using standard regression techniques and cross-section data defined across individuals at a single point in time. Holding all other things constant, an increase of one year in an individual's schooling would be expected to raise $ln\ Y$ by $b$. Since $\Delta ln\ Y$ approximately equals the proportional change in $Y$, it follows that $(1 + b)$ approximates the ratio of earnings after the extra year of schooling to earnings before. If forgone earnings represent the sole cost of the extra year of schooling, then $(1 + b)$ is the ratio of a year's earnings after the extra education to the cost of that education. Hence $b$ must be what we defined above as the private rate of return on education.

Equation (3.2) can be amended in order to estimate separately the private rates of return to primary, secondary and tertiary education. This involves using cross-section regression methods to estimate the parameters of the equation

$$ln\ Y = a' + b'S_1 + c'S_2 + d'S_3 + eX + fX^2 \tag{3.3}$$

where $S_1$, $S_2$ and $S_3$ are binary dummy variables which take unit value if an individual has an educational attainment of at least primary, secondary and tertiary level respectively. For instance, an individual who has completed secondary school but who has not invested in higher education would have $S_1 = 1$, $S_2 = 1$ and $S_3 = 0$. The private rate of return to primary education can then be calculated as $r_1 = b'/N_1$, where $N_x$ denotes the number of years required to complete the $x$th level of education, $x = 1, 2, 3$. So if pupils attend primary school between the ages of 5 and 11 years, secondary school from 11 to 18 years, and if higher education programmes last for three years, then $N_1 = 6$, $N_2 = 7$ and $N_3 = 3$. The private rate of return to secondary education is $r_2 = c'/N_2$, and the private rate of return to higher education is $r_3 = d'/N_3$.

An obvious disadvantage of the earnings function approach is that it can be used only to calculate the private rate of return. Social costs cannot readily be incorporated into this method since reference is made only to the individual's earnings in assessing the gain due to education and the cost due to years of labour forgone. Moreover, the earnings function approach is only as good as the assumptions of human capital theory which provide its underpinnings. It assumes that attainment-specific age–earnings profiles are vertically parallel to one another once workers enter employment, and that workers never retire. Fortunately, though, the first of these assumptions is roughly in line with what we observe in the world; and given the length of people's working lives, the second assumption is of little empirical importance so long as interest rates remain non-negligible. So the earnings function method provides a useful check on the results obtained by the more elaborate algebraic technique, and may also enable estimates of the private rate of return to be obtained in countries where data considerations do not allow the use of the algebraic method.

While the algebraic and the earnings function methods of calculating rates of return are useful tools in the empirical analysis of the economic value of education as an investment, the reader should be aware of several caveats which must apply to any statistical measure of the rate of return to education. First, education has a consumption element as well as an investment element. It is conceivable that the consumption benefits of education are enjoyed not only during the course of instruction but over the rest of the consumer's life: for example, the skills of literacy allow one to enjoy the pleasure of reading throughout one's life. Since measures of the rate of return take account only of the investment element, the presence of a consumption element imposes on the estimates a downward bias. Moreover, educated workers may be able to choose occupations which provide relatively substantial non-pecuniary benefits. Second, if labour markets are imperfect, there is no guarantee that the worker is paid her marginal product. If, for example, firms have a considerable degree of labour market power, the wage bargain could be struck at a level below a worker's marginal product. Estimates of the rate of return would, in such a scenario, fail to reflect the full extent to which education augments productivity. Third, estimated rates of return assume away the signalling and screening problems referred to in the last chapter: that is, they assume that earnings differentials between the educated and the uneducated are entirely due to education. This leads to an upward bias in the estimates if, to some extent, the observed wage gaps are due to differences in innate ability rather than to differences in educational experience.

The importance of the above caveats should not be underestimated. As was intimated earlier, rate of return analysis is potentially a very powerful tool which can be used to allocate government resources between different educational programmes, and even between the various functions of government, of which education is but one. The damage which biased estimates could cause is therefore significant, and it is not least for this reason that considerable care should be taken in evaluating rates of return.

In the next section the results of a wide variety of empirical rates of return analyses are considered. These enable us to consider how well the rates of return to education which may be observed in the world tally with the *a priori* expectations which we may derive from the theory of human capital.

## Empirical Estimates

An unusually high rate of return on any type of schooling would normally be expected to lead to an increase in demand for that kind of education. If supply responds to this increase in demand, then – after the appropriate lag – the availability of qualified workers in the labour market rises, thus pushing down the wage and reducing the rate of return. In this manner the rates of return for all types of education might be expected to converge upon one another. As Blaug *et al.* (1969) have commented, 'the first commandment of rate of return analysis is: thou shalt equalize rates of return in all directions!' However there are reasons why this might not be achieved.

Education is typically heavily subsidised by government. This leads to a discrepancy between the private rates of return (on the basis of which individuals base their demand for education) and the social rates of return (which are one of several influences on the provision of education by the state). The latter will not, in general, be allowed to fall below the average rate of interest available on the capital markets, since otherwise the government would be investing too much in human capital and too little in physical capital. If the private rate of return exceeds the social rate of return, an excess demand for education emerges. But if private education is not available at a price which can compete with state education (which is generally free at the point of delivery), then this excess demand cannot be met by an effective supply response. Even if private education is available, a further problem might arise owing to the imperfection of capital markets. This means that it may not be possible for some pupils to attend private schools because they cannot raise the finance to do so, even though the returns to their own education can be expected in the long run to exceed the interest payments on the loans which they are unable to secure. In effect this puts an upper limit on the demand for education at each level. Demand cannot then fully respond to differences in rates of return. It follows that differences in the rates of return to different levels and types of education can persist over long periods. In the remainder of this section these differences will be studied in some detail.

Estimates of both private and social rates of return to primary, secondary and tertiary education for a selection of countries appear in Table 3.1. In most countries the rate of return (both private and social) is greater for primary than for secondary schooling. So long as the rate of return to basic literacy skills remains relatively high, primary education should be expanded. But if all children have these skills, the rate of return to primary education must rise to infinity, since literacy is regarded as a prerequisite for productive employment. Expansion of primary education, though desirable if the rates

**TABLE 3.1**
**Returns to Education, Various Countries**

| Country or group of countries | Rate of return to education | | | | | |
|---|---|---|---|---|---|---|
| | Private | | | Social | | |
| | Primary | Secondary | Higher | Primary | Secondary | Higher |
| AFRICA | 45 | 26 | 32 | 26 | 17 | 13 |
| Ethiopia | 35 | 23 | 27 | 20 | 19 | 10 |
| Ghana | 25 | 17 | 37 | 18 | 13 | 17 |
| Kenya | 28 | 33 | 31 | 22 | 19 | 9 |
| Nigeria | 30 | 14 | 34 | 23 | 13 | 17 |
| ASIA | 31 | 15 | 18 | 27 | 15 | 13 |
| India | 33 | 20 | 13 | 29 | 14 | 11 |
| Taiwan | 50 | 13 | 16 | 27 | 12 | 18 |
| Thailand | 56 | 15 | 14 | 31 | 13 | 11 |
| LATIN AMERICA | 32 | 23 | 23 | 26 | 18 | 16 |
| Mexico | 32 | 23 | 29 | 25 | 17 | 23 |
| INTERMEDIATE | 17 | 13 | 13 | 13 | 10 | 8 |
| Greece | 20 | 6 | 6 | 17 | 6 | 5 |
| Israel | 27 | 7 | 8 | 17 | 7 | 7 |
| Spain | 32 | 10 | 16 | 17 | 9 | 13 |
| ADVANCED | * | 12 | 12 | * | 11 | 9 |
| Canada | * | 16 | 20 | * | 12 | 14 |
| France | 16 | 12 | 10 | * | 10 | 11 |
| Japan | 13 | 10 | 9 | 10 | 9 | 7 |
| Netherlands | * | 9 | 10 | * | 5 | 6 |
| UK | * | 11 | 23 | * | 9 | 7 |
| USA | * | 19 | 15 | * | 11 | 11 |

Note: The rate of return figures for groups of countries are unweighted mean estimates which include not only those individual countries listed here but others as well. The data for individual countries are based on estimates conducted at various points in time from 1958 onwards, and so cross-country comparisons should be treated with caution. Data for control groups of uneducated workers are not available for all advanced countries and so the rate of return to primary education cannot be calculated; these are indicated by an asterisk in the table.

Source: Psacharopoulos (1985), Tables 1 and A-1.

of return to it are relatively high, may not therefore be sufficient to equalise rates of return.

The estimates reported in Table 3.1 indicate that both the private and social rates of return are higher in the less developed countries (LDCs) than in the intermediate and advanced economies. This can be explained by observing that access to education is relatively limited in the LDCs, and this maintains a low supply of qualified labour. Those who succeed in acquiring qualifications in this environment can benefit from substantial rewards in the labour market. Although the social returns to education are high in these countries, the imperfection of capital markets (exacerbated by high national debt burdens) causes persistent underinvestment in human capital.

In many countries the private rate of return to higher education exceeds that for secondary education. This result is at first sight surprising. On closer inspection, though, the increase in private returns is due primarily to the heavy subsidisation of higher education. Evidence for this is provided by the observation that the social rate of return is typically lower for higher than for secondary education.

A major exception to the above rule concerns the advanced countries, where the social return to higher education is frequently higher than is the social return to secondary schooling. This is consistent with the hypothesis that higher education is rationed in many of these countries. Such rationing might persist partly because, despite being efficient, government spending on higher education is perceived to exacerbate inequities.

In the LDCs the difference in social rates of return between primary and tertiary education is particularly marked. This has implications for the optimal allocation of the finite resources which are available for education in the LDCs. Many observers have used this evidence to argue in favour of a reallocation of resources away from higher education and towards the primary schools, since the social benefit of the marginal pound is higher in the latter than in the former use (Psacharopoulos, 1985).

The private rate of return, as expected, almost always exceeds the social rate of return. The former is not, therefore, tied to the opportunity costs of public investment in education (that is, the rate of interest). The costs to society of educating individuals at the taxpayers' expense serve to reduce the social return to a level substantially below the private return to education. The most rigorous estimates of the social rate of return make allowance also for the beneficial external effects of education. Thus the impact which one person's education can have on the welfare of others – through, say, a reduction in delinquency and an improvement in standards of social responsibility – ought to be included in the calculation of the social rate of return. It is possible, therefore, but unusual, to find that social returns exceed private returns.

Throughout the advanced countries the social returns to education lie in the region of around 10 per cent. The numbers are reasonable, in that this is the return which would be required on an investment in education in order to cover the opportunity costs. The popularity of human capital models of education owes much to the fact that such reasonable estimates should be so consistently achieved.

Time series for the returns to higher education in the UK and the USA are given in Table 3.2. In the UK the return to higher education fell during the recession of the early 1980s as new graduates accepted offers of low-wage jobs for which they would normally be considered overqualified. During the recovery of the mid-1980s, however, graduates were in short supply, and this resulted in a very rapid rise in their relative earnings. Moreover, a combination of industrial change and tax policy encouraged the widening of the earnings distribution in Britain at this time; a fact which further served to raise the returns to higher education.

The behaviour of rates of return over the trade cycle can be observed also in the American time series, although (for a reason which remains unclear) the pattern differs from that observed in Britain (King, 1980). In the USA, rates of return typically rise during times of high unemployment, as those with relatively little education are more prone to joblessness than are others. Here the estimates are fairly low, reflecting the extent to which the existence of a flourishing private sector in higher education has liberalised the system in that country. The slight dip in rates of return during the mid-1970s fuelled concern that Americans were being overeducated (Freeman, 1976). This is an idea which we shall investigate further in the next section.

Abstracting from purely cyclical variation, the average rate of return to education over the long run appears to be remarkably stable both in the USA and the UK. It appears, therefore, that the long-run supply of education responds to labour market changes so that the amount of public investment in education remains close to its efficient level.

**TABLE 3.2**
**Time Series Estimates of the Private Returns to Higher Education, UK and USA**

| Year | UK | USA |
|---|---|---|
| 1971 | n/a | 9.2 |
| 1972 | n/a | 8.5 |
| 1973 | n/a | 8.9 |
| 1974 | n/a | 8.5 |
| 1975 | n/a | 8.9 |
| 1976 | n/a | 8.3 |
| 1977 | n/a | 8.5 |
| 1978 | 28 | 8.5 |
| 1979 | 28 | 7.9 |
| 1980 | 39 | 8.3 |
| 1981 | 22 | 8.7 |
| 1982 | 46 | 10.2 |
| 1983 | 92 | n/a |
| 1984 | 65 | n/a |
| 1985 | 81 | n/a |

Note: The figures for the UK are the percentage differential between those who left full-time education at 21 years and those (otherwise identical) persons who left full time education at 15 years. Since no allowance is made for forgone earnings and any private costs of education (that is, there is no unit of investment), these cannot be interpreted as *rates* of return. The data for the USA are rates of return to college education *vis-à-vis* completion of high school. The two columns are not, therefore, comparable, and the first column is not comparable with the rates of return reported for the UK in Table 3.1.

Sources: Moghadam (1990), Table 5.5; Willis (1986).

Variations in the rate of return can be observed across subject areas within higher education. Subject-specific estimates for a variety of countries are reproduced in Table 3.3. International variation in these estimates is quite pronounced, as might be expected given differences in industry mix and in the institutional constraints imposed upon the education systems. Nevertheless, a tendency can be observed for courses which are expensive to run (such as agriculture and engineering) to have relatively low social rates of return. Vocational subjects in which tuition can be provided at

**TABLE 3.3**
**Rate of Return to Higher Education by Subject Studied**

| Subject | UK | | Colombia | | Greece | | All countries (social) |
|---|---|---|---|---|---|---|---|
| | Private | Social | Private | Social | Private | Social | |
| Agronomy | | | 22 | 16 | 3 | 3 | 8 |
| Arts | 26 | 7 | | | | | |
| Economics | | | 33 | 26 | 5 | 4 | 13 |
| Engineering | 32 | 6 | 34 | 25 | 12 | 8 | 12 |
| Law | | | 28 | 23 | 14 | 12 | 12 |
| Medicine | | | 36 | 24 | | | 12 |
| Sciences | 38 | 7 | | | | | 8 |
| Social Science | 48 | 11 | | | | | 11 |

Note: Data for the UK, Colombia and Greece are for the years 1971, 1976 and 1977 respectively.

Source: Psacharopoulos (1985), Table A-3.

relatively low cost, such as economics and law, have comparatively high social rates of return.

This begs the question of why governments, as the main suppliers of education, do not seek to equalise the social rates of return across subjects, thereby increasing efficiency. Certainly if the rate of return on social science in Britain, say, were to remain very high, while that on engineering remained low for a prolonged period, there might be a case for government intervention to divert resources from the latter to the former field. In practice, though, such differentials tend not to be long lived. As we shall see in the next chapter, the manner in which labour market signals feed through to shape the demand for higher education by prospective students often ensures that the supply of various forms of instruction moves in the direction suggested by the equalisation of rates of return.

Early evidence surveyed by Psacharopoulos (1973) throws light on the returns to higher education separately at both initial and higher degree level. In Britain, the private rate of return to a bachelor level degree during the 1960s was estimated at 12 per cent. The private rate of return on a doctorate was 16 per cent. The corresponding social rates of return were, respectively, 8 and 5 per cent. The high cost of personal supervision and (in many disciplines) of research tools accounts for the fact that, for doctoral students, the social rate of return is relatively low, while the private rate of return is relatively high.

There is evidence to suggest that the type of school attended by an individual exerts an impact on future earnings quite separate from the level of educational attainment achieved. Layard (1977) uses the earnings function approach to demonstrate that, in Britain in 1971, those who attended a selective entry secondary school achieved an earnings premium of some 11.6 per cent over those who did not. Using data for graduates, Dolton, Makepeace and Inchley (1990) find that the earnings of males are boosted by 9 per cent if they attended an independent school, all other things being equal. But these figures are not rates of return since they make no allowance for the (often considerable) fees paid for private schooling.

Suppose that school fees amount to £3000 per annum, and that after attending an independent school for five years a worker can in perpetuity earn £2000 more per annum than an otherwise identical worker who attended a public sector school. If the interest rate is 10 per cent, the net return to private education is zero, since the discounted costs exactly offset the discounted benefits. If consumers of private education are rational, they will invest in private education only up to the point at which this is the case. So theory would lead us to expect that the net return to investment in private education is zero at the margin. The figures used in the above example are not wholly unrealistic, but – despite the early work of Psacharopoulos (1987) – it is a pity that more rigorous studies of this problem have yet to be carried out.

# Overeducation

The fall in the measured rate of return to higher education in America during the mid-1970s served to heighten awareness of the potential problem of overeducation (Freeman, 1976). At the same time college enrolments fell, with many secondary school leavers choosing not to proceed to higher education on the grounds that the market for graduate labour had become depressed. Thus, between 1969 and 1974, the number of 18- and 19-year old men entering American institutions of higher education fell by some 10 per cent, even though the population of this age group grew by 20 per cent over the same period. This reversed a trend of increasing enrolment which had lasted many decades. Freeman's explanation of this reversal lies in changes in both demand and supply sides of the graduate labour market. On the demand side, the massive research and development effort of the race to the moon, together with the escalation of the cold war, had, during the 1960s, produced a large but temporary positive shock. At the beginning of the 1970s, meanwhile, the supply of graduates to the labour market increased as the returns to postgraduate education fell. These trends are illustrated in Figure 3.1, which shows movements of the ratio of labour market demand to supply of new graduates. As can be seen from the graph, a chronic shortage of graduates suddenly ended in the late 1960s, and was replaced by an equally severe glut.

Further evidence of an increasing oversupply of educated labour during the 1970s is provided by Rumberger (1981). Separately for 1960 and 1976, he has derived the distributions of skill requirements defined across a ranking of occupations. As can be seen from Table 3.4, the distribution of labour market skill requirements matched that of the labour force educational attainment reasonably well in 1960. But by 1976, the distribution of educational attainment had shifted to the right, while little change can be observed in the pattern of labour market needs. Thus the interim period seems to have been one in which expenditures on education (as an investment in human capital) exceeded the efficient level. Of course the flip side of this coin is that the labour market might have been underutilising the human resources which were available during the 1970s, so that over this transitional period the USA was not fully exploiting its comparative advantage in 'knowledge based' industries. This view is underlined by the racial decomposition of Rumberger's results; although blacks were more overeducated than whites in both 1960 and 1976, the degree of overeducation amongst blacks declined over this period as the severity of labour market barriers declined.

The above analysis certainly supports the thesis that the supply of highly trained human resources exceeded demand in the USA during the 1970s. As we have already seen, though, the low rates of return for graduates proved to be short lived. Indeed, Freeman's forecasts suggested that the glut of graduates would disappear during the 1980s, when there would be 'a substantial boom in the market for new college trained workers' (p.73). It is not at all clear, then, whether

**FIGURE 3.1**
**Demand:Supply Ratio for New College Entrants**

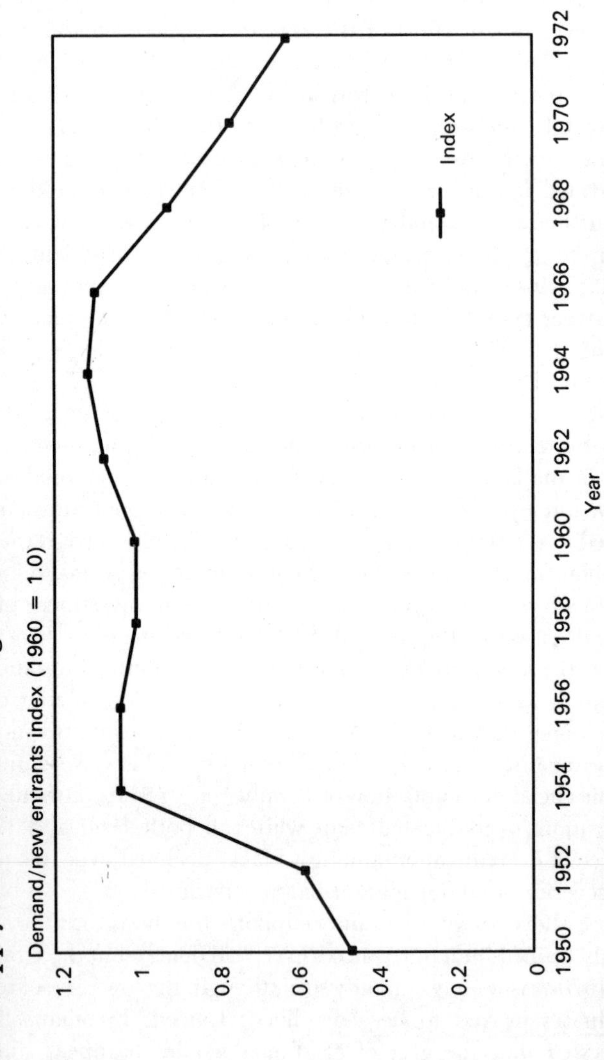


Source: Freeman (1976).

**TABLE 3.4**
**Distributions of Job Skill Requirements and Educational Attainment of the Employed Population, USA, 1960 and 1976**

| Years of schooling | % of employees with this education | % of jobs requiring this education |
|---|---|---|
| *1960* | | |
| 0–4 | 4.8 | 2.2 |
| 5–7 | 11.0 | 13.5 |
| 8–10 | 29.6 | 35.1 |
| 11–12 | 34.4 | 33.6 |
| 13–16 | 16.2 | 11.0 |
| 17–18 | 4.0 | 4.3 |
| *1976* | | |
| 0–4 | 1.8 | 1.6 |
| 5–7 | 4.1 | 13.2 |
| 8–10 | 16.8 | 29.8 |
| 11–12 | 44.7 | 35.4 |
| 13–16 | 25.8 | 16.1 |
| 17–18 | 6.8 | 3.6 |

Note: The percentages refer to the proportion of the employed population for whom the indicated level of education or skill is the highest attained, and the proportion of jobs for which the indicated skill level is the highest needed.

Source: Rumberger (1981).

the American experience of the 1970s truly represented overeducation; it may rather have been a temporary blip, necessary to supply the graduate labour market of the 1980s.

Sicherman (1991) takes a more direct route to investigating overeducation during the 1970s. Using data from the Panel Study of Income Dynamics (PSID), the extent of overeducation experienced by an individual can be measured directly. This involves comparing the years of education received with the minimum years of education required for the post currently held by the individual. Some 40 per cent of the sample were, by this measure, overeducated. Two features stand out from this analysis. First, overeducated individuals are significantly more likely than others to change both their occupation and their employer. This suggests that their tenure of a job for which they are overqualified is transient, and that they might choose short-term employment in such a job in order to gain experience which will better equip them for more advanced work in the future; this is a case of *reculer pour mieux sauter*. Second, over-educated workers are more likely than others to be promoted to a higher status occupation. In some firms, workers destined to become managers are required to spend a period 'on the shop floor' in order to gain experience of the business in all dimensions. While such workers are overeducated for the jobs which they currently hold, they can in due course expect to be promoted to positions outranking those held by less well-qualified workers.

The implication of much work on overeducation has been that a worker whose qualifications exceed those required in a given post is typically no more productive, and therefore earns no more, than an otherwise identical worker whose qualifications exactly match the employer's requirements. In other words, the return to overeducation is implicitly assumed to be zero. This view has been debunked by the work of Duncan and Hoffman (1981), who use PSID data to investigate separately the returns to required education and to surplus education. They use regression analysis to estimate a simple Mincerian (log-linear) earnings function in which the years of schooling variable is split into three components: the first is the years of required schooling; the second is the years of overeducation received by the individual (and is set to zero if the worker is not overeducated); the third is the years of undereducation (which, likewise, is set to zero for all workers who are not undereducated). The coefficients of interest are reported in Table 3.5, with separate regression equations estimated for the four gender–race groups. These are highly significant and lie within the bounds suggested by theory. For all four groups the returns to each year of over-education are about one half as great as the returns to each year of required education. So surplus education has a positive economic value, although its presence does suggest that the resources devoted to education could be allocated in a more efficent manner.

The theory of job competition developed by Lester Thurow (1975) throws some light on the phenomenon of overeducation (Tsang and Levin, 1985). In Thurow's world, wages are determined by the characteristics of a job, not those of a worker who occupies that job. Hence there is no Walrasian auctioneer in the labour market, and wages are rigid. This means that jobs cannot be allocated amongst

**TABLE 3.5**
**Private Returns to Required Education and Overeducation**

| | Black women | White women | Black men | White men |
|---|---|---|---|---|
| Required education (years) | 0.105 | 0.091 | 0.076 | 0.063 |
| | (15.0) | (18.2) | (10.9) | (15.8) |
| Surplus education (years) | 0.047 | 0.052 | 0.040 | 0.029 |
| | (4.7) | (6.5) | (5.0) | (4.8) |
| $\bar{R}^2$ | 0.413 | 0.314 | 0.261 | 0.279 |
| Number of observations | 662 | 1187 | 798 | 2034 |

Notes
1. The coefficients are obtained from a log-linear earnings function (see text).
2. The regressions included also a number of explanatory variables not reported here. These were: deficit education, labour force experience, experience squared, city size, and a dummy variable for residence in the southern states.
3. The numbers in parentheses are *t* statistics.

Source: Duncan and Hoffman (1981), Table 4.

workers according to the wage at which each worker supplies her labour, so there must be some other mechanism. This mechanism revolves around the training and education process. Using (imperfect) information about individuals' characteristics – age, innate ability, educational attainment, and so on – employers rank job applicants according to the expected cost of the training needed to bring them up to an acceptable level of performance in the job. Those with the lowest expected training costs are hired first. This type of fix-wage labour market might be appealing to firms in the long run, even though it is restrictive in the short run, since it guarantees a supply of trained workers into the future.

Now this model of job competition has dramatic implications for the education system. Under wage competition, a high-school pupil who considers whether or not to proceed to higher education does so on the basis of the wage premium which she expects to attach to a degree. If more of her contemporaries enter higher education, then the rate of return to such education will fall and make attendance at university less appealing. In the job competition model, though, the opposite is the case. The decision on whether or not to go to university now depends upon the probability of finding a job. If more of the pupil's contemporaries acquire tertiary level qualifications, she will find herself lower down employers' labour queues and will therefore find it harder to get a job, unless she too attends university. Since wages in each job are assumed rigid, the rate of return to college education falls as the number of college graduates rises only to the extent that some graduates enter jobs for which they are overqualified. However, since the allocation of jobs is competitive, a premium always attaches, *ceteris paribus*, to those who achieve relatively high educational qualifications. Consequently there is an inbuilt tendency to overeducation when job competition, rather than the flexibility of wages, determines the allocation of jobs amongst workers.

# Conclusion

The calculation of rates of return is an important prerequisite of successful planning – both by individuals and by the authorities – in the market for education. An awareness of the returns to education is crucial in the determination of the demand for it. Moreover, where the public supply of education obfuscates free market signals, those responsible for planning education must, for efficiency's sake, base their supply decisions upon rates of return analysis.

Efficiency requires the rate of return on all types of education to be the same. If this is not the case, then the transfer of investment resources from a type of schooling with low returns to one with the highest will increase overall returns. In many countries we have seen that there are wide disparities between the rates of return to primary, secondary and tertiary education. In particular, the return to primary schooling in many LDCs is especially high. Thus economists urge such countries to direct more of the resources which they dedicate to education in the direction of primary schools.

Movements in the rate of return over time can be the result of cyclical fluctuations or of longer term trends. Where the rate of return falls to low single digit levels and stays there for a lengthy period, overeducation might be the cause. In this case, resources might be more efficiently devoted to investment in physical rather than human capital. Those in favour of expanding (or even maintaining) the public provision of education under such circumstances must appeal to benefits of education other than the economic ones, and these might include the value placed on the development of the individual: a value which is too rarely included in economic assessments.

# Human Resource Needs 4

## Introduction

The rate of return to human capital is a major determinant of the demand for schooling. In an unregulated world, the supply of education might be expected to respond to demand variations, so that at the equilibrium price there exists sufficient provision of educational services to clear the market. More realistically, since education is provided largely by the state, the authorities determine provision. In either case it is necessary to investigate how well the system responds to variations both in the human resource requirements of the economy and in the demands of the potential consumers of education. Two questions are pertinent in this context. First we need to establish how labour market signals reach potential students and influence their decisions, and second, how the suppliers of education services respond to the needs of the economy and to the demands of potential students.

The answers to these questions throw light on the extent to which the market can be trusted efficiently and equitably to supply education of the right kind and in the right measure. If it turns out that the market responds too slowly to the needs of industry, there may be a role for the government to play in forecasting the future human resource needs of society, and cutting the education cloth to suit. This is the function of human resource planning (HRP).

In this chapter we shall first develop a theoretical model which examines how labour market signals can influence the demand for education. Later, empirical work on the response of the education sector to the needs of the labour market will be considered. Finally, the role of HRP will be assessed.

## Overlapping Generations

Since education takes time, it is inevitable that fluctuations in labour market demand for educated workers with particular skills should realise a supply response only after a lag. The demand for and supply of education therefore adjusts to labour market change according to an adjustment path which implies a period of disequilibrium. Once changes in the labour market throw the education market out of rest, it takes an unspecified period of time for stability to be restored. If the period of disequilibrium is lengthy, then the behaviour of the education market over this period is of considerable importance. Of especial concern is the question of whether the propensity of potential students to invest in education always moves in the intended direction in response to wage signals from the labour market.

A convenient means of studying the above problem is to use models based upon overlapping generations (OLG) of economic agents. The modelling technique of OLG was developed by Samuelson (1958), and more recent developments have put the method at the forefront of advanced research in the microeconomic foundations of macroeconomics (Balasko and Shell, 1980). The use of an OLG framework in the present context enables the simple model of dynamic adjustment in the labour market (Arrow and Capron, 1959) to be refined so that allowance is made for the time taken to acquire human capital.

Assume that in each generation there exists a single economic agent, and that this agent will live for two periods. She trains and works while she is young, but does not consume anything at this stage in her life. The proportion of time spent in training by the young worker in period $t$ is denoted by $k_t$, and this is chosen by the worker during youth in order to maximise lifetime utility, $U$. Time not spent in training, $(1-k_t)$, is spent at work. Work is rewarded by a wage which is allowed to vary across time periods. When she becomes old, the agent works and consumes, but she does not train. The productivity of the worker when old – and so also her remuneration – is greater than it was when she was young, and the extent of this age premium is related to the amount of training undertaken during youth. We shall focus on cases where there are positive, but diminishing, marginal returns to education. Since there is no training available for older workers, all the time available during old age is spent at work. Utility is derived only from consumption, $C$, and the ability to consume during old age is constrained by the real value of lifetime earnings. In common with other OLG models, a zero interest rate is assumed. In the absence of a sudden change in the returns to education, all agents are assumed to have perfect foresight of future prices. Money exists as a means of transferring resources from youth to old age; the nominal money supply is assumed fixed at $m_0$. Agents produce a single type of good, and this good is perishable, so that within any period the youth is producing output for consumption by the older person. The price of the good is allowed to vary from period to period in order to ensure that the demand for the good always equals supply; thus price $p_t$ may or may not equal $p_{t+1}$. A zero profit condition is assumed, and (since labour is the only factor of production) this implies that the current real wage (defined per unit of effective effort) equals unity at all times. The nominal (efficiency) wage in period $t$ can therefore be represented by $p_t$.

The OLG model can now be formally stated and solved. Utility can be measured by lifetime consumption, and lifetime consumption depends on the real value (in old age) of lifetime earnings. Hence

$$U = C_{t+1} = p_t(1 - K_t)/p_{t+1} + \alpha\, lnk_t + 1 \tag{4.1}$$

The first term on the right-hand side represents the real value of savings to which older workers have access, while the second term reflects their earnings in old age; the latter are a function of training undertaken in youth, since training augments productivity.

Each economic agent maximises utility with respect to her decision, made in youth, about how much education and training to acquire. There is a non-negativity condition on consumption, and $k_t$ is constrained to lie within the unit interval. During a period of price stability, the first order condition for $k_t$ implies

$$k^* = \alpha \tag{4.2}$$

From the assumptions listed above, we know that the nominal stock of money in the economy, $m_0$, is fixed by government at the level required to ensure that agents can transfer all their earnings from youth into old age. This also ensures that the demand for goods produced by youths equals the supply of such goods within each period. Hence

$$p_t(1 - k_t)/p_{t+1} = 1 - k_{t+1} = m_o/p_{t+1} \tag{4.3}$$

To close the model, one further assumption is necessary. To keep matters simple, a particularly restrictive closure is chosen here. To be specific, we prescribe the pattern of adjustment for prices during periods of disequilibrium. A perturbation of the system might be caused by a change in the wage premium associated with educated labour. In other words, $\alpha$ may change during period $t=0$, say from $\alpha_0$ to $\alpha_1$. For simplicity, it is assumed here that, following a disturbance, prices adjust towards their new equilibrium level according to the process

$$p_{t+1} = p_t + \beta(p^* - p_t) = p^t + \beta[m_o/(1 - \alpha_1) - p_t] \tag{4.4}$$

where $\beta$ is a constant reaction coefficient lying somewhere between zero and one, and where $p^*$ denotes the final equilibrium value of price.

The solution to the first order difference equation (4.4) is given by

$$p_i = m_o\{(1 - \beta)^i + \sum_{j=0}^{i-1}(1 - \beta)^j \beta\}(1 - \alpha_1) \tag{4.5}$$

Routine manipulation of (4.3) yields

$$k_{t+1} = 1 - m_o/p_{t+1} \tag{4.6}$$

and substitution of (4.5) into (4.6) yields the solution for the time path of the training propensity, (4.7).

$$k_i = 1 - (1 - \alpha_1)/\{(1 - \beta)^i + \sum_{j=o}^{i-1}(1 - \beta)^j\beta\} \tag{4.7}$$

Suppose that initially both price, $p$, and training propensity, $k$, are in equilibrium, there having been no recent change in the returns to education. Equation (4.2) provides the steady state value of $k$, and the corresponding value of $p$ is $m_0/(1-k)$. An increase in the returns to education and training may be represented by a rise in $\alpha$. If the labour market signals a need for more trained labour – that is, if $\alpha$ increases – the economy adjusts as follows. Both the price level and the training propensity will be thrown out of equilibrium, and will follow adjustment paths defined by (4.5) and (4.7) respectively. The demand for education, $k$, will rise towards its new equilibrium value, so that training propensities rise as the returns to education increase. Meanwhile, the price level will also rise; this needs to happen in order to equate demand and supply of the perishable good over the period of adjustment.

In order to fix ideas, consider the following numerical example. Suppose that the money supply, $m_0$ is 1, and the returns to education, $\alpha_0$, initially equal 0.5. It follows from (4.2) that the initial steady state value of the training propensity, $k_0$, is 0.5, and from (4.3) it is easily seen that the price level, $p_0$, equals 2. Suppose further that the reaction coefficient, $\beta$, is set to 0.5. This set of values represents a steady state, since there is no inbuilt tendency to change. Now let the exogenous returns to education rise so that $\alpha_1$ is 0.75. This sets in motion a disequilibrium process which moves $k$ and $p$ to their new equilibrium values. The movement of $k$ and $p$ over time is illustrated in Figures 4.1 and 4.2 (pp. 52–3) respectively. As time passes, $p$ tends to its new steady state value of 4, while $k$ rises to its new equilibrium of 0.75.

The OLG model described above generates an extremely simple set of dynamics. The difference equations produce monotonic convergence of the training propensity, $k$, to its new equilibrium values in response to any disturbance. The model is appealing in that the responses of the key variables are plausible: as the returns to education rise so does the demand for education, $k$, and the general price level rises too in order to choke off the temporary boost in the demand for consumer goods.

The simple dynamics exhibited by $k$ in the above example follow from the use of a very simple and restrictive closure to the OLG model, namely equation (4.4). It is not difficult, however, to think of alternative closures which would yield much more sophisticated (and less reassuring) adjustment patterns. One interesting possibility which has received a measure of empirical support is that $k$ initially overshoots its new equilibrium value and then bounces back, so that its adjustment process follows a 'cobweb' pattern (Freeman, 1976). This possibility will be considered in more detail in the next section.

Recent developments in non-linear dynamics suggest that even a cobweb model may oversimplify the true path of adjustment. Particular interest attaches to cases where the system generates disequilibrium behaviour which – far from converging on a unique equilibrium – appears to lack any pattern at all. Such behaviour is referred to as *chaos* (Gleick, 1988). Chaotic dynamics can be generated even by very simple OLG models (Grandmont, 1985), and it is therefore possible that the (optimal) response of the demand for education to labour market signals is considerably less straightforward than is suggested by the models described earlier. While empirical work has not till now identified any such complexity in the way that the demand for education responds to labour market signals, the possibility of chaos in education is an intriguing one.

The application of the OLG method to the field of education is a recent development, and there is an urgent need for research into the practical importance of these ideas. In particular, how do price mechanisms in the education sector serve to match the supply of suitably trained workers to the ever-changing demands of the labour market? Do the prices move in the 'right' direction, or is there a need for human resource planning by the authorities in order to remove failures of the market? Could it even be the case that the signals behave chaotically? These are empirical issues; the remainder of this chapter therefore examines the empirical evidence.

## Education and the Labour Market

This section is concerned with two main questions. First, do the consumers of education receive labour market signals sufficiently clearly to make efficient decisions about how much education to consume? Second, do the signals arrive in good enough shape to allow consumers efficiently to decide on their fields of specialisation? Underlying both these questions is a third issue: that is, even if the labour market signals arrive safely, do the consumers of education respond to them, or do they respond rather to non-price data?

Some light is thrown on these issues by a study of school-leaving decisions conducted by Pissarides (1981). He uses data from England

**FIGURE 4.1**
**Training Propensity Dynamics**

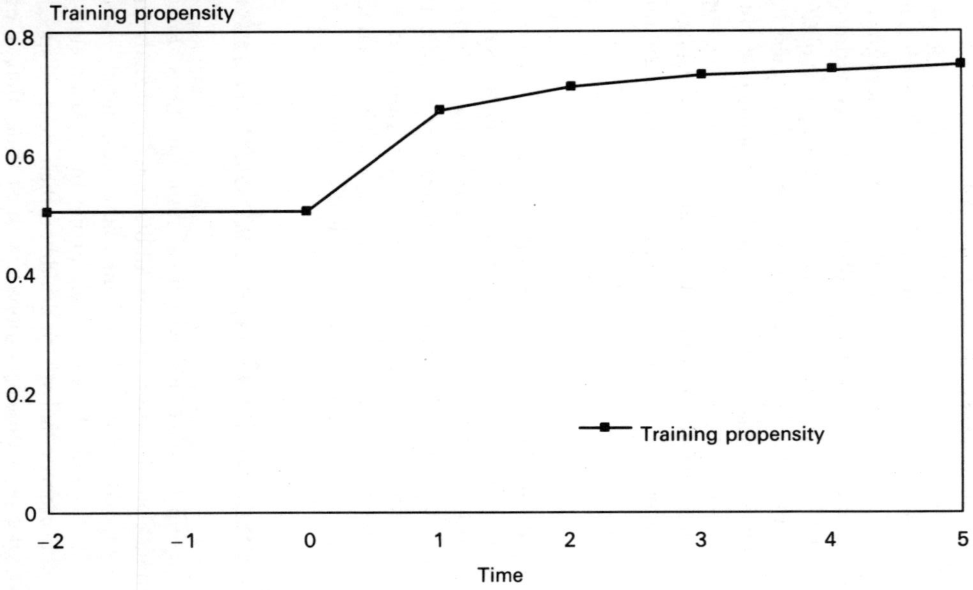

**FIGURE 4.2**
**Price Dynamics**

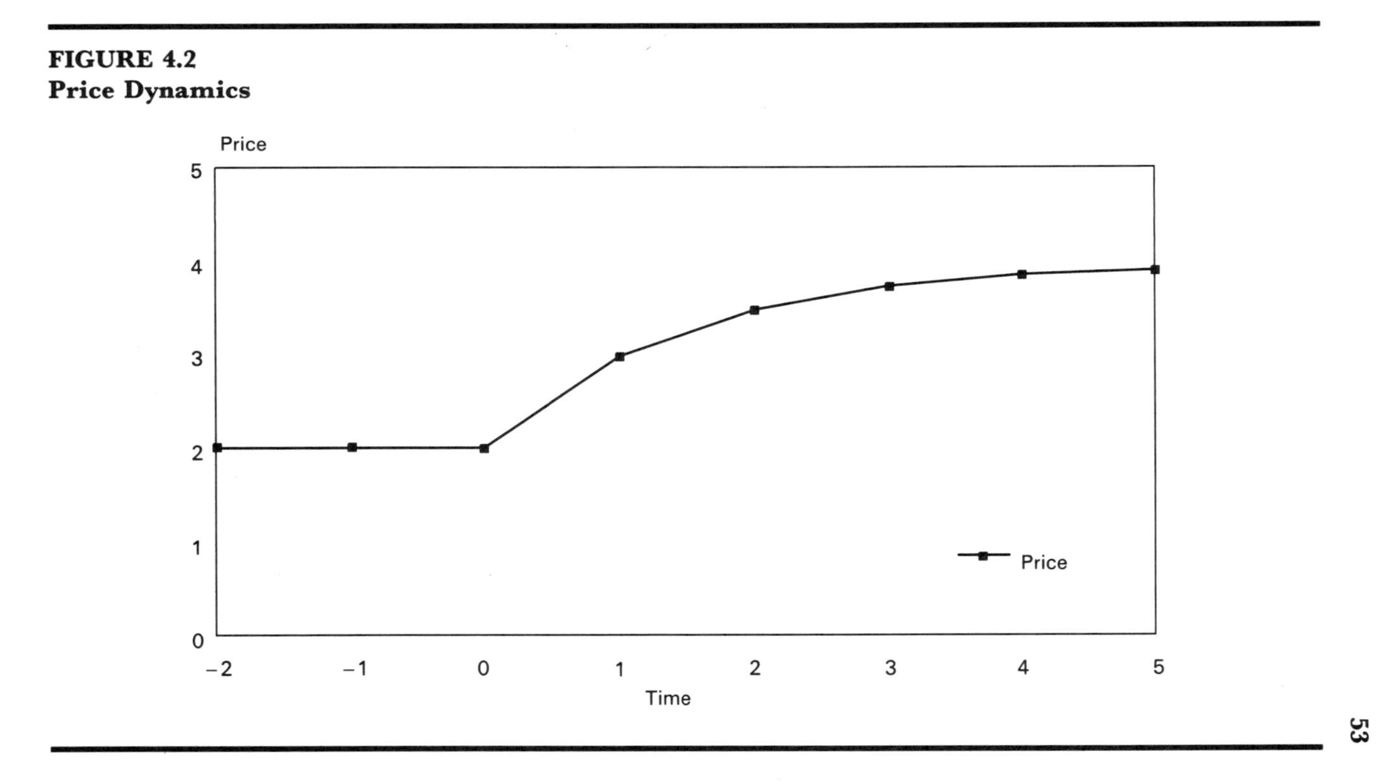

and Wales for the years 1973–8 in order to construct an empirical equation explaining the determinants of the staying-on at school rate. The dependent variable in his analysis is the logit, $ln[S/(1-S)]$, of the probability, S, of staying on at school; the use of the logit specification guarantees that the values of $S$ predicted by the equation will, as common sense dictates, lie within the unit interval.

The staying-on decision is modelled as a function of a number of explanatory variables. These include the following: real weekly earnings of youths, *WYOUTH*; real weekly starting salaries of university graduates, *WGRAD*; the adult unemployment rate (which indicates the state of the labour market which youths would be entering if they left school), *UYOUTH*; the percentage of university graduates who are unemployed six months after graduation, *UGRAD*; and a *RAGBAG* of miscellaneous variables.

All explanatory variables enter the equation in logarithmic form. This enables the relevant elasticities easily to be calculated by multiplying the relevant coefficients by the mean value of the school-leaving rate (in this case, 0.619).

For boys, the estimated regression equation is

$$\begin{aligned} ln[S/(1-S)] = &\underset{(0.4)}{-0.69} - \underset{(3.1)}{1.50}WYOUTH + \underset{(3.7)}{2.20}WGRAD \\ &+\underset{(3.7)}{0.33}UYOUTH - \underset{(1.3)}{0.093}UGRAD + RAGBAG \end{aligned}$$

A similar equation is estimated for girls. The fit of the equation is good, as is indicated by the $R_2$ value of 0.99, with 15 degrees of freedom. The $t$ statistics reported in parentheses above show the coefficients on *WYOUTH*, *WGRAD* and *UYOUTH* are significantly different from zero. Put simply, labour market signals feed through into school-leaving decisions in exactly the way that economic theory would predict.

For boys, this has the following implications. An increase in the earnings available to young school leavers increases the probability of leaving school at the age of 16 years; the elasticity of the probability of staying on at school with respect to the mean weekly real wage paid to youths is –0.93. The flip side of this coin is that an improvement in the salaries available to university graduates lowers the probability of leaving school. A 1 per cent rise in real mean graduate earnings leads to a rise of 1.36 per cent in the probability of staying on at school. It is worth noting that this estimate is broadly in line with those of other studies both in the UK and the USA (see, for example, Freeman, 1975; Dolphin, 1981; Mattila, 1982). Unemployment likewise has an impact upon school-leaving decisions: the elasticity of the staying-on probability with respect to the overall rate of unemployment is 0.21; with respect to the rate of graduate unemployment (six months after graduation), the elasticity of the staying-on probability is −0.06, and this estimate is insignificantly different from zero.

In the case of girls, the unemployment elasticities are insignificant, but the earnings elasticities of the staying-on decision follow the same pattern as is observed for boys. The elasticities of the staying-on probability with respect to youth earnings and graduate earnings, respectively, are −0.31 and 0.23. While these are both significantly different from zero, they indicate that the decisions of girls are considerably less elastic than are those of boys with respect to labour market variables.

The impact of youth unemployment on the decision to leave or stay on at school has also been documented by Rice (1987). More recent analysis by Micklewright, Pearson and Smith (1990) confirms that pupils tend to leave school earlier in low unemployment regions (the South East and East Anglia) than in the relatively high unemployment regions of the geographical periphery (Wales, Scotland), but find no *direct* evidence of an unemployment effect.

In the USA, research into the school-leaving decision has not been so successful. Mare (1980) provides an early analysis of the issue, but his emphasis on sociological rather than economic variables limits the usefulness of his study in the present context. Further limited evidence on the effect of local labour market variables on the decision to consume education is available from the work of Borus and Carpenter (1984). Their study of the factors influencing the decision by high school drop-outs to return to school included a measure of the local unemployment rate. The influence of this variable on the return-to-school decision was, however, statistically insignificant.

Although the studies referred to above throw some light on the relationship between the labour market and pupils' decisions to leave or to stay on at school, the empirical evidence on this subject really is quite frugal. Research on the labour market for school leavers has typically assumed the number of school leavers to be exogenous but variable over time, and has concentrated upon the impact of supply fluctuations on the youth wage. Clearly more research is needed in order to consider models which endogenise the school-leaving decision. In this way the decision of individuals to leave or stay at school beyond the compulsory age can be studied as a response to, as well as a determinant of youth labour market conditions. As we shall see below, somewhat more is known about the links between educational choice and the labour market at the higher education level.

Freeman (1976) has developed an interesting cobweb model which links the supply of graduates to the labour market with their starting salary. Focusing on the case of engineers, Freeman argues that the supply of graduates in year $t$ depends on the remuneration of graduates some four years earlier, since in the USA it takes this long for those attracted to degree courses by high salaries to graduate. Within the short run, the supply of graduates (within any vocational discipline) is fixed. A shortage of graduates in year $t-4$ must therefore lead to an increase in salaries in that year, as firms compete against each other for the fixed pool of qualified labour. The high salaries in this period will attract many entrants into higher education so that in period $t$, other things being equal, there will be a glut of graduates and the level of remuneration will be pushed down. This, in turn, creates a shortage of graduates in year $t+4$, and the disequilibrium process continues indefinitely.

The empirical analysis proceeds in three steps. The first stage involves a regression of the number of entrants into higher education against (amongst other things) the (relative) starting salary paid to engineering graduates. As expected, the number of entrants responds positively to increases in the relative wage. Second, a regression which explains the number of graduates as a function of entrants four years earlier (plus some control variables) yields a coefficient which is not significantly different from one. So (percentage) changes in graduate numbers mirror (percentage) changes in entrants to higher education four years earlier. Finally, a regression of current starting salaries against the number of new graduates (plus some control variables) indicates that, as hypothesised, downward pressure is exerted on the wage as the supply of new graduates expands. So the loop is closed, and the cobweb theory outlined above is supported by the evidence.

A more concise statistical representation of the theory can be achieved by solving the simultaneous system to yield a reduced form equation for entrants. This equation explains engineering enrolments as a function of a vector of exogenous variables. Since salary is an endogenous variable, it does not appear on the right-hand side of the reduced form equation. The reduced form equation is called the cobweb supply equation, and may be written

$$\begin{aligned} ENT = 12.7 &- \underset{(3.2)}{0.35GRAD} + \underset{(2.9)}{0.32RD} + \underset{(1.3)}{0.19DUR} - \underset{(2.3)}{0.90ASAL} \\ &+ \underset{(4.0)}{0.83ENT_{-1}} - \underset{(1.4)}{0.26ENT_{-2}} \end{aligned}$$

which is the estimated function for the years 1948–72. In this equation, *ENT* denotes new enrolments in engineering courses at institutions of higher education, *GRAD* is the number of new engineering graduates, *RD* is federal research and development expenditure, *DUR* is national output of durable goods, and *ASAL* is the average salary earned by workers other than those employed in engineering. The dynamics of the model are generated by the lagged dependent variable terms, $ENT_{-1}$ and $ENT_{-2}$, on the right-hand side of the equation. All variables are in natural logarithm form. The figures in parentheses are *t* statistics, and the overall goodness of fit is confirmed by a high $R^2$ value of 0.95.

The performance of this equation in predicting turning points in engineering course enrolment can be checked by reference to Figure 4.3. This shows the actual time path of *ENT* up to 1972, followed by the equation's forecasts up to 1985. Here it is assumed that *RD* grows by 3.7 per cent per annum, *DUR* grows by 4.1 per cent annually, and *ASAL* increases by 2.8 per cent each year. Fluctuations in the forecast values of *ENT* are therefore generated purely by the cobweb process. As the graph shows, the equation forecasts marked ups and downs in enrolment which follow neatly from the oscillations of earlier years.

The formal tests of the cobweb model referred to above are based upon US data. The fluctuations noted here probably appear in other countries too. In particular, Williams and Fulton (1980) report that there is 'plenty of casual evidence' that cobweb cycles exist also in Britain.

**FIGURE 4.3**
**US Engineering Course Enrolment**

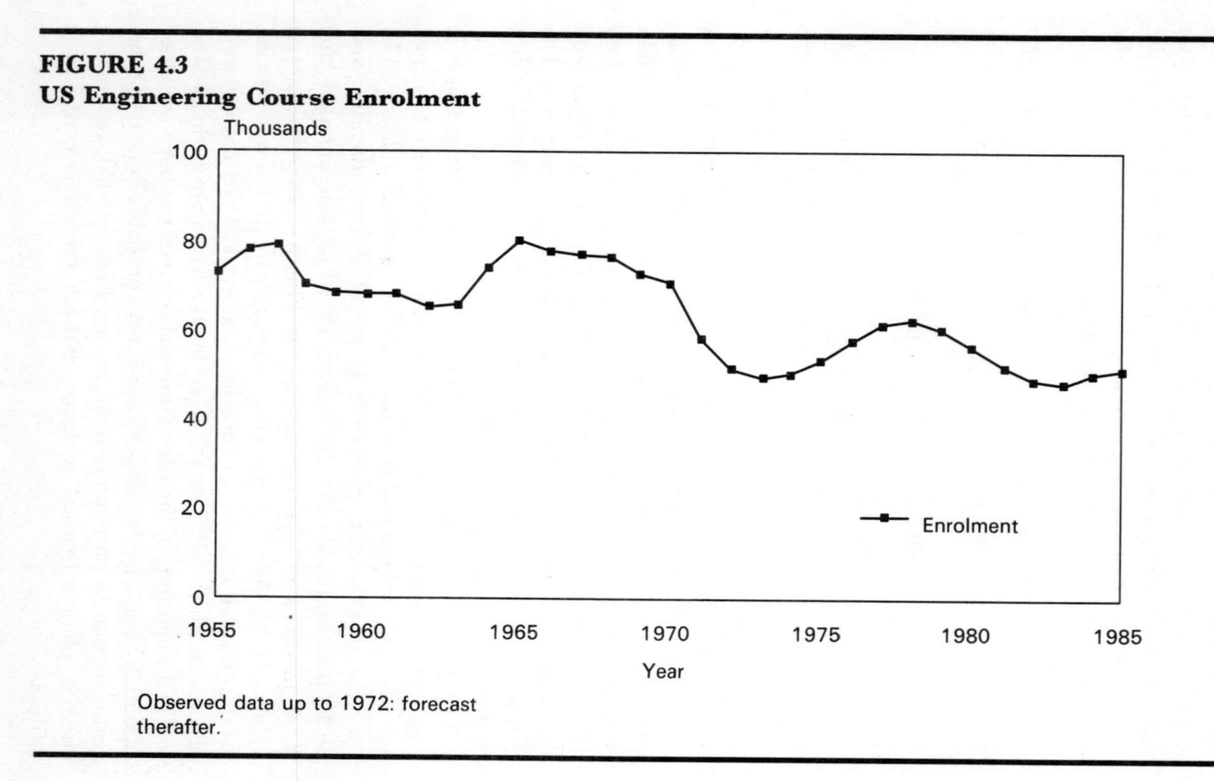


Observed data up to 1972: forecast therafter.

The cobweb model assumes that entrants into higher education fail to form rational expectations of the starting salaries which will obtain four years hence. Otherwise, they could predict the full effect of labour supply changes on the wage, and would build this into their own labour supply decision. However, the empirical evidence indicates that expectations are – for whatever reason – not formed in this way (or that the costs of acquiring full information outweigh the benefits).

In Britain, the responsiveness of the demand for higher education to labour market trends has been investigated by Guerney (1987). His study uses data on university application numbers from the Universities Central Council for Admissions (UCCA) and figures on graduate unemployment (six months after graduation) collated by the Universities Statistical Record (USR). These data refer to the years 1971–83, and separate information is available for each of eight broad subject areas. Regression analysis is then applied to these data in order to explain changes in UCCA application numbers (by subject) as a function of subject-specific graduate unemployment rates and of the overall rate of graduate joblessness. As expected, a deterioration in labour market conditions for graduates of any specific subject leads to a decrease in the number of applications for that subject area. Moreover, given the labour market conditions faced by graduates of subject A, a deterioration in labour market conditions for graduates of subject B leads to a switch in demand from B towards A. Thus the response of the demand for education to changes in the labour market seems to work in favour of market clearing.

The results do, however, indicate some differences between subjects in the degree of responsiveness to labour market conditions. In particular, the demand for places on science and engineering courses is much more sensitive to market forces than is the case for arts and social studies. The relevant elasticities, while small, are all statistically significant. In the case of arts and social sciences, a 1 per cent increase in the subject-specific unemployment rate results in a decline of 0.11 per cent in applications. The corresponding figure for agriculture, engineering and science is 0.28 per cent. Subject areas differ also in their responsiveness to the employment opportunities in other disciplines: that is, the cross-elasticities are non-zero. For instance, a 1 per cent increase in other subjects' graduate unemployment rates, *ceteris paribus*, raises applications for arts and social science courses by 0.11 per cent. The corresponding figures for agriculture, professional subjects, and science and engineering are, respectively, 0.25, 0.06 and 0.4 per cent. It is noticeable that the influence of labour market signals on the demand for courses is stronger for agriculture, science and engineering than is the case for programmes in the arts, social science or professional disciplines. This might be expected to cause particularly strong Freeman cobweb effects in the former group of subjects; it is interesting to compare this result from Britain with Freeman's choice of engineers as a group prone to cobweb cycles in America. It may be speculated that the relative lack of sensitivity to labour market conditions shown by arts and humanities students (as opposed to prospective engineers and scientists) is due to a relatively high consumption element in the demand for such courses.

Further evidence on the manner in which labour market signals feed through into the demand for education is provided by Bosworth and Ford (1985a, 1985b). These studies rely on data collected from a sample of entrants to Loughborough University in 1982. The respondents answered questions concerning their perceptions of the labour market, and the way in which these perceptions affected their decisions in the market for education. Their perceptions of income streams and social status of occupations appear to be fairly accurate. However, the importance which potential students attach to the financial returns of study is not, in general, as great as the weight they assign to non-pecuniary aspects, such as academic interest and personal satisfaction. This is especially true for women and for students of the arts. Students of engineering, business and finance are more likely than others to deem the financial returns to their study important. It is, of course, no surprise to find that those who value future remuneration most highly select the subject areas which, in that respect, promise the greatest reward.

Overall, therefore, the available evidence suggests that labour market signals do feed through into the demand for education. Both the quantity of education demanded and the form of education required vary with labour market events. It is unlikely, however, that this process occurs rapidly or smoothly enough completely to obviate the need for supply side management in the education sector. Those who elect to study in fields which are not attractive to graduate recruiters do so at least partly because they attach great weight to non-pecuniary considerations, not just because economic signals from the labour market fail to arrive. As Bosworth and Ford (1985b) state:

**for a substantial number of respondents, the level of financial returns is not a prime consideration. While such people may hold a considerable degree of information about the labour market, the extent of its influence in structuring student preferences is at least open to question.**

## Human Resource Planning

We have seen that the influence of labour market change upon the demand for education may not be sufficiently strong to ensure that applications to education courses (particularly in higher and further education) follow a pattern geared to the needs of employers. If this is the case, then there is a role for the suppliers of education to play in matching the availability of courses to the needs of society.

In practice this means that the supply of student places in courses whose graduates become relatively unappealing to employers can be cut. To match demand and supply for such courses, the 'price' of admission – that is, the entry qualifications requirement – is raised. This is exactly what has happened recently in the field of biology in the UK; graduate employment opportunities have declined, the provision of student places at universities has fallen, and the A level entry requirement has risen. Conversely, in engineering – a field in which labour market shortages were reported during the early 1980s – entry requirements have remained relatively low.

This kind of supply management in the education sector is an example of HRP. Essentially, HRP involves the coordination of education supply in the present so as to match the future output of qualified individuals to the human resource requirements of the labour market. HRP is used as a means of informing the supply of education in many countries, and was, until recently, known as 'manpower planning'; the change in terminology is due to the swings of fashion and to the somewhat sexist connotations of the word 'manpower'.

To match the current provision of education to future human resource needs, it is obviously necessary first of all to have an idea of what the future needs will be. The initial stage of any programme of HRP is therefore to produce an official forecast of the economy's human resource needs over the next five to ten years. This forecast consists of an estimate of the numbers of workers which will be demanded within each broad occupation category, and it is made conditional upon a set of assumptions about the desired growth rate of the economy and about how this growth is to be achieved over the forecast period. In the UK, forecasts of this kind are regularly produced by the Institute for Employment Research at Warwick University (see, for example, Wilson, 1990). Similar forecasts are, of course, produced elsewhere too; those for the USA have usefully been reviewed by Bailey (1991).

The next stage involves a comparison of the current occupational structure with that of the forecast. Bearing in mind that over the forecasting period a proportion of workers will leave the labour force, the number of new workers needed within each broad occupation group can be estimated. Once this is known, the implications of the human resource requirements forecast for the desired output of the education system can be evaluated. Hence, if a rise in the demand for managers is predicted, an increased provision of student places on management courses would be desirable; likewise, a rise in the demand for craftsmen requires an expansion of training provision in those areas. Since few occupations are very specific in terms of educational requirements, the plan must be painted with a very broad brush. In particular, the plan should use as categories the 'several levels and branches of the educational system' (Parnes, 1964). It should inform the authorities on the likely required size of each major sector of education (especially post-compulsory secondary, further and higher education sectors) and of each of the vocational fields of study; detailed projections of the output of non-vocational courses are not needed, however, since workers trained on such courses are relatively mobile across occupations.

The use of the HRP method is not uncontroversial, and objections have come from two camps (see Teichler, Hartung and Nuthman, 1980). The first group of critics argues that the supply of education should not be tethered to the demands of industry, but should respond instead purely to the tastes of consumers. According to this view, when there exists a mismatch between the requirements of employers and the human capital inventory of the labour force, industry should adjust its behaviour to match the human resources at its disposal, not (as with HRP) the other way around. This philosophy underlies the absorption approach to educated labour, in which the government has twin responsibilities: to guarantee the supply of education, and to ensure that sufficient jobs exist to employ the educated workforce (Hinchcliffe, 1987; Levin, 1987; Glytsos, 1990b). The absorption approach is likely to produce surpluses of educated labour: the case of overeducation discussed in the previous chapter. In this situation some workers possess qualifications over and above those required to perform their jobs. This situation may be equitable insofar as it guarantees equal access to post-compulsory education and training for all those who want it. It is not efficient, though, since it does not encourage workers to choose the jobs in which they are most productive.

The second group of objectors to HRP, unlike the first, do not question the philosophy of regulating the supply of trained labour to meet the future demands of industry. Their objections are based on practical considerations. To be specific, they believe that the market is more competent than planners in predicting and adjusting to the human resource requirements of employers.

The ability of economic forecasters accurately to predict human resource requirements more than about five years into the future is, of course, open to doubt. Dynamic forecasts of aggregate demand – and so also of labour demand – are prone to inaccuracy. Little is known about occupational mobility, so it is difficult even to predict which jobs those who are already working will occupy in, say, five years' time. This criticism of HRP misses the point, however. Even in the absence of HRP, consumers of education make their own forecasts of human resource requirements in order to arrive at the demand-side decisions which they consider optimal; the implicit judgement of an economics student about her future employment prospects, for example, informs her decision to study that subject. Now planners may have access to more complete information than do individuals, or they may have more time in which to process the information at their disposal; so they may be able to produce forecasts of the human resource needs of society which – while not precise – are nonetheless on average more accurate than those made by individual agents. The planners' forecasts do not need to be perfect; in order to be useful they need only to be better than the forecasts implicitly made by the consumers of education. In other words, it would be misleading to compare real world imperfections in planners' forecasts with an unrealistic ideal where individual consumers of education (unlike the planners) enjoy perfect foresight. Moreover, even if all agents were to have perfect foresight, the weight attached by workers to non-pecuniary factors suggests that the supply side needs to adopt more than just a passive role in matching human resources to the requirements of industry.

The unreliability of predictions of human resource needs may raise problems, however, in that the range of plausible forecasts may be very wide. It is possible, then, that the confidence interval of the forecast includes an outcome similar to that which would obtain in the absence of any supply-side regulation. If this happens, the planner would have no concrete evidence with which to justify intervention. The potential benefits of HRP would, in such a scenario, be scuppered by the poor quality of the forecast.

Despite the difficulties outlined above, HRP continues to be used, in one form or another, in many countries. A series of books by Bikas Sanyal and various collaborators, published by the United Nations Educational, Scientific and Cultural Organization (UNESCO), surveys the use of HRP techniques in a variety of countries, including Bangladesh, Poland, Germany, the Philippines, Egypt and Zambia. The study of HRP in the Federal Republic of Germany, by Teichler and Sanyal (1982), is typical of these. This draws heavily on the results of various reports compiled in the mid-1970s by the Federal Ministry for Education and Science (Bundesminister für Bildung und Wissenschaft, or BBW). The BBW predicted that by 1990 there would be an oversupply of highly qualified workers trained in the engineering and natural science disciplines. The extent of this oversupply was unclear, though: the most optimistic view forecast an excess supply of 63 800, while the most pessimistic scenario produced a figure more than five times that amount. In the case of economics, jurisprudence and social sciences, a less extreme oversupply of graduates was predicted for 1990; if demand for graduates turned out to be at the top end of the forecast range while supply was at the bottom end, however, it was conceivable that the market for this type of graduate could clear, but a more likely outcome would be an oversupply of around 70 000.

Glytsos (1990a, 1990b) has investigated the market for graduates in Greece. The impact of a number of exogenous variables on both the demand for and the supply of graduates can be assessed quantitatively by means of regression methods. The exogenous variables themselves are assumed to trend linearly over time, and so their expected future impact on graduate demand and supply can be predicted straightforwardly. The rather crude nature of this forecasting method is compensated for by checking that the results of the exercise remain reasonably robust even when extreme values of the exogenous variables are used.

A number of variables are identified which might influence the demand for graduates. These include national output growth, changes in the nation's occupational structure, and the absorption of graduates in clerical jobs. If output growth is slow, if the occupational mix of employment develops along lines unfavourable to graduates, and if few graduates find employment in clerical work, then over the ten years to 1995, Glytsos estimates that there will be some 121 000 job openings for graduates. If, on the other hand, the out-turn coincides with the forecasts of these three variables which are most optimistic for graduate demand, then there will be some 301 000 job openings over the same period. The most realistic scenarios imply a demand for about 160 000 graduates.

Factors influencing the supply of graduates include the demand for student places and the net international migration of graduate labour. Low enrolment and high emigration implies that, over the ten year planning period, there will be 204 000 graduates seeking work. High enrolment and low rates of out-migration would imply that some 293 000 graduates will be needing jobs. Thus, although the most bullish scenarios would permit a demand and supply equilibrium to obtain, there is expected to be a substantial excess supply of graduates in Greece over this period. Consequently, it might be expected that the graduate–non-graduate wage differential will fall, the quantity of higher education provided will decline, and the absorption of overqualified graduates into clerical jobs will increase.

In the UK, official attitudes to HRP have varied over time. In general, the need for some form of supply management has been accepted, while the limitations of HRP in general, and human resource forecasting in particular, have been recognised. Moser and Layard (1964) give a good early overview of the issues. Despite the more libertarian policies adopted over the last fifteen years, forecasts of both human resource needs (Wilson, 1990) and graduate supply (Department of Education and Science, 1986) abound still.

The current British view on the management of higher education has been described thus:

**Allocation of resources across courses and institutions is broadly determined by the pattern of student demand but**

> **extra incentives to study particular subjects and some control over subject balance is allowed. Student demand should be informed by whatever market signals are available, although the normal sub-text is that these signals are pretty poorly defined and contradictory. There should be no attempt at manpower planning.** (Tarsh, 1987)

In other words, the development of higher education should, in the main, be entrusted to market forces. The needs of the labour market will – given good information flows and a simple set of dynamics – feed through into the demand for education. In this way, labour market shortages in certain specialisms will raise relative wages and lower unemployment propensities for graduates of the relevant disciplines. Applications for student places on these courses will then increase. However, information flows are imperfect, and (as we saw in the section on OLG above) it may take a long time for the demand for education to respond to signals from the labour market; moreover, the labour market itself generally operates imperfectly. All this being so, there may be scope for the authorities to speed things along by providing extra incentives for certain subject areas. So institutions may be encouraged to raise (or cut) their provision of student places in subject areas which the authorities deem to be fields of growth (decline), so that by lowering (raising) entry requirements, student demand can be stimulated (dampened). This is reminiscent of human resource (manpower) planning, but clearly the philosophy is that such control should be exercised lightly and sparingly.

# Conclusion

The links between the labour market and the demand for education are complex. Signals are transferred from one market to the other imperfectly, and are subject to lags. Although these links have vitally important implications for the free operation of the market for education, still relatively little is known of the way in which they operate. A substantial research programme into the dynamics of the education market is urgently needed.

Nevertheless, we can at this stage draw some tentative conclusions. First, the markets for labour and education are closely related one to the other, so that fluctuations in the demand for labour cause changes in both the demand for and the supply of education. Second, the prices which act as lubricants between the two markets are only partially successful in doing their job. Parts of the machine work quite well: the demand for student places on management courses has risen in line with managers' salaries. But other parts of the machine are quite rickety: for instance, teachers in the numerate disciplines are in chronic short supply. Third, while markets lead wisely when they work, the reservations mentioned above suggest that it may not be appropriate for the authorities to allocate substantial education expenditures guided *solely* by the vagaries of demand fluctuations.

A straw man who saw no role at all for HRP would, in essence, be advocating an approach which cramps the style of the market, since he would be allowing demand-side considerations complete influence at the expense of the supply side. Few, if any, observers would volunteer to have one of their hands tied behind their backs in this way. Furthermore, equity considerations suggest that it would be undesirable to bar access to education to some individuals on the grounds that there will always be a demand for relatively unqualified labour. An eclectic approach, allowing the demand side of the market to lead, but recognising that the supply side – through planning – may occasionally need to nudge the system in one direction or another, seems to offer the greatest benefits.

# 5 Private or Public Sector?

## Introduction

In Chapter 2 it was seen that while the arguments in favour of significant state *funding* of education are persuasive, this need not imply that the state should necessarily *provide* that education. This is analogous to the argument that while public money may be used to build roads, the contractors who actually do the work can come from the private sector. In the present chapter this issue is further investigated. Attention is focused on the privatisation programme in general, and on the place of education within that programme. The relationship between the public and private sectors within the education industry is also analysed. The theory of social choice is a cornerstone throughout this analysis, highlighting, as it does, the manner in which society's preferences for non-rival goods can be determined; for this reason social choice theory is extensively used in this chapter to guide the discussion.

## Efficiency and Equity in Education

The concepts of efficiency and equity are familiar to any student of the economics of public choice. Put simply, they refer to the size of the nation's cake and the fairness with which it is distributed amongst the country's citizens (McMahon, 1982).

Efficiency can conveniently be split into two components. The first is *allocative efficiency*. This occurs if given resources are allocated between alternative uses in such a way as to maximise social welfare. It is the type of efficiency addressed by the three Paretian marginal conditions. The second type of efficiency is known as *x-efficiency*. This refers to inefficiencies such as overmanning or managerial waste, and occurs whenever it is possible to produce more output without necessitating any change in the allocation of inputs. An economy which is producing within, rather than on, its production possibility frontier, is experiencing x-inefficiency; an economy which is producing on the frontier, but which is not at the socially optimal point along that frontier is experiencing allocative inefficiency. Both types of efficiency are fostered by a competitive environment, and neither provides a justification for the production of educational services by either a private or public monopoly producer.

The justification for the public provision of education, if there is one, must therefore rely on equity grounds. While a widely accepted definition of efficiency exists, the same cannot be said of equity. Value judgements cannot be avoided when outcomes must be deemed fair or unfair. Nevertheless, for concreteness we adopt here the utilitarian view that equity can be achieved by maximising the sum of individual utilities. That is, each individual's utility is assigned equal weight (Arrow, 1971).

Suppose that each individual's utility, $U$, is defined across ability, $A$, and education, $E$, by the function

$$U = A^{\alpha}E^{1-\alpha} \tag{5.1}$$

The assumption of a straightforward Cobb–Douglas utility function guarantees the usual properties: that is, utility rises with both the arguments of the function, but is concave so that the marginal returns to both ability and education are declining. This being so, the utilitarian view of equity defines a fair allocation of educational expenditure to be one which ensures that the rate of change of utility with respect to education is constant across all individuals.

An education policy requires that the government should determine an (equitable) allocation of educational resources amongst individuals of differing abilities. Educational expenditures, $E$, therefore vary with ability, $A$, although the sign of the first derivative of $E$ with respect to $A$ is not prescribed. If it is positive, then educational policy is said to be input-regressive, since this means that more resources are devoted to those with greater innate ability than to those with less. If, on the other hand, $E$ varies negatively with $A$, then the policy is said to be input progressive.

Just as the concept of equity – along with progressivity and regressivity – applies to the allocation of inputs, so must it apply to the outputs of the education system. An outcome where individuals' utility, $U$, varies positively with their ability, $A$, is said to be output-regressive. One in which $U$ varies negatively with $A$ is termed output-progressive. Rewriting equation (1) in full, we get

$$U = A^{\alpha}[E(A)]^{1-\alpha} \tag{5.2}$$

and differentiating with respect to $A$ yields

$$\frac{\partial U}{\partial A} = \alpha[E(A)/A]^{1-\alpha} + (1-\alpha)[A/E(A)]^{\alpha}\,\partial E/\partial A \tag{5.3}$$

It follows immediately from equation (5.3) that, if the right hand side of the equation is to be non-positive, then $\partial E/\partial A$ must be negative. In other words, in order to achieve an output allocation that is not regressive, we *must* have input progressivity; more resources should be devoted to the education of those with less ability than to that of more able pupils.

This is a startling result. The conventional allocation of resources in education, where the greater part of expenditure is devoted to the schooling of those with most innate ability, clearly produces an inequitable outcome. For reasons of efficiency this may be desirable, since if initially all individuals received the same education the gain in productivity achieved by a marginal increase in the education of an able individual would be relatively high. Moreover, the above theory implies that an equitable outcome cannot be achieved by sole reliance on the free market; this is because equity of outcomes (individual utilities) and equity of inputs (the income sacrificed by individuals to buy education) could not, in the absence of redistributive policies, simultaneously be achieved. Equity of outcomes is therefore likely to conflict with the goal of efficiency. If both efficiency and equity are deemed to be desirable, there must be a role for the government to play in getting the economy to (and keeping it at) the socially optimal position on the efficiency–equity trade-off.

This does not, however, mean that efficiency and equity are necessarily best served by complete control of the education sector by government. While some element of government involvement is needed to guarantee equity (however defined), the optimal extent of this involvement is a subject of debate. Furthermore, while government finance may be necessary to ensure a measure of equity, this does not imply that the government should itself produce educational services. Many initiatives in recent years have sought to increase the efficiency of the education system while minimising the impact on equity. Such moves have typically involved an increase in the role played by the private sector, and form part of the more general privatisation programme. An analysis of the merits and demerits of such an approach forms the subject of the next section.

# Privatisation

Privatisation, strictly speaking, refers to the sale to private shareholders of over one half of a new company which has been created to perform roles previously undertaken by a government body. In this chapter a broader definition will be used: privatisation is an increase in the exposure of state-owned functions to market forces. The means by which this can be achieved, as we shall see later, are several; first we must consider why privatisation might be desirable.

The five primary objectives of privatisation have been defined by Kay and Thompson (1986). The first is to improve the economic performance of the industries which are privatised. The belief is widespread that nationalisation has blunted the efficiency of organisations by protecting monopoly positions, obfuscating goals and providing a guarantee against losses. The mechanism by which privatisation improves a firm's efficiency varies from case to case, but frequently involves the introduction of competition and other incentive devices such as shareholder pressure for profit. Of the five goals of privatisation, this is the most pertinent in the case of education.

Second, the relationship between government and the nationalised industries has frequently been uneasy, and privatisation removes the source of this strain. Private sector managers can plan in response to shareholders' profit motives, and can be assured that these motives remain reasonably stable even though the owners of the shares may change. In the case of the public sector, though, a general election can signal substantial and discrete changes in the objectives of the 'owner' of the firm; such sea changes make management difficult, and inevitably generate stress.

Third, it has been argued that the British government has seen privatisation as a means of reducing the power of the trade unions in the public sector. Lengthy disputes during the late 1970s and early 1980s in industries such as coal, steel, and the public services had involved these unions. Where privatisation involves allowing, for the first time, a multiplicity of independent suppliers to operate in the market, industrial relations can be decentralised, thus increasing competition in the market for labour.

Fourth, where privatisation involves a sale of assets by the state to the private sector, the proceeds of the sale are made available to the exchequer. This enables the current tax burden to be reduced. It should be noted, though, that in a world of perfect information, the price of equity should equal the net present value of all future earnings of the firm. Consequently, the gain to the exchequer at the time of the sale is offset by a future reduction in exchequer revenue, because the profits made by the privatized firm accrue to shareholders rather than to the exchequer.

Fifth, privatisation has been used as a means of promoting wider share ownership. The political ideal of a property-owning democracy has enjoyed widespread support during the privatisation era; during the early and mid-1980s this was no doubt helped by the bullish nature of the stock market which (along with the pricing policy adopted for the new issues) helped many investors in the newly privatised industries to realise windfall gains.

Three broad classes of privatisation activity can be defined (Kay and Silberston, 1984). Although only one of these involves a direct sale of assets by the government, all three are likely, over a long period, to promote the growth of the private sector at the expense of the public sector.

The first type of privatisation is *liberalisation*: the introduction of competition to areas of activity where hitherto monopoly privileges have been protected. Liberalisation need not involve any transfer of ownership from the state to the private sector; publicly owned suppliers must, after liberalisation, compete with private sector firms. Of course, if they fail to do so effectively, they may go out of business, leaving their assets to be bought by their competitors. But the aim of liberalisation is more modest than that: it is merely to introduce competition and thereby to reduce x-inefficiencies to which monopolies (public or private) are prone. One example of liberalisation in Britain is the deregulation of express coach transport in 1980, which allowed private operators to compete with the National Bus Company. A second example is the training credits scheme introduced in some parts of the UK in 1991. Under this scheme, students wishing to undertake vocational training are given a voucher to spend at the college or training centre of their choice; rather than be allocated a fixed number of students per year, suppliers of training must therefore compete with one another for students in a competitive market. (The voucher system is studied in greater detail in Chapter 7.)

The effectiveness of liberalisation policies is predicted by very simple economic theory. In general, competition is more efficient than monopoly, since the competitive firm produces at the lowest point of its unit cost curve, while the monopolist does not. Liberalisation is most appropriate in cases where private goods are supplied and where scale economies are limited, so that no natural monopoly situation arises.

The second type of privatisation involves a more blatant *transfer of ownership* of assets. In the UK, it is this type of privatisation which has led to the major share issues of firms such as British Telecom, British Airways and the utilities companies (gas, electricity and water). The sale of the Rover car group to British Aerospace is another example, although this did not involve a public sale of equity. The aim of the transfer of ownership from the state to the private sector is to increase efficiency. It is worth pausing at this stage to consider why this should be so; since the management of a firm whose ownership is transferred from public to private sectors is generally the same before and after the transfer, it is at first sight curious that the switch to private ownership should be deemed of itself to generate increased efficiency.

One possible explanation focuses on the divorce between ownership and management in large firms. Vickers and Yarrow (1988) argue that differences in the way the owners of the firm communicate their wishes to the managers can lead to efficiency differences between the public and private sectors. In each sector the owner (that is, the collective of shareholders in the private sector, or of taxpayers in the public sector) must devise an efficient means of rewarding the manager of the firm, so that the manager (who may have her own goals) has every incentive to pursue the owner's objectives. The incentive must be effective even though the owner's information about the manager's activities is imperfect. This problem of designing appropriate incentives commonly arises in economics, and has come to be known as the principal-agent problem (Ross, 1973; Rees, 1985; Strong and Waterson, 1987). The owner is the principal, and the manager is the agent.

To formalise the above ideas, consider a world characterised by uncertainty. Three possible states of nature can exist, and each is equally likely. The principal (the collective of owners of the firm) has imperfect information in that it cannot observe which state of nature obtains at any time. These states are denoted $s_1$, $s_2$ and $s_3$. The agent (the manager) must decide how much effort, $e$, she will put into her job. For simplicity it is assumed that she may either work hard, in which case $e=1$, or she may shirk, in which case $e=0$. Both luck (the state of nature) and craft (the manager's effort) determine the profit, p (gross of the manager's salary), which the firm makes in any given period. Since the principal has access only to imperfect information, it cannot tell whether the performance of the firm in any period is attributable to luck or to craft. The owners of the firm therefore have the problem of designing a reward system for the agent which (at minimum cost to the principal) ensures that the agent has every incentive to work hard. This involves the design of a strategy which defines the salary, $s$, paid to the agent under a variety of scenarios.

Suppose initially that the principal is the collective of like-minded shareholders of a private firm and that its utility is defined by

$$U_p = p - s \tag{5.4}$$

and that the agent's utility is given by

$$U_a = s^{0.5} - e \tag{5.5}$$

Thus the principal gains utility from profit, net of the agent's salary. Meanwhile the agent enjoys her salary (subject to the usual diminishing marginal utility considerations) but dislikes effort. We also assume that the agent could, if not employed in this firm, obtain work elsewhere, and therefore has a reservation utility of 10 units. In other words, she will not work for this principal at all unless she expects to earn enough to give her at least 10 units worth of utility per period.

Let the profits matrix be given by Table 5.1. The expected profit (gross of the agent's salary) is clearly greater if the agent works hard than otherwise. In order to design an efficient fee payment mechanism, the principal must ensure that two conditions are satisfied. First, the agent should be paid no more than is necessary to satisfy her reservation utility constraint. Second, the payment to the agent should be structured in such a way as to ensure that the utility derived from working hard (and getting paid for it) is at least as great as that derived from shirking. This involves setting a basic salary plus a performance bonus which is paid to the agent only if the gross pay-off is 300. Denoting by $s_b$ the basic salary and by $s_p$ the performance related bonus, these conditions may algebraically be represented by the following two equations respectively.

$$0.67(s_b + s_p)^{0.5} + 0.33{s_b}^{0.5} - 1 = 10$$

$$0.67(s_b + s_p)^{0.5} + 0.33{s_b}^{0.5} - 1 = 0.67{s_b}^{0.5} + 0.33(s_b + s_p)^{0.5}$$

In these equations, the probabilities (0.33 and 0.67) represent the agent's chances of achieving a bonus payment under high effort, $e = 1$ (in the first equation and the left-hand side of the second equation), or low effort, $e = 0$ (right-hand side of the second equation). The first equation thus says that the utility gained from expected remuneration must (at least) match reservation utility; the second equation says that the expected utility gained from working hard is (at least)

**TABLE 5.1**
**The Profits Matrix**

| | | State of nature | | |
|---|---|---|---|---|
| | | $s_1$ | $s_2$ | $s_3$ |
| Agent's action | $e = 1$ | 300 | 300 | −100 |
| | $e = 0$ | 300 | −100 | −100 |

as great as that obtained by shirking. Solving this pair of simultaneous equations yields $s_b = 81$ and $s_p = 63$. Implementation of this reward structure ensures that $e = 1$, and it gives the principal a net profit of 43.67 units (that is, $0.67 \times 300 - 81 - 63) + 0.33 \times (-100 -81))$.

Now suppose that the principal is the government, and that its utility function is no longer determined by profit, but still varies negatively with the agent's salary. There is now no reason for the principal to build an incentive system into the agent's salary structure. The only condition which must be satisfied in the determination of $s$ is that the agent's utility should at least equal her reservation utility. In this case the solution to the problem will be given by $s = 100$, and the agent has an incentive to shirk.

From the above example, it is easily seen that the principal–agent relationship fails to secure efficient management if the profit motive of private sector firms is absent. Vickers and Yarrow's model is considerably more complex and richer than that reproduced here; for example, they identify situations in which public ownership provides more efficient monitoring of managers' actions than does private control. Nevertheless, the essential argument remains: differences between the public and private sectors in the nature of the principal–agent relationsip mean that 'ownership matters'.

So much for the theory. The empirical evidence on the importance of ownership (as opposed to competition) is mixed (Millward, 1982; Pryke, 1982; Kay and Thompson, 1986). Pryke compares (erstwhile) public and private sector operators within industries (for example, British Airways versus British Caledonian, Sealink versus European Ferries, Electricity Board Showrooms versus Currys and Comet). He concludes that in each case the nationalised firm 'performed relatively poorly in terms of its competitive position, has used labour and capital inefficiently and has been less profitable'. It is possible, though, that sample selection effects biased his conclusion; inevitably the private sector firms used in the comparisons are successful ones which have survived. Millward's results suggest that Pryke's findings might reflect a pattern peculiar to the UK: in terms of unit costs, evidence from North America reveals '*no* broad support for private sector superiority'.

The transfer of ownership, like liberalisation, is most appropriate in the case of private goods. According to the Vickers and Yarrow story, however, it may be beneficial to transfer to the private sector the ownership of natural monopolies as well as industries in which the gains from scale economies are more limited. This is because the advantage of transfer of ownership does not derive from competition but from the clarity of communication between owner and manager in the private sector.

If a major aim of privatisation is to secure funds for the exchequer in the short term, then privatisation must involve the transfer of ownership. Since monopolies have a higher expected stream of future profits than do more competitive industries, it is against the government's interests to introduce liberalisation policies when it is transferring ownership to the private sector. If it were to do so, it would reduce the price at which it can offer the new company for sale. It is therefore unlikely that the transfer of ownership will be accompanied by increased competition, at least in the short term. Likewise, it is unlikely that the management of the company would support privatisation if this meant increased competition. Consequently the means of privatisation which is most attractive to both government and the firm's management – the transfer of ownership – is one which automatically resists the introduction of the liberalisation policies which could do most to enhance efficiency. Kay and Thompson (1986) have called this the *paradox of privatisation.*

The third type of privatisation involves the *encouragement of private provision* of services which hitherto have been supplied predominantly by the public sector. In some areas of economic activity there exist institutional features which put the private sector at a competitive disadvantage in relation to the public sector. This is especially the case in health and education, where consumers who wish to buy services from the private sector must typically pay twice, once to the private firm and once through the tax system. The removal of barriers of this kind is a form of privatisation since it encourages the transfer of activity from the public to the private sector of the economy. An example of such encouragement in the UK is the set of incentives given to taxpayers to contract out of the State Earnings Related Pension Scheme (SERPS) in order to join private schemes.

To illustrate these ideas in a more formal manner, consider the following model which draws on the seminal contribution of Stiglitz (1974). Suppose that the economy consists of three individuals, $i = 1, 2, 3$. Each is endowed with the same initial wealth, $W$, and may not borrow on the strength of future earnings. The individuals differ in terms of their innate ability, $A_i$, and for simplicity suppose that

$A_i = i$. That is, individual 1 has 1 unit of ability, individual 2 has 2 units of ability and individual 3 has 3 units of ability. The government taxes these people on the basis of their wealth, so that public education can be financed. Government spending on education is denoted by $G$, so each taxpayer contributes $G/3$ as a tax payment. Individuals may if they wish buy education from the private sector to supplement the education which they receive from the government. The amount spent by the ith person on private education is denoted by $P_i$. It is assumed that education has no immediate effect on earning power; education is therefore demanded either because it yields consumption utility in the present or because it is an investment, the return on which is future earnings which cannot presently be accessed.

Suppose that the utility derived by the *i*th person is a function of her consumption of education (both public and private) and of her consumption of private goods other than education. Suppose further that ability enhances the potential of any individual to benefit from education, and that the productivity of the marginal pound spent on education differs across the public and private sectors. It is convenient now to specify a form for the utility function which incorporates these assumptions; hence the utility, $U_i$, of the *i*th individual is given by

$$U_i = i(G^2 + P_i)^{0.5} + W - G/3 - P_i \qquad (5.6)$$

Each individual chooses the amount of private education she wishes to consume by maximising this function with respect to $P_i$ to give

$$P_i = i^2/4 - G^2 \qquad (5.7)$$

Thus the demand for private instruction rises with ability, but falls as the extent of government provision increases. These results accord with intuition.

People do not only have influence over private consumption, however. Through the political system, they determine also the level of public provision. Clearly the individuals in this model would not agree with one another about the ideal level of government provision, $G$. Those with more ability would like more public education than would those with less. This is because they stand to benefit more from it than do the less able, even though the cost is evenly spread across all abilities. The median voter – individual 2 – therefore plays a key role, since it is her preferences for government spending that can carry majority support. (Her preference would be the second choice of both 1 and 3; the level of government spending favoured by 1 could attract no support from 3; likewise the level of provision desired by 3 would be too high to gain support from 1.) So individual 2 maximises her utility function with respect to $G$ to give

$$P_i = (9i^2 - 1)G^2 \quad (5.8)$$

Equations (5.7) and (5.8) can simultaneously be solved for $i = 2$ to give the solution for government expenditure, $G = 1/6$.

Substituting the chosen value of $G$ into either equation (5.7) or (5.8) yields the person-specific levels of expenditure on private education. Hence $P_1 = 8/36$, $P_2 = 35/36$, and $P_3 = 80/36$. So all individuals choose to consume some private education in order to supplement the publicly funded provision. This result, which appears curious at first sight, follows from the differences in productivity of the public and private sectors.

Despite its simplicity, the above model has much appeal. It clarifies the reasons why the demand for private and public sector education should co-exist. It suggests that those with more ability consume more private education than do those with less, and it provides a link between the demand for private education and the level of government provision. Alternative models which also throw light on the demand for publicly funded education include those of Bruno (1976, 1977) and Ulph (1977).

The encouragement of private provision is an appropriate form of privatisation where a basic level of provision of a private good is supplied by the government, and where individual consumers may wish to top this up from their private resources. Such a scenario exists where the state provides a necessity as a means of income redistribution, or as a means of alleviating harmful externalities. Pensions, health and education services are obvious examples. It may also be possible to obtain private sponsorship of some activity within industries which produce public goods. The classic example of the latter is advertising and sponsorship on the commercial broadcasting services. Such sponsorship may be desirable because it enables Pareto gains to be made; while the sponsors benefit from publicity, the public benefits from the service which needs to accompany the publicity material in order to attract viewers. It is this broad class of privatisation measures that is most germane in the context of education.

Within the sphere of education, a number of provisions are available which are designed to encourage private provision (Pring, 1988). The first of these is the subsidy by government of places in private schools for able pupils whose parents have limited financial means. The Assisted Places Scheme in the UK is a step in this direction, although it is likely that many of the beneficiaries of the scheme in its early years would have attended private schools even in the absence of the subsidy.

A second means whereby the private sector of the education industry is supported by the exchequer is through tax breaks. Private schools enjoy charitable status, and as such they benefit from tax relief on covenanted fees. Third, certain needs of pupils within the public sector are supplied by buying in specialist services from the private sector; for instance, some local education authorities cater for pupils with special educational needs in this way. Fourth, government personnel who are required to work abroad may – on account of their frequent international mobility – be entitled to receive from the government private school fees to pay for their offspring's education. This applies to certain employees in the armed forces and in the diplomatic service.

Fifth, certain variants of the voucher proposal for education would involve a large subsidy to private education (Friedman, 1962). If pupils were allocated education vouchers which could be spent at *any* school – state or private – voucher expenditures on private sector schools would represent a significant new transfer of public money into that sector. Since this is discussed at length in Chapter 7, it will not be treated in any greater depth at this juncture.

In addition to policies designed to promote the private provision of services in competition with the public sector, the privatisation effort in the education system has included numerous schemes aimed at the promotion of the private provision of services *within* the public sector. This includes the sponsorship of teachers, buildings and equipment by private sector firms; such firms may view the sponsorship as effective advertising or, where the firms are dominant employers in the local labour market, they may regard it as a means of improving the quality of their future workforce. Other means whereby private resources could be released for use within public sector schools include charges which schools might make for tuition in certain subjects, such as in playing musical instruments, or in art, or in sports. These are all subjects where the consumption element of education is relatively high. Finally, the talents and time of pupils and parents could be used to the benefit of the school if some aspects of regular maintenance (such as decorating) were carried out by volunteers.

The private provision of some services within the state education system has a close parallel in the health service; many patients, despite being covered by state insurance schemes, choose to undergo elective surgery in the private sector. If the propensity to opt for private provision varies significantly from area to area, there are implications for the socially optimal geographical pattern of public expenditure. For instance, a district whose residents have a relatively high propensity to buy private (health or education) services requires less spending on state services per head of the population in order to achieve parity with other districts (Nicholl *et al.*, 1984).

## The Public Sector and Crowding Out

In many areas of debate on the role of the public sector, concern is expressed about the possibility that public sector activity might crowd out private sector investment. This may be because the increase in public sector borrowing raises interest rates and so lowers the rate of capital accumulation by private sector firms, or it might be because a tax change not only affects consumption but also influences the demand for money. For instance, a tax hike shifts the IS curve rightwards and – so long as the demand for money depends upon disposable income – the LM curve moves to the left, thus leaving the overall impact upon national income uncertain (Mankiw and Summers, 1986). But a third explanation of crowding out might be of more direct relevance in the case of education. This explanation assumes an inelastic demand for education, and suggests that any shortfall in the provision of public education will be met by private sector provision.

Casual observation provides some support for the idea of crowding out. Consider first those countries where the government guarantees the availability of primary and secondary education which is free at the point of delivery. Private sector schools are sure to find the going relatively tough in these countries, since they can compete only by providing a service which is perceived to be of higher quality than that of the state system. Elsewhere, where state-funded education cannot be guaranteed for all children, there are market gaps which the private sector can fill. In the latter countries, quality is not such an important characteristic of private sector schools.

In LDCs the coverage of state education systems is typically incomplete. There is considerable scope for the growth of a private sector in education which, rather than competing with the public sector, exists to plug the gaps. The private sector can therefore flourish without the need for government subsidy or interference. High quality instruction is expensive to provide and is imperfectly observed by consumers; this being so, and since competition between schools encourages cost-cutting, there is an inbuilt tendency for quality to be sacrificed. Though they offer diversity in curriculum content, with a few exceptions private sector schools in LDCs are in general of inferior quality (James, 1991).

It follows that governments in the LDCs face a trade-off between quantity and quality. Improvements in the quality of private sector education can be achieved by way of regulation, but since such improvements are expensive they will likely be realised at the cost of a decline in the quantity of private sector provision. (An upward shift of the marginal cost curve of firms in a competitive industry forces some firms out of business and reduces the quantity supplied to the market.) The existence in LDCs of a quantity–quality trade-off is in marked contrast to the experience of developed countries. In the latter, the quantity of provision is given, since the state typically guarantees universal free access to education.

In the developed countries the private sector struggles to compete, since its patrons must, in effect, pay twice for education: once through the tax system and once directly. While this may be justified on equity grounds – it resembles an extra degree of tax progressivity which the rich *volunteer* to pay – it renders the maintenance of a large private sector difficult. The private sector in such countries has tended to flourish only when significant subsidies are available from the state. These subsidies might include the tax benefits of charitable status, the availability of low-interest loans, the provision of state financed scholarships, the subsidy of teacher training, the provision of some equipment, or even the provision of some teachers. To many of these subsidies are attached conditions and regulations. For example, minimum standards may be imposed on buildings, schools may be required to enter their pupils for national examinations or follow a national curriculum, tuition fees or teachers' salaries may be stipulated by the government, or the school might be required to operate as a not-for-profit organisation.

These regulations which tend to accompany subsidies to the private sector serve to increase the influence of government in private provision. Thus it tends also to reduce the diversity, innovation and competition which adherents of the private sector claim as its primary benefits. As James (1984) argues, the private sector of education becomes 'quasi-governmental; as the private sector grows, through governmental subsidies, it becomes more like the public sector'.

The discussion in this section so far has been rather abstract and it is useful at this stage to illuminate the analysis by studying some data. Table 5.2 shows the share of private spending in the total national expenditure on education across several countries. This table illustrates the tendency for private spending on education to be particularly high in LDCs, although this pattern is by no means without exception. In Kenya, for instance, the coverage of the state education system at primary level is wide, and this accounts for the low percentage of all education expenditures due to private spending.

**TABLE 5.2**
**Share of Private Spending in Total National Expenditure on Education**

| Country | Year | Per cent |
|---|---|---|
| Australia | 1986 | 16.4 |
| Colombia | 1983 | 28.6 |
| France | 1985 | 5.1 |
| India | 1985–6 | 50.3 |
| Kenya | 1980 | 8.6 |
| Netherlands | 1986 | 3.5 |
| Thailand | 1986 | 26.5 |
| UK | 1986 | 10.1 |
| USA | 1986 | 24.1 |
| Zimbabwe | 1985 | 26.5 |

Source: UN, National Accounts Statistics, 1986, Tables 2.1 and 2.5.

In the USA, meanwhile, the private sector receives extensive subsidies, and these help explain the high figure in the table for that country.

The differences between developed countries and LDCs in the access of individuals to state education is illustrated further in Figure 5.1. In this diagram, Lorenz curves are shown for the two groups of countries. These show the share of public educational spending accounted for by various groups of the population, where the population is ranked along the horizontal axis according to their terminal level of education. The point at which the Lorenz curve leaves the horizontal axis tells us the proportion of the population which has no access at all to public education. The reading on the horizontal axis below the first kink in the curve tells us the proportion of the population which receives at most primary education; the corresponding point below the second kink tells us the proportion which receives at most secondary education. The height of the kinks indicate the proportion of public education expenditures which are devoted to the relevant group of pupils; hence in both developed and less developed countries, between 30 and 40 per cent of public expenditures on education is spent on higher education (although the proportion of the population enjoying access to education at this level is only 6 per cent in the LDCs as against 20 per cent in the developed countries). Since the Lorenz curve for the developed countries lies entirely within that for the LDCs, we may conclude that the distribution of public education resources is more equitable in the former group of countries than in the latter.

While, on the surface, it appears that public sector activity crowds out the private sector in education, it is clear from the above discussion that extreme caution needs to be exercised in interpreting the evidence. The education systems in developed countries and the LDCs differ in important respects, and it is important to avoid naive comparisons. Three points stand out. First, the governments of LDCs face a trade-off between the quantity and quality of education services provided to their citizens, while those of developed countries do not. Second, the private sector in LDCs can flourish without government assistance, whereas in the developed countries government subsidies are essential to the survival of a private alternative. Third, the greater are these subsidies, the less distinct are private sector schools from those in the public sector.

**FIGURE 5.1**
**Lorenz Curves for Education Expenditure**

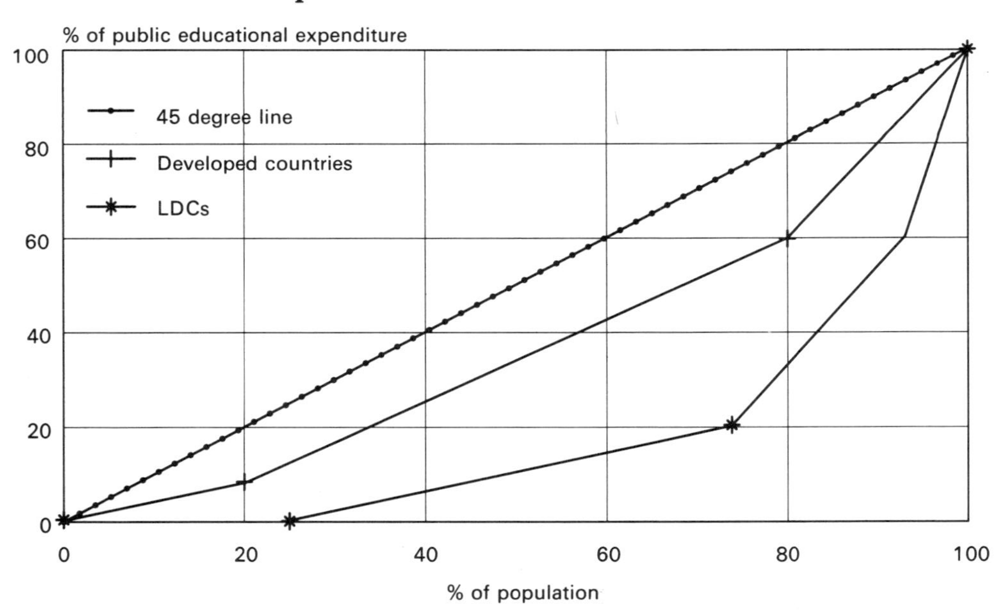

# Conclusion

Gains are possible from a privatisation programme, and these gains can be secured in the field of education as elsewhere. The benefits of privatisation, broadly defined, in the education sector include the following: increased competition between schools, clearer incentive mechanisms which encourage enhanced performance from those working in education, and a more flexible system of provision where each pupil can choose the amount and type of education which best suits her requirements.

None of this denies the role that the state has to play in financing education. We all gain if our neighbours have been educated to act as responsible citizens, and if they are literate and numerate. To this extent, education is a public good, and must therefore be funded by the state. Government also has a clear role to play in enforcing minimum standards. But none of this necessitates government control of the supply of education. If there were no benefits attached to state control of education supply, though, privatised systems would be ubiquitous. Clearly there are certain benefits attached to control which need to be weighed against the costs. The monitoring and enforcement of standards is likely to be easier under a nationalised system than under a private system. The objective of schools under a nationalised system could be clearly defined; no monitoring would be necessary in order to ensure the compatibility of objectives of the government and the owners of private schools.

Equity requires at least partial state funding for the education system. The experience of LDCs suggests that government control – or regulation so tight that it approximates control – is necessary in order to preserve high standards. While there may be benefits to privatisation, therefore, there are costs too. The optimal balance of private and public sector activity may change over time, and can only be sought by a process of trial and error.

# 6 The Costs of Provision

## Introduction

Changes in the practice of educational administration could conceivably allow the provision of a given level of educational service at reduced cost. The desirability of this scenario has led to a keen concern about the nature and determinants of school costs. The recent growth of interest in these issues has been due in part to the widespread devolution of managerial functions towards individual institutions. More people working within the education industry now have to worry about the financial implications of their decisions than has ever before been the case. Partly for this reason, a considerable amount of recent academic research has been generated on the determinants of costs in educational institutions.

In this chapter the impact of the devolution of managerial responsibility upon the roles played by school managers will be considered, with special emphasis on the financial aspects of management. In particular, the cost structures of institutions will be studied, thus throwing light on the factors which influence the costs of operation of a school or an institution of higher education. An understanding of these influences is necessary if managers in education are to be able to control costs.

## The Devolution of Managerial Responsibilities

The UK Education Reform Act of 1988 represents part of an international trend away from centralised planning in education. In some countries, such as the USA, schools have for many years enjoyed a considerable measure of autonomy. In many others, particularly in Europe, the move towards local management has accelerated over the last decade.

In France, for example, the role of headteachers has been extended so that they are now expected to liaise with local interest groups and be responsive to their needs. The interest groups include teachers, parents, local employers and unions, as well as the general public in the community. Nevertheless, a strong central bureaucracy remains.

Meanwhile, the Swedish system has become increasingly decentralised, with considerably more decisions than before being taken at district level, and central control being limited to matters of strategic planning. The Swedish experience, however, has not been aimed at giving schools autonomy. School heads in Sweden are typically specialists in routine administration and manage not just one school each, but several; consequently it has been to the school district rather than to the individual school that managerial authority has been devolved from the central bodies. Throughout, the goal is to increase flexibility within the system so that schools become increasingly responsive to local needs (Spreadbury, 1989).

In Britain, schools now undertake managerial roles which previously were adopted by the local education authority (Cave, 1990; Glennerster, 1991). These include financial management, human resource management, and marketing in an increasingly competitive environment. The aim of the reform is to make schools more responsive than was previously the case to the needs of parents and pupils in their local area, while at the same time freeing schools to choose their own suppliers of materials and labour. Since the old decision-making authorities faced no competition, they were widely believed to be wasteful, inflexible and bureaucratic. The efficiency gains secured by way of the extra flexibility and freedom should, it is hoped, more than offset the duplication of administrative effort which is implied by the replacement of centralised decision-making by a multiplicity of school-specific decision-making processes (Stenner, 1987, 1988).

The UK Education Reform Act 1988 has given financial control to all state secondary schools and to all primary schools with more than 200 pupils. All local authorities in Britain are now required to formulate and publish a set of rules which determine how funds are to be allocated between schools within their jurisdiction (s. 42 of the 1988 Education Reform Act). The authority first determines its total expenditure on education; this is termed the General Schools' Budget (s. 33). A proportion (currently up to 7 per cent) of the General Schools' Budget may be retained by the authority to cover overheads. The balance, called the Aggregated Schools' Budget (s. 33), is then distributed amongst the schools according to the Resource Allocation Formula (s. 38), ensuring that due allowance is made for pupil numbers (weighted by age), and for any pupils with special educational needs. The governors of the schools themselves then control the allocated monies, although they may devolve this responsibility to the headteacher (s. 36).

An immediate consequence of this is that decision makers – and more generally the teaching staff – within these schools have needed to become increasingly aware of the structure of costs. At the same time, they have become responsible for management in a much broader context than was previously the case; they must now ask of themselves questions such as: what is the function of our institution? What programmes does it provide? Why does it provide them? Does it need to provide all of them? Should we introduce new programmes? If so, how? Can we operate more efficiently? If so, how?

The answers to these questions define the direction in which the institution seeks to move. Those responsible for management within the school will then need constantly to appraise the institution's performance and act upon the information thus acquired, in order to ensure that it continues to fulfil its stated goals.

A key problem facing school managers involves the reconciliation of conflicting goals amongst interested parties. For instance, while governors will be interested largely in the efficiency with which resources are used, parents will be mainly interested in the levels of academic achievement, and the local public will be keen to ensure (amongst other things) that the labour market needs of the area are well served (Strain, 1990). Such a multiplicity of goals presents management with a major challenge, and the associated problems are ones which economic analysis can help resolve (Turner, 1989).

The existence of distinct groups with an interest in the school's activities, each of which has its own set of goals, raises an economic problem frequently encountered in the theory of social choice. The aggregation of preferences across groups or across individuals is fraught with difficulty. In particular, this is a situation where the impossibility theorem of Arrow (1951) applies (see Appendix 1 to this chapter). Arrow's great achievement is to show that *no* voting system can be devised which *guarantees* that a non-authoritarian decision-maker can meaningfully aggregate preferences across groups. This leaves decision-makers in education – as elsewhere – in something of a quandary. Indeed, many of the problems faced by management in any sphere involve finding ways around Arrow's impossibility theorem. Often this involves violating the non-dictatorship condition in a manner which minimises the long-term damage to the organisation.

It should be noted, though, that Arrow's analysis does not imply that the aggregation of preferences across groups is never possible; all it shows is that no *method* of aggregation is failsafe. Typically, agreements can be reached between the various groups concerned with a school without recourse to dictatorial methods. For example, it will generally (though not always) be possible for the various groups involved in the school to bargain with one another over the feasible allocations of resources. If bargaining occurs in an efficient manner, the outcome will lie on the 'core' of efficient solutions (see Appendix 2 to this chapter). The core is the set of allocations of the available resources which satisfy the Pareto rule that no group can be made better off except at the expense of others. While it is clear that allocations away from the core are inferior (in the traditional welfare sense) to those which lie within the core, it is not possible, without making value judgements, to prefer one point in the core to another. The solution to the bargaining process depends upon the bargaining strengths of the groups involved, or upon the judgement of the arbiter and ultimate decision-maker.

However conflicts of the kind referred to above are resolved, the outcome should enable each school to form a budget plan which is consistent with the overall aims of the institution, and which respects the constraints imposed by the limited resources available. Performance targets should be clearly stated, and the means whereby achievement is measured and rewarded should be made unambiguous (McAlister and Connolly, 1990). Put bluntly, a school should, when formulating its annual budget plan, fix the goalposts and ensure that they cannot be moved during the planning period.

Once the plan is in place, tasks must be delegated within the organisation. Those to whom duties are allocated accept responsibility for the success or failure of their obligation, thus facilitating the realisation of the institution's goals.

In constructing its budget plan, an institution has a number of options available. The budget could, for instance, build upon past practice, with only marginal changes made in departmental allocations from year to year. Such an approach, known as incremental budgeting, is attractive in that its demands on the time of administrators are limited. It does, however, suffer the disadvantage that inefficiencies are likely to be perpetuated from year to year. An alternative approach to budgeting might be to start from scratch each year, and compel each department annually to justify its proposed expenditures in their entirety. While encouraging efficiency, this method of zero-based budgeting is costly in terms of administration time; this approach might also frustrate long-term planning by introducing discontinuities into the system. A third possibility, which seeks to capture the benefits of both incremental and zero-based budgeting, might be to opt for a half-way house between the two extreme approaches.

Each of these forms of budget planning aims to do two things. First, the output goals of the school are to be explicitly stated. A school is deemed to be effective if it realises a given set of goals. Second, those output goals are to be achieved with the least possible expenditure on inputs. A school which succeeds in doing so is deemed to be efficient. As an example, consider a school which aims to ensure that all its pupils pass at least five GCSE examinations. Such a school is effective if it succeeds in that goal, and is efficient if it does so with the use of the minimum possible resources. Effectiveness is therefore a prerequisite for efficiency. (This means that if one school operates at a lower per pupil cost than another, the former school can be deemed to be the more efficient only if it is at least as effective as is the latter.)

The above discussion has been rather abstract, but its importance in the context of the local management of schools should be clearly appreciated. Headteachers and others involved in managing schools face numerous problems, many of which stem from the conflicting objectives of those with whom they work. Given that some groups' objectives include the efficient operation of the school, and given that resources are in any event limited, it may not be possible always to reconcile the warring goals of different members of the school body without resort to authoritarian tactics. Where possible, however, a dictatorial approach is best avoided, since full consultation encourages a movement towards the core of (Pareto) efficient solutions. The art of management inevitably requires prudent use of subjective judgement; the discipline imposed by economic analysis can inform both the manner in which that judgement is exercised and the observer's understanding of the decision-making process.

The increased devolution of responsibility to schools has raised awareness of the cost implications of managerial decisions. At the same time, the policy of decentralisation is likely to have an impact on the structure of costs in education. As the provision of education is freed of regulation, thereby becoming increasingly competitive, administrators become more keenly aware of the extent and nature of the costs involved. The remainder of this chapter, therefore, is devoted to an examination of the determinants of costs in schools and other institutions of learning.

## Optimal School Size

A crucial determinant of costs is that of school size. This issue often generates considerable controversy and is therefore worth considering separately from the other influences on costs. The closure of a small rural school on the grounds of high operating costs generally causes public concern. Certainly schools in such areas generate externalities – meeting rooms, sports facilities, community spirit – whose value to local residents is rarely included in calculations which balance costs against benefits. At the other end of the scale, large schools are sometimes criticised for being impersonal.

If schools were all privately run profit maximisers, then competition would ensure the survival of the fittest, and size would be one determinant of fitness. Where schools are predominantly owned and operated by a monopoly – the state – competition cannot be relied upon to drive the size of the representative school towards the optimum. For this reason it is particularly important that studies of costs be conducted in order to ascertain what conditions minimise costs at any given level of service.

Total costs consist of overheads and variable costs. The proportion of total costs accounted for by overheads might reasonably be expected to vary across types of school. In particular, fixed costs might (in relative terms) increase with the age of the pupils catered for by the school. Thus in primary schools, fixed inputs consist largely of buildings and furniture. In secondary schools, fixed costs include also more extensive laboratory equipment, and facilities for craftwork and computing. In the case of the tertiary sector, the costs associated with specialist equipment might reasonably be expected to be higher still.

By spreading overheads across many students, the burden of fixed cost per student declines. If fixed costs vary across the primary, secondary and tertiary sectors as hypothesised above, then the cost saving associated with increasing (from a given base) the size of the institution is most marked in higher education, and is least important in the case of the primary schools. In other words, operating educational establishments at minimum efficient size requires that secondary schools be larger than primary schools, and that institutions of higher education be larger than secondary schools.

Economies of scale may, of course, be overtaken by diseconomies as size increases beyond a certain limit. It would not be efficient to teach all teenagers in the country in a few massive schools. To do so would impose vast costs of commuting and/or boarding. It would lead to administrative difficulties and a substantial bureaucracy, and would result in time being wasted as teachers and pupils walk from one part of the school to another. It might also cause discipline problems. Such a school would be suffering diseconomies of scale.

The existence of both economies and diseconomies of scale suggests that there can be defined an optimal size (or an optimal range of sizes) for a school, at least in the primary and secondary sectors. Based upon the above arguments, it is expected that the optimal size for a primary school should be lower than that of a secondary school. Much empirical work has been conducted on this topic, especially in the USA; the results of several statistical studies are discussed below.

An important caveat attaches to the results reported in the remainder of this section. The work on optimal school size assumes that scale of operation can be measured by the number of pupils on the roll. No reference is made to differences in the quality of tuition, or indeed to any of the alternative measures of school performance which will be discussed later in the book (in Chapters 9 and 10). If the aim is to minimise school costs, given current levels of effectiveness, then this approach is valid. If, however, the aim of the exercise is to investigate the nature of the trade-offs between throughput, quality and scale, a more comprehensive approach is required. Such an approach would consider not only scale of operation as a determinant of costs, but would include also a range of measures of school performance. This would help policy-makers to decide on the most appropriate mix of school size, effectiveness and costs. It would enable them to define the size of school which provides the best education or the cheapest education or any desired combination of the two. The goal of the present section is, however, considerably more modest than that: here the aim is to hold quality constant, and thereby establish the cost-minimising size of schools in the primary, secondary and tertiary sectors.

In Britain, evidence on the existence of scale economies is provided by Coatesworth (1976), who studied a sample of primary schools in the mid-1970s. He concluded that cost per pupil varied little from school to school in the sub-sample of schools with enrolments of 70 or more pupils. In the case of smaller schools, however, he found that unit costs rose substantially as school size diminished. This result does not imply the existence of an optimal school size, but it does indicate that the minimum efficient size of a typical primary school is about 70 pupils. This result tallies well with the earlier finding of Cumming (1971) that in primary schools, unit costs fell as school size rose up to (but not beyond) a roll of 80 pupils. Hough (1981) also finds evidence of scale economies in primary schools, and confirms that, in general, unit costs do not turn up once they have reached their minimum. Many small primary schools in remote areas may survive despite high costs of operation, because it may be cheaper to keep these schools open than to transport pupils daily to the nearest town.

The findings reported above for Britain have been replicated in a number of other countries. The desire to exploit economies of scale in primary education led to the closure of thousands of small rural schools in the Soviet Union during the 1960s (Coombs and Hallak, 1972). A useful survey of school costs in LDCs is provided by Tsang (1988). In Australia, Hind (1977) has found that instructional expenditures per pupil in the primary school sector are related to enrolment, $Q$, according to the rule $AC = 173 + 3452/Q$. Thus average costs flatten out considerably above an enrolment of 100, and fall to within 10 per cent of their asymptotic minimum when enrolment reaches 200 pupils.

At secondary school level, a number of pioneering American studies are of interest. Many data on school costs in the US are collected at school district level, and information is not therefore available on individual high schools. This problem has been bypassed by Riew (1966), who investigated a sample of 109 school districts in Wisconsin; each of these school districts was unusual in that it contained only one senior high school. Since the data for each of these districts refer to a single school, they can be used in an analysis of school costs. Riew conducted a regression of operating expenditures per pupil, $AC$, against linear and quadratic terms in enrolment, $Q$, and a vector of miscellaneous variables. These included teacher salaries, the breadth of the curriculum, recent change in number of pupils, recent construction of buildings at the school, and the average number of courses taught by each teacher. The regression equation thus obtained was

$$AC = 0.00012Q^2 - 0.402Q + 10.31 + \ldots$$

Differentiating $AC$ with respect to $Q$ and setting the result to zero provides the first order condition for minimum average costs. This occurs with an enrolment of 1675 pupils.

Riew's method of analysing school districts in which there is only one high school has been employed also by Cohn (1968), who used data on over 370 school districts in Iowa. The results of this study are broadly in line with Riew's conclusions, in that the optimal school size turns out to be between 1500 and 2200. Further confirmation of this result is provided by Osburn (1970), who finds optimal enrolment near the top of this range. Kenny (1982) also finds evidence of substantial scale economies in US high schools.

The most thorough study of secondary school costs in Britain has been that of Hough (1981). His study of the secondary sector distinguished various types of school (grammar, secondary modern, comprehensive, high, middle and upper) within each of four (anonymous) Local Education Authorities. Various specifications of the total cost function were tested, including the linear, quadratic and cubic forms. In each case regression analysis was used to estimate the parameters of the total cost equation. The quadratic and cubic functional forms both enable a minimum average cost to be defined. Hough's findings include strong evidence of scale economies within the secondary sector.

The evidence on the existence of an optimal school size is more ambiguous. While the quadratic and cubic specifications of the total cost function work well, it is not clear that they provide significantly better fits to the data than does the more parsimonious linear specification. For those cases where a minimum of the average cost curve can be defined, optimal school size varies from 624 to 1765; in most cases the figure is fairly close to 1200. A typical example of the quadratic total cost function estimated by Hough is the following, which uses 1974–5 data for all secondary schools in Local Education Authority 'C':

$$C = 0.05Q^2 + 93.87Q + 68489$$

This generates an average cost curve with a minimum at $Q^* = 1170$ pupils, as shown in Figure 6.1.

Butel and Atkinson (1983) have conducted a statistical analysis of the relationship between costs and size in a sample of 48 British comprehensive schools, all of which lay within the jurisdiction of a single Local Education Authority. They used a regression analysis with total costs as the dependent variable, and included linear, quadratic and cubic versions of school size as explanatory variables. Dividing both sides of the estimated equation by school size provides an estimate of the average cost curve. The minimum of the average cost curve occurs when the school enrols some 1147 pupils. However, the evidence pointing to scale diseconomies is weak; consequently, while confident about the presence of economies of scale, Butel and Atkinson are more cautious about their estimate of optimal school size.

The optimal school size estimates obtained for secondary schools in the UK are therefore somewhat lower than is the case in the USA. This illustrates a danger in applying results of cost studies conducted in one country to the case of a second country. A number of reasons may explain why optimal school size appears to be higher in the USA than in the UK. First, overheads may be higher in the USA; this may be so if laboratories contain more expensive equipment, or if sports facilities are more extensive, or if the local management of

**FIGURE 6.1**
**Costs in UK Secondary Schools, 1974–75**

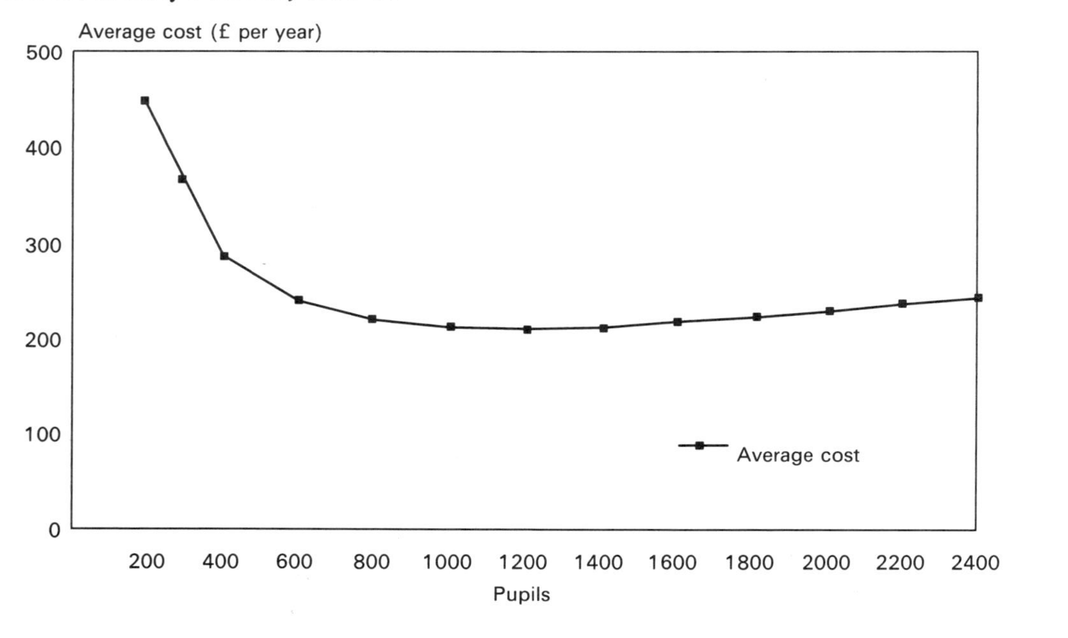

schools requires greater managerial expenditure at school level. Second, average variable costs may follow a country-specific pattern; if relatively large plots of land are cheaply available in the USA, then schools may cover a relatively large area, thus alleviating capacity constraints. Finally, estimates of the enrolment consistent with minimum unit costs can be sensitive to small changes in the estimated coefficients; if the coefficients have high standard errors then too much significance should not be attached to the precise estimates of optimal school size.

At tertiary level, two British studies are of interest. Layard and Verry (1975) find evidence to support considerable scale economies in the universities. Their preferred specification of the total cost function is linear; this is restrictive in that it does not allow the unit cost curve to bottom out. Let the subject-specific total cost, $C$, be a linear function of undergraduate student places, $Q_1$, postgraduate numbers, $Q_2$, and a measure of research activity, $R$, so that

$$C = a_0 + a_1 Q_1 + a_2 Q_2 + a_3 R$$

Fixed costs within the subject area thus equal $a_0$, while the marginal cost associated with an additional undergraduate student is constant and is defined by $\partial C / \partial Q_1 = a_1$. Given $Q_2$ and $R$, the average cost of an undergraduate falls as $Q_1$ rises and is given by $a_1 + (a_0 + a_2 Q_2 + a_3 R)/Q_1$.

Estimates of the parameters, $a_0$, $a_1$, $a_2$ and $a_3$ are obtained by the weighted least squares regression method, using cross-section data for 1968–9. The analysis is conducted across six broadly defined subject areas. Each university represents a single data point in each of the six regression runs (so long as that university has departments working in the relevant subject area). This gives a sample size of between 42 and 57.

Annual fixed costs varied considerably across subject areas. While insignificant in the case of the physical sciences, fixed costs amounted to (on average) over £9000 in the social sciences (at 1968–9 prices). The increase in cost associated with the enrolment of an additional undergraduate student on a course also varied according to subject area, but the linear specification of the total cost schedule constrains marginal cost to be constant with respect to the number of students registered on each course. Marginal cost was lowest for mathematics (at about £120) and highest in engineering (at around £440). In the case of postgraduates, marginal cost was found to be considerably higher. This varied from about £420 in the arts to around £1500 in the case of the physical sciences.

More recently, Osborne (1989) has repeated the Layard and Verry exercise using pooled time series and cross-section data for 30 British polytechnics from 1978 to 1986. In this case, neither subject-specific data nor information about research activity are available, however. The estimated total cost curve is $C = 4464834 + 3194Q$, where $Q$ measures full-time equivalent (FTE) students. Marginal cost is therefore constant at £3194 (at 1986 prices), and average cost falls as $Q$ rises to yield the curve shown in Figure 6.2. Average costs fall to within 10 per cent of their asymptotic minimum as enrolment rises towards 14 000 students.

The optimal size of institution at tertiary level has also been investigated in a number of other countries. In the USA, studies on the viablility of colleges have found that tertiary sector schools with low enrolment of FTE students are relatively likely to suffer financial distress (Andrew and Friedman, 1976; Gilmartin, 1984). The World Bank (1986) found that substantial scale economies exist in the tertiary education sector in China, up to an enrolment of about 1000 students. Their equation was

$$AC = 2.42 - 1.048Q/10^4 + 4.368Q^2/10^9 + 0.129SSR$$
$$(11.4) \quad (1.2) \qquad\qquad (0.6) \qquad\qquad (5.3)$$

where $SSR$ denotes the student:staff ratio. The determination coefficient, at 0.53, indicates a reasonably good fit, but the $t$ statistics (in parentheses) on the scale variables indicate that little confidence can be placed in the observed non-linearity of the unit cost function in this case.

In a cross-section study using data across 143 countries, Lee (1984) found a similar pattern of unit costs in universities and colleges; average costs decline significantly as enrolment rises up to 10 000 students. The pattern of costs in higher education therefore appears to be fairly robust across national boundaries.

In this section we have seen that scale effects matter in the determination of costs in all sectors of education. While some country-to-country variation in the optimal size may exist, the broad pattern which emerges is remarkably robust across numerous

**FIGURE 6.2**
**Costs in UK Polytechnics, 1978–86**

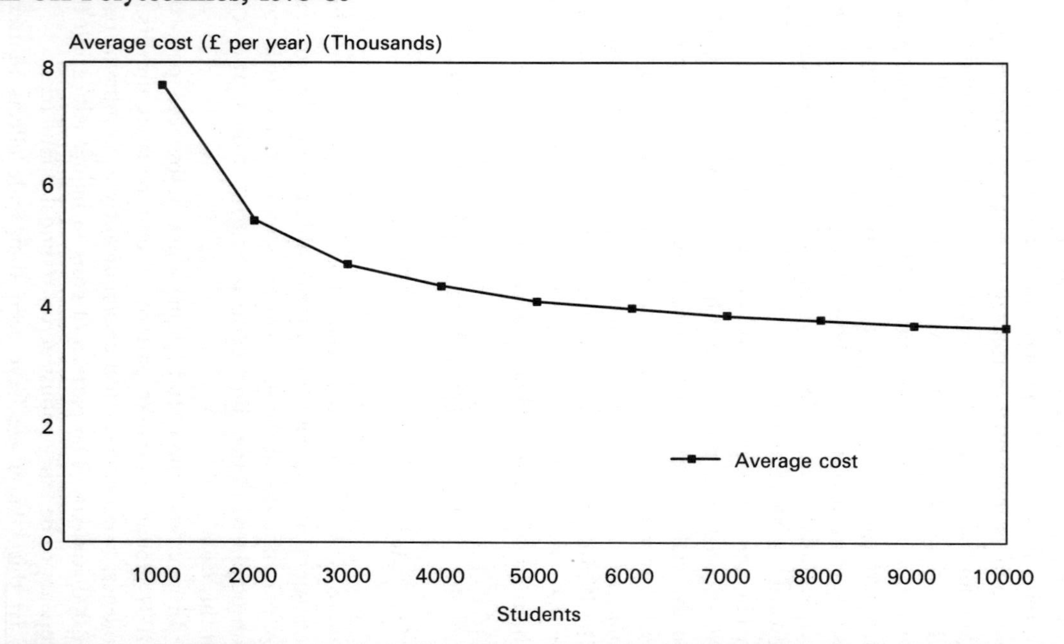

studies conducted in many countries. A definite pattern of scale effects can be indentified which distinguishes the primary, secondary and tertiary sectors of education. Primary schools can realise substantial scale economies up to an enrolment of about 80 pupils; thereafter costs level off. Secondary schools experience economies of scale as enrolment rises towards the cost-minimising level, but suffer diseconomies beyond this point. The optimum appears to vary somewhat across national boundaries; in the UK it is about 1200 but it is somewhat higher in the USA. Finally, substantial (long run) scale economies can be exploited in the tertiary sector, where the optimal size is likely to be 10 000 students or more.

# Other Determinants of Costs

Scale of operation is, of course, only one of many determinants of school costs. Most of the studies referred to above include in the analysis a variety of control variables, each of which also exerts an impact on the cost of operation. These variables form the subject of the discussion in the present section.

Early work in the USA has unearthed a tendency for the unit costs of education to be relatively high in large urban areas (Levin, Muller and Sandoval, 1973). This is largely a function of labour costs: teachers working in the cities tend to be more experienced and better qualified than those employed in rural areas. Moreover, there is a greater demand in the cities for teachers who cater for special needs such as remedial tuition. The premia paid to such teachers raise unit costs in these areas. Extra compensation may also need to be paid to teachers working in uncomfortable environments, or to those facing the relatively high living costs of the city. In the inner cities, special programmes designed to offset the educational disadvantage conferred by poverty can also serve to raise expenditure. Higher overheads might be incurred if disciplinary and administrative problems are associated with city size. In addition to these labour costs, the high price of land in urban areas adds to the fixed costs faced by the school.

Since education is, in many countries, financed largely by local government, the affluence of the area surrounding a school can positively influence the level of education expenditure. James, Kelly and Garms (1966) have found a positive association between the average wealth of a district's residents and the cost of educating a representative pupil at the local schools. This does not necessarily mean that schools in such areas are inefficient, however, since they may be providing each pupil with a greater quantity of educational services than is available to pupils in other localities.

Cumming (1971) stresses the role of subject mix as a determinant of unit costs. Partly as a consequence of typical class sizes, partly owing to systematic inter-subject differences in the qualifications and seniority of teaching staff, and partly because of hardware requirements, the unit costs attached to tuition vary across subjects. At secondary school level, the inter-subject variation is wide. Staffing costs per pupil-year varied from £3.26 for music to £31.25 for the classics (at 1968–9 prices). Small class sizes account in large measure for the high costs attached to the teaching of classics. Amongst the more popular subjects, modern languages and English had unit costs more than twice as high as history and geography. It is likely, therefore, that differences in curriculum (between, say, grammar and secondary modern schools) explains much of the observed differences in costs across schools.

Other factors which are likely to influence average costs of school operation include the type of heating fuel used, the frequency of cleaning, and the extent of evening, weekend and vacation use by outside organisations. The age of the school buildings also influences the level of maintenance expenditure. As we saw in the last section, fixed costs also tend to rise along with the age group of the pupils for whom the school caters.

An interesting view of the determination of education costs – and in particular the costs of higher education – has been proposed by Bowen (1980). This approach assumes that institutions of higher education seek to maximise not profits but prestige. Prestige, $P$, is a function of the quantity and quality of the teaching, $T$, and research, $R$, activity undertaken by the institution. But teaching and research both cost money. The cost of each unit of teaching may be denoted by $c_t$, and the cost of each unit of research may be given by $c_r$. In order to maximise its prestige, 'each instituion raises all the money it can' and 'each institution spends all it raises'. Total costs therefore must equal the budget, $B$, and are limited only by the institution's ability to raise funds. The implication of this model is that costs are not defined by technology as is the case in profit-maximising competitive industries; instead, costs are limited only by the means of those (legislators, firms and students) who provide institutions with money.

Bowen's model can usefully be formalised as follows. The maximand is prestige, and this may be assumed to take the form

$$\max_{R,\,T} \quad P = RT \tag{6.1}$$

The constraint is

$$c_r R + c_t T = B(P) \tag{6.2}$$

where

$$B(P) = P^{\alpha} \qquad 0 \leq \alpha \leq 0.5 \tag{6.3}$$

Using standard Lagrangian methods to solve the problem given by (6.1)–(6.3) yields the solution for research

$$R = [(c_r/c_t)^{\alpha}/2c_r]^{1/(1-2\alpha)} \tag{6.4}$$

and for teaching

$$T = c_r R/c_t \tag{6.5}$$

Consider cases where $(c_r/c_t)^{\alpha} > 2c_r$. It is clear from (6.4) that a rise in the willingness, $\alpha$, of donors to give money to the institution will raise research activity. From (6.5), it also raises teaching provision. Prestige and costs are therefore constrained by the limits to donors' willingness to give. If $\alpha$ tends towards 0.5, then prestige and costs will tend towards infinity. This special case is of particular concern to Bowen, since it implies 'ever-increasing expenditure'.

More generally, Bowen's model of the determination of output and costs in higher education implies a vicious circle of high prestige, high levels of giving, and high costs. This does not necessarily lead to the endless acceleration of costs above (a vicious spiral). But it does suggest that institutions of higher education may not be subject to the market disciplines imposed upon competitive, profit-maximising firms. To the extent that this is so in practice, the costs of higher education are likely to lie above the Paretian welfare optimum. The model does not subject research and teaching to diminishing returns, so there is no inbuilt limit on institutions' activity. Whether or not this is realistic is, of course, an empirical matter.

Brinkman (1981) presents a study of the variables which determine unit instructional costs in American universities. He divides the influences on costs into two broad categories, namely 'input variables' and 'output variables'. The former group consists of factors which might influence costs given the level of educational services provided; the latter group is made up of variables which capture differences in the quantity of education produced. Multicollinearity problems emerge when both input and output variables are used on the right-hand side of the regression equation (not surprisingly, since inputs typically determine outputs). When input variables alone appear as explanatory variables in the unit cost regression, the following exert significant influence (at 5 per cent): the ratio of academic staff (faculty) to FTE students, the average salary paid to academic staff, and the per capitum level of personal incomes in the county within which the university is located. The last of these variables is intended to represent the salaries paid to non-academic staff. A fourth input variable – the ratio of non-academic staff to FTE students – is significant only at the 10 per cent level. As expected, all these input variables positively influence unit costs.

The output variables used in Brinkman's analysis are generally more powerful in explaining variation in unit costs than are the input variables. The statistically significant output variables used are (at 5 per cent): total FTE enrolment (used as a proxy for the number of graduates), the proportion of postgraduates in the student body, and the diversity of the university's curriculum (measured by the number of degree programmes on offer per 1000 students). An increase in either of the latter two variables serves to raise costs. The scale variable (FTE enrolment) affects unit costs in the non-linear fashion suggested by the results of the last section. A fourth output variable, measuring research emphasis, also influences costs – institutions which are more active on the research front tend to have higher unit costs than others – but this is significant only at the 10 per cent level.

In Britain, Johnes (1990) has analysed costs using a cross section regression based upon data for 45 universities. The data set used in this study enables an evaluation of the impact on unit costs of inter-university differences in the mix of subjects taught. As Peston (1985) has argued, there are substantial differences in unit costs across subjects, so a university which concentrates its activity in more expensive subjects (such as medicine or physics) will tend to have higher overall costs than one which specialises in, say, law or accountancy. Johnes calculates (for each university and across all subjects) a weighted average of the national mean subject-specific unit costs (where the weights are the proportion of FTE students in each subject); this is a measure of the unit cost which each university can expect to face on the basis of its subject mix. Some two-thirds of inter-institution variation in cost per FTE student is explained by differences in this variable alone. Two other variables significantly affect unit costs; the first is the proportion of postgraduates in the student body, and the second is the ratio of (full-time) academic staff to FTE students. As was the case in Brinkman's study of the USA, unit costs proved to be positively related to both of these explanatory variables.

# Conclusion

The investigation of the determinants of costs in the field of education has, as is clear from the foregoing discussion, occupied the time of many researchers. The structure of unit costs, and especially the question of optimal school size, has been of particular concern. Yet the problem remains, what is a unit of education?

Should the output of a school be the number of pupils passing through its roll (including truants and those who pass no examinations), or should it be the number of pupils who leave with good examination results (however defined)? Or should it be the number of pupils who have learned to become 'good citizens' through their attendance at school? Since the value added by education varies from pupil to pupil, defining the yardstick by which educational service is measured is difficult. Measuring the educational service provided by each school against such a yardstick is harder still.

The studies surveyed in the present chapter bypass this difficulty by assuming the pupil to be the unit of measurement. Now it is clear that costs per pupil could be reduced simply by reducing the standard of provision of education. If the standard of provision of education declines as school size increases, then it may be the case that costs per unit of educational service do not decline as the quantity of educational services provided increases. In other words, the finding that economies of scale exist in education could be due entirely to the use of an inappropriate indicator of educational output.

To illustrate this, note that cost per pupil declines as class size increases (Cumming, 1971). At the same time, it has been established that pupils' academic achievement is greater, *ceteris paribus*, the smaller the size of class (Finn and Achilles, 1990). There is certainly no clear-cut evidence here to support the existence of economies of scale.

A comprehensive analysis of unit costs in education should take these issues into account. A variety of yardsticks needs to be used to measure the provision of education. The best of the studies referred to above include controls such as examination performance as explanatory variables in the cost function. This mitigates the problem to some extent, but (given enrolment) much remains to be learned about the nature of the trade-offs between costs and the quality of provision.

# Appendix 1: Arrow's Impossibility Theorem

To illustrate the operation of Arrow's impossibility theorem in the case of a school, consider an example in which limited resources can be put to one of three uses. The school may invest in a shop which sells goods bearing the school crest (call this option $x$); or the school may hire an extra careers adviser (option $y$); or the school may hire an extra economics teacher (option $z$). Suppose further that there are three groups with an interest in the school: governors, parents, and the local public. Except by acting dictatorially, the decision-maker has no decision-making mechanism at her disposal which simultaneously satisfies all of the following rules.

1. If all groups in the 'society' of the school express a preference for a given use of the resources (over and above a given alternative use), then society too has this same preference.
2. The preferences of each group, and those of society, must be transitive. In other words, if a group prefers $x$ to $y$ and prefers also $y$ to $z$, then the group must prefer $x$ to $z$.
3. Society's ranking of alternative uses for the available resources depends only on the uses under consideration. Other alternatives (such as, in our example, the construction of a new classroom) are not allowed to

influence a group's preferences defined across the uses being considered ($x$, $y$, and $z$). If, when no new classroom is to be built, governors prefer $x$ to $y$, for example, and also prefer $y$ to $z$, then a decision to build a new classroom can have no impact upon this preference ordering. This rule is frequently summarised as the independence of irrelevant alternatives.

4. The mechanism must work for all logically possible orderings of preferences by the groups constituting society.

Majority voting clearly satisfies rules 1 and 3. It cannot, however, satisfy the remaining conditions. This is because of the possible occurrence of a paradox which was first analysed by Condorcet (1785). Suppose governors' preferences are given by $xPyPz$, where the operator $P$ denotes 'is preferred to'. Suppose further that, for the local public $yPzPx$, and for parents $zPxPy$. Although the majority of groups prefer $x$ to $y$, and the majority of groups prefer $y$ to $z$, it is also the case that the majority of groups prefer $z$ to $x$. Any social ranking which emerged from majority voting in this example would therefore be intransitive.

Consider, then, an alternative to majority voting, namely rank order voting. In this voting system each group expresses its preferences across all alternatives by placing '1' against its preferred alternative, '2' against the next best option, and so on. The votes received by each option are then added across all groups, and the alternative with the lowest score wins. In the example considered above, this would lead to a three way tie between the options $x$, $y$ and $z$. Each option would pick up 6 votes. But consider what would happen if the public decided that they prefer $z$ to $y$, while they still prefer $y$ to $x$. Concentrating on options $x$ and $y$, $z$ now should be an irrelevant alternative: society's preference ordering between $x$ (the shop) and $y$ (the careers advisor) should not be affected in any way by a change in one group's view of the importance of an extra economics teacher (option $z$). However, since after this change in preference $y$ receives only 5 votes, while $x$ still receives 6, the change in the public's perception of option $z$ results in a change in society's preference ordering between $x$ and $y$. In other words, the rank order voting scheme violates the rule of the independence of irrelevant alternatives.

The majority voting and the rank order voting schemes discussed above are merely examples. Arrow has gone much further than this, however, to show that *no* voting scheme can be conceived which can always enable the meaningful aggregation of groups' (or individuals') preferences. He has therefore generalised Condorcet's paradox, so that the result applies to all possible voting systems, not just majority voting.

# Appendix 2: The Core

Suppose that the three groups identified in Appendix 1, namely governors ($g$), parents ($p$) and the local public ($l$) each have utility defined across the three goods, $x$, $y$, and $z$. The prices of these three goods are given by $p_x$, $p_y$

and $p_z$ respectively. The school's budget, $B$, for spending on the three goods is fixed. The utility enjoyed by the three groups are defined respectively by $U_g$, $U_p$ and $U_l$, where

$$U_g = x^{\alpha}y^{\beta}z^{\gamma} \tag{A.1}$$

$$U_p = x^{\beta}y^{\gamma}z^{\alpha} \tag{A.2}$$

$$U_l = x^{\gamma}y^{\alpha}z^{\beta} \tag{A.3}$$

and where $\alpha > \beta > \gamma$ and $\alpha + \beta + \gamma = 1$ for simplicity.

Pareto optimality requires that an allocation of $x, y$ and $z$ be found which satisfies the rule that no group's utility can be raised without harming the utility of any other group. The set of Pareto optimal allocations of $x, y$ and $z$ consists of all points on the budget constraint within the area defined by the following coordinates:

$$x = \alpha B/p_x\gamma[1 + (\alpha + \beta)/\gamma];\ y = \beta B/p_y\gamma[1 + (\alpha + \beta/\gamma];\ z = B/p_z[1 + (\alpha + \beta)/\gamma] \tag{A.4}$$

$$x = \beta B/p_x\alpha[1 + (\beta + \gamma)/\alpha];\ y = \gamma B/p_y\alpha[1 + (\beta + \gamma)/\alpha];\ z = B/p_z[1 + (\beta + \gamma)/\alpha] \tag{A.5}$$

$$x = \gamma B/p_x\beta[1 + (\alpha + \gamma)/\beta];\ y = \alpha B/p_y\beta[1 + (\alpha + \gamma)/\beta] \therefore\ z = B/p_z[1 + (\alpha + \gamma)/\beta] \tag{A.6}$$

These coordinates represent respectively the preferred positions of groups $g, p$ and $l$.

Suppose, for concreteness, that $p_x = 5$, $p_y = 10$ and $p_z = 15$. Assume further that $B = 150$ and that $\alpha = 0.5$, $\beta = 0.3$ and $\gamma = 0.2$. An initial allocation of $x = y = 1$ and $z = 9$ would yield utilities of $U_g = 1.55$, $U_p = 3.00$ and $U_l = 1.93$. This is not an efficient solution, however, since an alternative allocation of the available resources between $x, y$ and $z$ could increase the utility of all groups. For example, an allocation of $x = 9, y = 6$ and $z = 3$ would yield $U_g = 6.34$, $U_p = 4.79$ and $U_l = 5.29$, thus increasing every group's utility in relation to the initial position. This latter allocation is in the core: no further transfers of expenditure between the three goods can yield Pareto benefits. An infinity of other Pareto efficient points form the rest of the core; these include allocations such as $(x, y, z) = (8, 5, 4)$ and $(x, y, z) = (9, 3, 5)$.

The core can usefully be interpreted as the set of points in $(x, y, z)$ space within which the final solution will lie if bargaining between the parties is efficient. It is analogous to the familiar contract curve of Edgeworth box analysis. Indeed, the existence of a core indicates that 'there is something to negotiate about' (Colman, 1982). Economic theory cannot predict where in the core the final solution will lie; this must depend on the relative bargaining strengths of the parties involved, or on the judgement of the arbiter. But any efficient solution to a bargaining problem – if one exists – must lie within the core. Of course, it would be possible to move from one point to another within the core. Such a move would not be Pareto efficient (since at least one group would be made worse off), but it would not leave potential gains unexploited (as would an allocation outside the core). Economists cannot, therefore, without making value judgements, comment on point to point moves within the core.

Arrow's impossibility theorem says that a solution to the problem of aggregating preferences across groups may not exist. Likewise there is no guarantee that the core exists. That this is so can be seen easily by replacing the Cobb–Douglas utility functions used above by Stone–Geary functions which specify that utility can only be positive if more than a (group-specific) minimum provision of a good is available. Impose also a constraint on the model that the utility of all groups should be strictly positive in the core. If the cost of providing the minimum quantity of $x$ required by (say) the governors plus the minimum amount of $y$ required by (say) the parents exceeds $B$, then no core exists. There is no scope for Paretian bargaining. The ability to tell whether a core exists and (if it does) where it is located is therefore an important attribute for any managerial decision-maker.

# 7 Auctions, Vouchers and Loans

## Introduction

The finance of education has been the subject of close scrutiny in the recent past. Many changes in the education system, while desirable, have not come cheap; these include postgraduate teacher training, comprehensive education, the raising of the school leaving age, the widening of access to higher education, and the purchase of computing and other modern equipment. However, radical new proposals have been developed and put into practice which promise to revolutionise the manner in which education is funded. Running through these proposals are two common themes: sources of finance other than the state should be sought out, and the education system should be encouraged to become more efficient.

In this chapter, three of the new ideas will be analysed in detail. The first of these is the system introduced by the higher education funding councils in the UK, whereby institutions bid for students as if they were bidding in an auction. In discussing this proposal it is useful to appeal to the extensive economic literature on the theory of auctions. The second is the voucher system which has been tested in schools in the USA and as a means of financing vocational training in the UK. This system imposes upon schools the discipline of the market by extending parental choice; parents (or students) are allocated education vouchers which they may then spend at the school of their choice. The proposal is therefore analogous to the popular luncheon voucher scheme which is offered as a perquisite to many employees. The third proposal discussed in this chapter concerns the maintenance allowance given to students in higher education; the issue of grants versus loans will be considered, and the new Australian graduate tax will also be analysed.

## Auctions

The theory of auctions has generated considerable interest amongst both theoretical and applied economists in recent years. The seminal work of Vickrey (1961) was followed – albeit after a long lag – by a large volume of research during the 1970s and 1980s. This is usefully surveyed in papers by McAfee and McMillan (1987) and by Milgrom (1989).

There are two basic types of auction. Variants of each type exist, but here we concentrate only on the simple models. These are the *first-bid* auction and the *second-bid* auction. In the case of the first-bid auction, independent bidders simultaneously submit their bids in confidence to the auctioneer. The auctioneer then awards the contract to the bidder offering the best price. The price paid is the price bid by the winning bidder. The second-bid auction differs from the first-bid auction in that the contract is awarded at the price offered by the second-best bidder. This guarantees the winner a positive economic surplus.

Under weak assumptions, the first-bid auction is formally equivalent to the Dutch auction, and the second-bid auction is equivalent to the English auction. In a Dutch auction, the auctioneer starts the bidding process by offering the lot at a price which he is sure no bidder will accept. He then gradually moves the price in a direction favourable to the bidders. The first bidder to accept the price offered by the auctioneer is successful, and the price paid is the price bid by the successful bidder. Thus only the 'first' bid matters. In an English auction, on the other hand, the auctioneer starts the bidding process by offering the lot at a price which he deems to be acceptable to many bidders. The bidders then compete against each other by moving the price in the direction which is unfavourable to themselves. The successful bidder is the one who stays in the race the longest. The price paid by the winner is the best price offered by the last of her rival bidders to survive; that is, the price is determined by the 'second' bid.

English auctions are commonly used in the sale of artwork, antiques and wine; in these cases the seller is a monopolist. Dutch auctions are used for selling goods such as cut flowers in the Netherlands. However, the Dutch auction tends to be more commonly used in the context of monopsony. In particular, government procurement contracts are frequently settled by first-bid auction.

Since (at least) two types of auction are available, it is important when considering the introduction of an auction scheme into a new context to determine which is the more efficient method. In other words, is it the first-bid or the second-bid auction which produces the greater surpluses to the buyer and seller? The rather surprising answer to this question is that – under reasonable assumptions – it makes no difference! A particularly simple example which serves to demonstrate this result is given below.

Suppose that two bidders are buying lots of fixed size and that, for the representative lot, each bidder sets a reservation price (or valuation) above which she derives no surplus. The representative bidder will bid in a fashion governed by her reservation price and by the rules of the auction. Assume that reservation prices follow a uniform distribution over the (0,1) interval. Each bidder knows both her own reservation price and the shape of the probability distribution, but is uncertain about her rival's valuation. Let the auction rule be given by the formula

$$P = \lambda W + (1 - \lambda)L \tag{7.1}$$

where $W$ is the first (winning) bid, and $L$ is the second (losing) bid. The weight, $\lambda$, may be interpreted as follows: if $\lambda = 0$, then the rules of the second-bid auction apply; if $\lambda = 1$, the rules of a first-bid auction apply; and if $0 < \lambda < 1$, then the hammer price is given by some weighted average of the first and second bids. The surplus enjoyed by the winning bidder is therefore

$$S^* = V^* - \lambda W - (1 - \lambda)L \tag{7.2}$$

where $V^*$ is the winner's valuation of the lot.

Given the assumption of a uniform distribution, the expected value of the losing bid is given by $L = W/2$. Moreover, since the distribution extends over the unit interval, the *ex ante* probability that the representative bidder, making a bid of $B$, wins the auction is given by $F(B) = B$. The typical bidder, whose reservation price is $V$, therefore maximises her expected surplus by choosing B to solve

$$\max_{B} \quad B[V - B(1 + \lambda)/2] \tag{7.3}$$

The first order condition is found by differentiating equation (7.3) with respect to $B$, and setting the result to zero. This implies that the representative bidder should set her bid so that $B = V/(1 + \lambda)$. Note that this implies that in the second-bid auction, the bidder will choose to bid up to her reservation price, while in the first-bid auction she will need to post a lower bid (namely $V/2$) in order to maximise her expected surplus. In both of these extreme cases, the surplus expected by the representative bidder (conditional upon winning the auction) is $V/2$. In the first-bid auction, this is because the winner (who is the price maker) optimally bids only half her valuation. In the second-bid auction, it is because the statistical expectation of the second bid (given that the highest bid is $V$) lies mid-way between zero and $V$. Since the bidder's surplus is robust with respect to auction type in this fixed lot auction, the price does not vary according to the scheme used either. On average, in this example, we would expect the winning bidder's valuation to be 2/3. Consequently, her surplus will be 1/3 and the price paid to the monopolist will be 1/3.

This result, known as the *revenue equivalence theorem*, is surprising because one might expect the first-bid scheme to yield lower surpluses to the bidder than does the second-bid scheme. This does not occur in the above model, however, because bidders take this into account when formulating their bidding strategy.

This being so, it is rather surprising to find that, in practice, the type of auction does seem to matter. The stylised facts are that while most auctions are of the second-bid type, procurement auctions are generally of the first-bid variety. Such distinct patterns of behaviour suggest that the revenue equivalence theorem fails to tell the whole story. As a result, much recent research into auctions has focused on the identification of conditions under which the theorem does not hold. An example of this literature is a paper by Robert Hansen (1988), which successfully explains the tendency for procurement auctions to follow the first-bid procedure.

The assumptions of Hansen's model differ from those used to generate the revenue equivalence theorem in only one respect. In the earlier model the lots were of fixed size; thus bidders in an art sale would make offers to buy one painting, and bidders for road construction contracts would make offers to build one road. We now change this assumption so that the quantity traded may vary with the bid price. The reservation price adopted by each bidder is assumed to be invariant with respect to quantity traded. Thus, the higher the price in an art auction, the more paintings will be supplied for sale within the same lot; likewise the lower the price in an auction for construction contracts, the more roads will the authorities demand within the same lot.

In the case of a second-bid auction, nothing changes. The successful bidder is a price-taker, since she cannot influence the value of the second-best bid which determines price. It is always optimal, therefore, for the bidder to bid her reservation price; this is because the price paid in the event of her winning will be more favourable (to the bidder) than the reservation price, thus ensuring that the winner secures a positive surplus. In the first-bid auction, however, the new assumption makes a difference, since the bidder's own actions determine the quantity traded (if she is successful). This means that there is an additional incentive for the bidder to bid more aggressively, since what she loses in terms of price per unit traded can be compensated for in terms of quantity traded. In sum, then, given the new set of assumptions, a first-bid auction will (compared to a second-bid rule) lead to a greater quantity being traded at a price less favourable to the bidder.

The above argument can be expressed in more formal terms as follows. Specifically, suppose that the quantity sold by the monopolist, $Q$, rises with price so that $Q = 1 + P$, subject to a constraint set by the bidder's reservation price. If $P > V$, then the bidder will choose not to buy any units of the good. This constraint is crucial to the argument. All other assumptions of the model stay as before. Under a second-bid auction the constraint operates, and the optimal bidding behaviour is to bid up to $V$. It follows that under a second-bid scheme, the outcome of the auction is the same as it was in the fixed lot size case. Under the first-bid auction, however, the optimal bid is now $B = (V^2 + 10V + 1)^{0.5}/6 - (1 - V)/3$. The expected winner's valuation is, as before, 2/3. The winning bid, and so also the price, is expected to be 0.36. The quantity traded is therefore expected to be 1.36, and the expected surplus obtained by the successful bidder now rises, since she sells more units than before. To be specific, expected surplus is $1.36 \times (0.67 - 0.36) = 0.41$. At the same time, the price received by the monopolist rises to 0.36 per unit. Both buyers and seller will therefore prefer to use a first-bid rather than a second-bid auction.

So long as the benefit to the bidder of increased quantity can compensate for the lower margin which she enjoys on each unit, the bidder will favour a first-bid approach to the auction. On the other side of the market, the monopsonist (or monopolist) will also benefit from the use of a first-bid scheme via an increase in consumer (or producer) surplus, so long as the demand function is concave (or not excessively convex).

It is often the case in auctions for procurement of government contracts that the government will buy services from the bidder offering the lowest prices in a quantity that varies negatively with the price. The Hansen model therefore explains why such auctions are typically operated according to a first-bid rule. This result is of crucial relevance in the context of auctions for procurement in the education sector, as we shall see later in this chapter.

Before ending the discussion of the theory of auctions, it is worth mentioning a phenomenon which many successful bidders discover only through bitter experience. This is known as the *winner's curse.* The winner's curse can be an outcome of either first-bid or second-bid auctions, and is an occurrence which may easily be explained by theory. Put simply, the winner's curse is this: when a bidder is successful at auction, and so wins a contract to supply services, her costs (on average) turn out to exceed expectations. Consequently, an organisation which wins an auction can end up making large losses.

The theoretical explanation for the winner's curse is simple. Suppose that each bidder makes an estimate of the costs attached to fulfilling a contract. These estimates will be subject to random error, but these errors are assumed unbiased, so that on average each bidder's cost estimates are accurate. Now, in spite of this lack of bias at aggregate level, in each auction the firm making the *lowest* bid (which is probably made by a different firm in different auctions) does so on the basis of a downwardly biased estimate of its costs. This is because some firms underestimate their costs while others overestimate them, and the successful firms at auction will in general come from the former group. Consequently the successful bidder will often find its costs turn out to be greater than expected. This is precisely the winner's curse result. Unfortunately, the only way to avoid experience of the winner's curse involves increasing the risk of losing profitable contracts by bidding cautiously.

In the next section we shall investigate auctions in education, and empirical observation will be related to the theory outlined above. In particular, the introduction of bidding systems as a means of encouraging greater efficiency in the production of educational services will be investigated, and evidence of the performance of such schemes will be considered.

# Auctions in Education

Auctions of various types have a long history as a means of price determination in the field of education. A common example of their use concerns tendering for research and consultancy contracts. In this section, however, we shall concentrate primarily on two of the more controversial proposals of recent years in the British education system. These are the schemes devised by the Universities Funding Council (UFC) and the Polytechnics and Colleges Funding Council (PCFC) whereby institutions bid against each other for students; institutions charging relatively low tuition fees are thus allowed to recruit disproportionately many students (UFC, 1989; J. Johnes and Taylor, 1990, pp.44–9; Turner and Pratt, 1990). The aim of the auction is to increase the cost effectiveness of higher education provision.

Public funding dedicated to the finance of undergraduate teaching activity reaches UK universities through two distinct channels. The first is student fees. These are typically paid for by the students' local authorities. Until 1990, these fees were set at levels far below the true cost of provision: in 1989/90, for example, the fee for a full time undergraduate was just over £600 for the year. Since then, fees have been increased substantially, especially for students studying more resource-intensive subjects (such as sciences or medicine). Even after these fee increases, fees still cover only about 30 per cent of the recurrent costs of undergraduate tuition.

Student fees for various subjects are determined by the government. In recent years the tendency has been to allow fees to vary positively with the costs of provision. There is no guarantee, however, that the government will in future refrain from adjusting the fee structure in a manner designed to favour certain subjects. Indeed, precisely such an adjustment was made in the wake of the 1992 Autumn Statement. This is curious in view of the government's declared goal of a market-driven system, and its declared hostility to HRP at the macroeconomic level.

The second channel through which public funds for teaching reach the universities in the UK is the block grant. The block grant is distributed by the UFC. Part of the block grant is intended to promote research activity; the allocation of this element depends in part on measures of universities' research performance. The remainder of the UFC block grant to universities represents payments made to cover the costs of undergraduate teaching. It is this latter element of the block grant that has recently been revamped by the introduction of an auction system. The auction scheme works as follows.

The UFC publishes 'guide prices' for student places in each subject area. These have initially been determined by the average cost of tuition in each subject area. Institutions are invited to bid for funded students at prices at or below the guide prices. Each university's bid in each subject area consists of an offer to provide services for a specific number of students at a specific price; both the bid number of students and the bid price are at the institution's discretion. In this respect the auction differs from any of those discussed earlier where the bidder is a quantity-taker. Subject to quality assurances, the UFC bases the allocation of students across universities on the bids received. Funds are thus allocated in a manner which, *ceteris paribus*, favours universities which submit low bids. The process therefore follows the principle of a first-price auction.

There are two scenarios in which institutions might undercut guide prices. First, institutions may, by way of efficiency gains, be able to lower their unit costs, thereby enabling them profitably to provide services at prices below the guide levels. Essentially, this scenario highlights the role of the auction process in providing an incentive to remove x-inefficiencies.

The second scenario, by way of contrast, assumes that the position of the institutions' cost curves is fixed, and that no x-inefficiencies remain. In this case, the marginal cost of provision may lie below the average cost, so that the institution might raise its surplus by taking on extra students at prices below the guide prices (that is, below average cost). In this manner, advantage can be taken of hitherto unexploited economies of scale.

Clearly, institutions cannot supply services to all students at prices which fall short of average cost unless further support is forthcoming to cover fixed costs. Such overheads can be financed partly through earmarked UFC grants for non-recurrent expenditures, and partly through private sector funding. The UFC can then allow the bidding process to determine the per capitum prices which may be below average cost.

The first run of the new UFC auction system occurred in 1990, and was intended to determine the allocation of student places across universities over the planning period from 1991/2 to 1994/5. The experiment did not run smoothly, however, and the process collapsed amid scenes of acrimony between the UFC and the universities. The UFC declared itself disappointed by the scale of economy offered by the universities, while the universities themselves argued that further economies would inevitably result in an unacceptable decline in standards.

The universities' perception that they are chronically underfunded contributed to the early failure of the UFC auction scheme. The collapse of the bidding process does not necessarily, therefore, indicate that the auction system itself is at fault. This being the case, the UFC's successor (the Higher Education Council for England) has introduced a variant of the bidding scheme which uses the principle of 'yardstick competition' (Johnes and Cave, 1993).

In the polytechnic sector, the bidding system was first used by the PCFC to allocate recurrent funding for 1990/1. The first tranche of bids was submitted by the polytechnics to the PCFC in October 1989. The PCFC system therefore predates the UFC scheme by one year. However, while the UFC set out to allocate the entire teaching component of the block grant in line with the outcome of the bidding process, the PCFC has been far more cautious in its approach. In the first year, some 5 per cent of recurrent funds in the polytechnic sector was retained by the PCFC for allocation according to the results of the auction process.

The method of operation of the PCFC auction scheme differs from that used by the UFC in one crucial respect. Like the universities, polytechnics submit bids for both quantity (number of students) and price (funding per student). The difference is that although lower bids are favoured, other things being equal, several other criteria are also considered in the allocation of student places. Non-price variables to which the PCFC attaches weight include quality, student demand, and the broadening of student access to higher education.

In the remainder of this section the first-price auction model discussed earlier is amended. This enables us to rationalise the distinguishing feature of the UFC scheme (namely, that bidders are required to bid quantities as well as prices).

Suppose as before that there are two bidders in the auction, but now they are bidding for the right to sell a variable quantity, $Q$. The bidding process follows the rules of a first-bid auction. The average cost of provision of the traded service is given by $V$, and this valuation rises as $Q$ rises according to the rule

$$V(Q) = \bar{V}Q \qquad (7.4)$$

In common with the models described earlier, we shall assume that valuations, $V$, are distributed uniformly across the unit interval: that is, between zero and one. The bidders therefore seek to maximise their expected surplus. This is calculated as the product of the *ex ante* probability of success, $(1 - B)$, the level of provision, $Q$, and the gap between expected price and valuation for the typical unit of output sold. As usual, the expected price equals the bid in the case of the first-bid auction. To maximise their expected surplus, bidders choose $B$ and $Q$ to maximise

$$\max_{B,Q} \quad (1 - B)\,Q[B - V(Q)] \qquad (7.5)$$

The partial derivatives of this expression with respect to $B$ and $Q$ are set to zero in order to satisfy the first order condition for a maximum. The optimal value of $B$ is chosen to satisfy

$$Q = (2B - 1)/\bar{V} \qquad (7.6)$$

and the optimal value of $Q$ requires

$$B^2 - B(1 + 2\bar{V}Q) + 2\bar{V}Q = 0 \qquad (7.7)$$

This pair of simultaneous equations can be solved to yield the reduced form solutions for B and Q. Hence

$$B = 2/3 \qquad (7.8)$$

and

$$Q = 1/3\bar{V} \tag{7.9}$$

(There is also a trivial solution where $B = 1$.)

A striking result which emerges from the above analysis is that differences in valuation (or average costs) across institutions do not produce differences in the prices bid. The number of student places offered, $Q$, may vary from institution to institution according to differences in valuation, but the bid price, $B$, does not. This probably explains the similarity across institutions in the prices bid when the UFC bidding process was run for the first time. This means that inter-university differences in costs are captured by the second dimension of the bidding process (namely student places, $Q$).

The intuition which underlies this result is that the institutions each realise that to win the auction they must submit the lowest bid price (but that their quantity bid does not matter). Each therefore bids at the price which it expects will win the auction, and allows quantity adjustments to ensure that expected surpluses (conditional upon success at the auction) are optimised. Since, by symmetry, all institutions have the same information about the distribution of valuations, the prices bid by all institutions will be the same.

The above model can be made more realistic by introducing demand constraints and by using more general specifications of the institutions' cost curves (G. Johnes, 1992). While these innovations weaken somewhat the central result noted above, it remains the case that under certain conditions all institutions will bid the same price, regardless of cost differences between them. This happens even in the absence of collusion between the sellers.

The aim of the auction mechanism is to encourage universities and polytechnics to find ways of improving the efficiency of their operations. So long as gains of x-efficiency or allocative efficiency can be made, institutions have the incentive to make them. Since the first-price auction system determines the price which universities charge for student places, the savings achieved in this way will reduce the cost to the exchequer of providing higher education.

By corollary, if no further gains can be secured, institutions will not be able to bid below the guide prices. The most obvious explanation for the collapse of the UFC system in 1990 is not that the principle of auctions is flawed, but that the auction scheme chosen by the UFC encouraged universities to compete in terms of quantities, not prices. The same argument does not apply to the polytechnics' bidding process, because the PCFC scheme allowed institutions to justify high price bids by reference to the quality of their courses; the above model does not incorporate such a refinement.

## Vouchers

In Chapter 2 it was argued that while the government should have a role in financing the education system, this does not of necessity mean that the government should own and operate all institutions of education. State funding is, in any conceivable circumstances, desirable in some measure. Children may, through ignorance, underestimate the value of education, and parents may be cautious in making short-term financial sacrifices for the uncertain long-term gain of their offspring. If capital markets are imperfect, potential pupils might be unable to afford education if their families are, by reason of poverty, unable to provide security for a loan. Moreover, there are positive externalities associated with education; these include the gain to industry of a literate, numerate and otherwise skilled workforce, and may also include cultural benefits. For all these reasons, state subsidies to education have merit. State *control*, however, is certainly not necessary and – since state control typically means monopoly control – it may not even be desirable.

In this section we shall investigate the possibility of introducing a scheme whereby the government can finance education while at the same time encouraging competition between the suppliers. Thus the sterility and inefficiencies associated with monopoly provision can be avoided. The essence of the idea is simple: instead of providing schools with a grant to provide education, the government gives each consumer (pupil or parent) an education voucher which can be used at the school of the consumer's choice. In this way, the government no longer dictates both price and quantity, but instead enables independently operated schools to respond to the market in typical surplus-maximising fashion. Schools which are better (as perceived by the market) will experience a rise in demand for their services and will, in response, increase their provision. Schools which are worse (again, as perceived by the market) will suffer a fall in demand and will therefore cut back their provision. The system provides incentives for all schools to optimise the standard and efficiency of educational services offered, but it maintains the government's financial support.

The greatest enthusiasm for the voucher proposal has come, not surprisingly, from economists who espouse free market principles. Milton Friedman (1955; 1975, Ch. 12) has been a vociferous supporter of such schemes in the USA. In Britain, supporters include Peacock and Wiseman (1964), West (1967a), Gorman (1986) and Kelly (1989). These proponents all regard the system as lending support to market forces, thereby increasing the economic efficiency of the education system.

A large variety of different types of voucher scheme can be identified. While a detailed consideration of each proposal lies outside the scope of the present book, it is useful to draw up a list of the various schemes which are available. A useful starting point is to concentrate upon the answers to the following questions.

1. Are schools which are currently independently owned and operated to be included in the scheme as well as those which are, at present, in the state sector?
2. Are schools free to raise or lower the fees which they charge pupils in response to demand?
3. Are additional 'compensatory' vouchers allocated to low income families and/or to otherwise disadvantaged pupils?
4. In the case of secondary and tertiary education, it would be possible to make the value of the voucher allocated to each student vary positively with performance in the examinations which serve as entry qualifications; is this done?
5. Are parents allowed to 'top up' the value of the voucher by spending their own money on additional educational services?
6. Does the scheme cover only types of education traditionally provided by the state, or are other forms included too? (Examples include driving instruction or music tuition).
7. Can schools vary their entry requirements? For instance, would some schools be able to restrict demand by raising the grade point average required for entry achieved by potential pupils in their previous school?
8. Are pupils constrained to spend the whole value of their voucher at one school, or may they spend some at one school and some at another? For instance, a pupil (or her parents)

may be dissatisfied with the teaching of mathematics at her school, and may therefore wish to employ tuition (at another school or at home) in that subject, while studying all other subjects at the school; may the voucher be split for use in such circumstances?

9. Is the value of the voucher subject to income tax?
10. Are schools which are included in the scheme required to offer scholarships to pupils from low income families?
11. Are schools allowed to charge higher fees to pupils suffering an educational disadvantage (such as dyslexia or other learning difficulties)?
12. Are schools whose staff are expensive to employ (for example, because of their average age) compensated for this by way of a block grant from government which operates separately from the voucher system?

If the answer to both 2 and 7 is 'no', then the school must (if demand exceeds supply) establish a mechanism to ration scarce places. This might involve some *ad hoc* rule (such as a geographical catchment area) or a random selection procedure.

Since each of the above questions has two possible answers, together they enable a typology of over 4000 voucher schemes to be derived. A considerably simpler but less detailed typology has been provided by Maynard (1975). He identifies eight broad classes of voucher scheme as follows.

1. The Jencks (1970) voucher: this group includes schemes which answer 'yes' to questions 2 and 3 above. The allocation of compensatory vouchers in such schemes explicitly enables them to discriminate in favour of low income and otherwise disadvantaged groups.
2. The Friedman (1955) voucher: this comprises schemes which answer 'no' to question 3, but alternative means of introducing positive discrimination are not precluded.
3. The Peacock and Wiseman (1964) voucher: this group is made up of schemes which favour poorer families by answering 'yes' to question 1.
4. The compulsory private scholarship voucher: such schemes answer 'no' to question 3 but allow a degree of progressivity to be introduced by answering 'yes' to question 10.

5. The effort voucher: this group consists of schemes which answer 'no' to question 2 and 'yes' to question 3.
6. The egalitarian voucher: this comprises proposals which answer 'no' to both questions 3 and 5.
7. The achievement voucher: such a scheme answers 'yes' to question 4.
8. The regulated compensatory voucher: schemes of this kind answer 'yes' to questions 3 and 11, but 'no' to question 2.

Clearly certain schemes could be designed which fall into more than one of Maynard's categories. For instance, any voucher proposal designed to cover all schools which makes the value of the voucher subject to income tax but which does not include compensatory voucher allocations to the disadvantaged is *both* a Friedman *and* a Peacock–Wiseman voucher. It may even also be an egalitarian and compulsory private scholarship voucher. The obstacle to the construction of a scheme which could encompass all eight of Maynard's categories is the issue of whether compensatory vouchers should be allocated on the basis of either family income or educational disadvantage. The answer to this question seems to be largely a matter of political opinion; right-wing observers tend to argue against, while more liberal advocates of vouchers argue in favour of compensatory vouchers.

The motivation behind all these proposals is that, by giving parents choice, they provide an incentive for schools to provide the type of education which the markets want, and to provide it well. As a by-product, the voucher system may encourage the growth of schools which aim to fill hitherto unoccupied niches in the market. Consequently a more diverse and truly comprehensive system would emerge.

The voucher scheme has not been without its critics, however. In particular, the emphasis on parental choice has come under fire. First, it has been argued that parents are not competent to assess the quality of education provided by a group of schools, and that such judgements should be made by professional educators (Vaizey, 1962). Supporters of vouchers counter that a paternalistic approach of this kind insults parents, and that the professionals are not free of vested interest. Moreover the judgements of the professionals are likely to be available for consultation by parents when making informed choices (see, for example, Clark and Round, 1991).

Second, choice is necessarily limited in rural areas, so that the advantages of the scheme will not be observed equally throughout the country. The same, of course, is true of the operation of the present system in areas which are geographically remote.

In certain variants of the voucher proposal, schools would be allowed to respond to a change in student demand by changing the price at which they provide their services. Thus, popular schools could, in the short term, raise their price, while unpopular schools could attract students by lowering their price (Wagner, 1974). Alternatively, differential academic entry requirements could be set, or some other rationing rule could be imposed (although these solutions are both unlikely to be adopted in view of the financial incentives which 'good' schools could exploit by charging differential money prices). In any of these cases parental choice is eroded, since some pupils will be discriminated against on the grounds of finance, ability or luck. This is the third main criticism of the voucher proposal. The key issue, of course, is whether the erosion of choice thereby caused is more or less severe than that which exists under other systems (including the system currently in being).

Voucher schemes which allow schools to vary their fees could result in a vicious circle where the poor can only afford to send their children to the 'worst' schools, while children of more affluent parents enjoy the 'best' education. It would be possible to counter this tendency by discriminating in favour of the poor in the allocation of vouchers (Jencks, 1970).

The Jencks proposal for a progressive allocation of vouchers based upon parental income has received widespread support. Friedman (1975), for example, expresses 'great sympathy for the proposed compensatory voucher', although he qualifies his support with the cynical observation that the strong middle-class political lobby for education expenditure may not support such a move. Moreover, the implicit assumption which underlies the invisible hand model of the competitive market economy – that the marginal utility of money is constant across individuals – is as suspect in the context of education as in any other. This observation provides further reason to give pupils from low income families vouchers of higher value than others.

The fourth criticism of vouchers follows immediately from the third. If discrimination on the basis of ability or income cannot be eliminated, then the scheme will tend to be socially divisive (Blaug, 1967). It would thus be subject to the same criticisms as applied in the past to the grammar versus secondary-modern school divide, and which today applies to the public versus private sector division. It should be remembered, though, that systems in which geographical catchment areas determine a school's enrolment have in the past encouraged wealthy parents to move house on the basis of perceived school quality, and that this has exacerbated the tendency for urban areas to be carved up into spatially distinct areas of affluence and poverty.

Fifth, teachers' unions have vociferously opposed the introduction of vouchers, largely on the grounds that the new schemes will threaten the employment prospects of their members (National Union of Teachers, 1983). Nevertheless, it is not at all clear that overall economic efficiency or equity is enhanced by protecting the jobs of teachers whose comparative advantage may lie outside the teaching profession.

Sixth, concern has been expressed about the possibility that schools which fail to attract sufficient pupils will have buildings and equipment lying idle. This criticism overlooks the role of the price system in the scheme, however. A school which the market considers to provide relatively poor services can raise the demand for its services simply by lowering its fees or by lowering its entry requirements. A school which cannot, after taking such action, cover its costs will release buildings and equipment for use by schools which more efficiently provide the type of education which consumers want.

Finally, if a constraint is imposed which requires that education should be available to all without charge, the value of the voucher may become difficult to set. Schools within an area may collude and raise their fees to a level well above costs, in the knowledge that this will force the authorities to increase the value of vouchers.

In its simplest form the proposal for vouchers has been present in the literature for a long time. Indeed, West (1967b) traces its origins back to the work of the eighteenth-century political commentator Thomas Paine (1915, pp. 246–52). Nevertheless, it is only since Friedman (1955) refined the idea that the proposal has received serious, albeit patchy, support. Empirical evidence on the performance of such schemes is limited, therefore, and is concentrated mainly on some experiments in the USA. Indirect evidence is also available from Britain, where the introduction of vouchers was, for a while, under consideration during the 1980s.

The most prominent of the early American experiments with vouchers in education started during 1972 for a sub-set of public sector schools in the Alum Rock area of the city of San Jose, California (Weiler, 1977). The rein allowed the free market in this experiment was limited in several ways. The Alum Rock scheme was a regulated compensatory voucher plan in which schools with supply constraints allocated scarce places by lottery. School tuition fees were all restricted to equal the value of the basic voucher, but schools attracting pupils eligible for the compensatory voucher could use the additional funds released by such vouchers at their discretion. Only a quarter of all schools in the district participated in the first instance. Teachers' job tenure and seniority rights were protected. Each participating school was encouraged to divide itself up into a number of 'mini-schools' in order to provide parents with extra choice.

Evidence on the success of the Alum Rock experiment is mixed. Parents generally felt more satisfied with their children's education under the new system than they had been before its introduction. Teachers were pleased to receive extra funds for discretionary use, but were unhappy with the increased workload caused by administrative complexities. The costs associated with the compensatory voucher were considerable and rendered the voucher system more expensive to the exchequer than was its predecessor; this was due in large measure to the high set-up costs of the scheme. There is no firm evidence to suggest that academic performance of pupils was affected in any direction by the introduction of the scheme. So, bearing in mind the very limited nature of the experiment, the Alum Rock experience does not help us much one way or the other in reaching a decision on the practical usefulness of vouchers.

Other early experiments in education vouchers have been conducted in various parts of New England (Sugarman, 1974). More recently, the 'parent power' programme initiated by the authorities in Cambridge, Massachusetts, has attracted considerable interest (Tan, 1990). This scheme, introduced in 1979, was originally designed to reduce the tendency for primary schools to be racially segregated. Since its introduction, parents have been allowed to rank their four preferred schools, one of which their children will attend. So long as the ratio of ethnic minority to ethnic majority student numbers does not violate predetermined limits, a student will, subject to availability, be allocated a place in her parents' most preferred school. The schools aggressively market their product. It is claimed that this programme has resulted on average in better academic performance by students, while at the same time promoting greater racial integration and a less divergent spread of performance across schools. It should, however, be borne in mind that Cambridge is one of the smallest urban school districts in the country (it has only one high school), and that the success of the scheme may be attributable in part to its size.

Another recent development in the USA was mooted in 1986 with the Remedial Education Program. This was intended to be a federally financed scheme enabling district authorities in areas with a high average poverty rate, should they so wish, to donate vouchers to the parents of pupils whose school performance was below average. This voucher could be spent at any approved school in order to top up the child's education with remedial tuition. The parents would determine the school at which the voucher was spent. The voucher value was intended to cover most (but not all) of the typical cost of remedial education. Parents wishing to top up the value of the voucher using their own resources would be allowed to do so. The proposed scheme met with considerable public dissent, however, and was eventually replaced by less radical proposals to enhance choice in the public sector school system.

The Dutch system of education has for many years operated along lines similar to a limited voucher scheme (James, 1984). In the Netherlands, some 70 per cent of both primary and secondary education is run by the private sector, primarily by religious denominations. The public sector finances the system by way of both capital grants (given by the municipality) and by way of a voucher system. Each pupil, in effect, receives a voucher whose value equals the per capitum cost of tuition in the local public sector school. She may spend this voucher at the public sector school or at a private school. The schools then claim the funding which the voucher represents from the state. The funding from government includes an allowance for teachers' salaries (which the government regulates in both sectors) on the assumption of a given student:staff ratio. Private sector schools have a limited right to charge supplementary fees, designed to cover facilities such as sports equipment or library books rather than the service of education itself. Thus pupils' families may be required to top up the voucher out of their own resources if they choose to attend such a school. Although the Dutch system has many favourable characteristics – the availability of choice within a competitive setting – government subsidies to the private sector have been accompanied by regulation to the extent that the distinction between the private and public sectors has become fuzzy.

In Britain, the Conservative government led by Margaret Thatcher considered the introduction of vouchers on a number of occasions. Early experiments in the county of Kent, predating the Thatcher era, generated considerable interest. In 1978, a feasibility study indicated that the operation of a voucher scheme in the Ashford district would be costly in terms of administration (Kent County Council, 1978). An acute difficulty would arise for schools with high staffing costs (because the average age of their staff is high, or because their pupil:teacher ratio is low) unless the authorities could arrange and finance appropriate compensation. The gains in terms of parental choice, meanwhile, may not be great; in about one in eight cases only would parents wish to change the school attended by their children.

Despite this, in 1982 a pilot study involving the use of vouchers was proposed for the Ashford area, but was scrapped after the resignation of the chairman of the county's education committee in November of that year. A similar pilot scheme was mooted for Sefton, but this too was scrapped before it could be introduced. By the middle of 1984, the government had withdrawn its proposal to introduce vouchers. Concern about the cost of the scheme was one reason for this: since parents of children who currently attend private sector schools would, for the first time, receive subsidies for their children's schooling, the scheme would initially raise the exchequer cost of education. It has also been speculated that the desire of civil servants to retain control over educational planning may have frustrated the progress of the voucher idea. Brief airings of the proposal occurred in 1986 and again in 1990, but in 1993 there are no plans to introduce education vouchers in the UK.

Nevertheless, the principle of parent choice has existed in Britain for a long time. Section 76 of the 1944 Education Act stressed that local education authorities should, as far as possible, take into account the wishes of parents. Unfortunately the wording of that section was clouded by ambiguity, and it was not until the 1980 Education Act that a serious attempt was made to clarify it. Section 6 of that Act states that

> **every local authority shall make arrangements for enabling the parent of a child in the area of the authority to express a preference as to the school at which he wishes education to be provided for his child in the exercise of the authority's functions and to give reasons for his preference.**

Moreover, subject to certain conditions (which were tightened in the 1988 Education Reform Act), 'it shall be the duty of a local education authority and of the governors of a county or voluntary school to comply with any preference expressed'. This being so, the current British system is formally equivalent to a simple type of voucher scheme, even though no vouchers actually change hands. If evidence of the operation of this system is favourable, more reforms can be expected which enhance further the flexibility of the system.

Education properly includes not only schooling but also vocational training. In this field Britain has already experimented with vouchers. The training credits initiative was announced in 1990 by the Secretary of State for Employment, Michael Howard (Hansard, 27 March). Pilot schemes started in April 1991 in several areas, operated by the local Training and Enterprise Councils (TECs) in England and Wales and by the Local Enterprise Companies (LECs) in Scotland (Howard, 1991). The scheme operates as follows. Training credits (or vouchers) are issued to 16- and 17-year olds leaving full-time education. The credit given to each youth has printed upon it a monetary value. The credit may then be spent by the young worker by presenting it to an employer who makes training available, or alternatively to a specialist provider of training (such as a further education college). The value of each training credit is determined by an allocation of funds from central government, but local employers, TECs or LECs may supplement this if they wish to secure more training services for youths covered by the scheme in their area.

The TECs and LECs are required to liaise closely with local education authorities, colleges of further education and the careers service. They must also ensure that all youths who are unable to secure employment are offered places on training schemes, and that the training offered is of adequate quality and relevant to the needs of industry. The pilot schemes are being closely monitored in order to evaluate their performance, but it is as yet too early to arrive at any firm conclusions.

It is appropriate to end our discussion of vouchers with a consideration of the words of a past British Secretary of State for Education, Sir Keith Joseph (1984):

> **I was intellectually attracted to the idea of education vouchers because it seemed to offer the possibility of some kind of market mechanism which would increase the choice and diversity of schools in response to the wishes of parents acting as customers. In the course of my examination of this possibility, it became clear that there would be great practical difficulties in making any voucher system compatible with the requirements that schooling should be available to all without charge, compulsory, and of an acceptable standard. These requirements . . . entail an involvement on the part of the state . . . which would be both financial and regulatory and on a scale likely to necessitate an administrative effort as great as under the present system . . . For these reasons, the idea of vouchers is no longer on the agenda.**

Any voucher scheme which does not, in some way, discriminate in favour of the poor must surely run into practical difficulties of the type identified by Sir Keith. Without such discrimination, it would be difficult to guarantee free education for all. The sheer variety of available schemes makes it likely that a voucher scheme could be devised which is sufficiently flexible and progressive in its impact to dispel the disquiet aroused by the prototypes. Whether the costs of administering such a scheme could ever be low enough to make its introduction a real possibility, however, is another matter.

## Grants, Loans and Graduate Taxes

As is clear from previous sections, the issue of how best to finance the provision of education has generated a considerable number of exciting and radical ideas. In many cases these have led to policy changes. This is certainly true of the case of student maintenance.

In the early 1990s, Britain introduced student loans which operate alongside the established system of grants, and Australia started to finance student maintenance by means of a graduate tax. The merits and demerits of each of these schemes form the subject matter of this section.

Before discussing student maintenance at length, we should consider whether it is a topic worthy of such consideration. In other words, before we ask whether students' living expenses should be met by a loan, graduate tax or grant, we should ask whether the government should be concerned about student maintenance at all. After all, students typically study at least partly so that they can augment their future earning power. Some students – especially postgraduates – already arrange their own loans through private sector banking facilities. Why not, then, let all students do this?

One reason, of course, is that banks are generally unwilling to make large advances to students who cannot provide security. Moreover, the higher education of an individual may confer positive externalities on the rest of society, and the Pigovian subsidy provided by state-sponsored schemes of student maintenance can, in such a situation, raise the demand for education towards the socially optimal level (G. Johnes and J. Johnes, 1992).

Although many variants exist, the most useful typology of student maintenance schemes divides the menu of choices into three main categories. These are grants, loans and a graduate tax. It is helpful at this stage to define each of these in turn.

Grants are awards given to students to help them pay their living expenses while engaged in full-time study. These awards may be given by government or by the institutions themselves (in the form of scholarships) or by private firms (in the form of sponsorships). Students are not formally required to pay back grants to the awarding authority upon completion of their studies.

A loans system also allows eligible students to claim support during their years of study, and (like grants) they may be provided by government, educational institutions or private firms (such as the banks). Unlike grants, loans must formally be repaid. The repayment regulations vary considerably from scheme to scheme and in some cases the repayment period is short, in others long; sometimes the government subsidises the interest payments, but this is not universally the case; some schemes allow loan repayments to be deferred (or even cancelled) if the debtor suffers a spell of low income, but others do not; and an interesting recent proposal by Darvish-Lecker and Kahana (1990) argues in favour of making the burden of repayments inversely related to the student's academic performance, so that effort can be rewarded.

The idea of the graduate tax was put forward by Glennerster, Merrett and Wilson (1968). This type of scheme is formally similar to a loan which explicitly makes the repayment dependent upon income. Graduates pay a surcharge on their income tax or national insurance contribution, either for part or for the whole of their working lives, in exchange for the support which they receive during their higher education (Lal, 1989). The graduate tax therefore explicitly builds into the loan repayment scheme a mechanism whereby the repayment of a debt cannot impose hardship on those suffering spells of low income. For many observers – including, no doubt, many prospective students – this makes the graduate tax preferable to a loan although, as we have seen, many loans systems link repayments to income, too. In some variants of the graduate tax, the total tax due by an individual is not linked to the level of course fees at all; in these cases the tax operates as a supplementary income tax, so that those graduates enjoying especially high incomes subsidise other graduates who are less successful in the labour market.

Most countries operate a mix of grants and loans as a means of supporting students (Woodhall, 1982). The grants-only system which operated in the UK was therefore unusual, as is the Japanese system of loans only. The loans component of student maintenance usually involves financial commitment by the government. This commitment may take the form of subsidised interest rates, or a loan guarantee which fully pays off the debt in the event of the graduate's death or illness, or a loan deferment if for any reason the graduate suffers a period of low income. In some countries (such as Sweden) the loan scheme is operated by the government itself; in other cases (including the Guaranteed Student Loan in the USA) the government merely supervises the provision of subsidised loans by the private sector.

The variety of different loan systems currently in being around the world is immense. In some countries (such as Canada and the USA) the maintenance schemes are partially administered by local government, and many colleges provide their own student aid programmes. This makes the variety and complexity of the schemes all the greater.

Indeed, the US system has received much criticism on these grounds. Morse (1977) has argued that educational administrators in America 'could scarcely . . . have devised a more confusing, more expensive or less efficient program than the one we now have'. Students may receive a grant (the Pell grant) which is income related. They may also qualify for a number of loans from various programmes. The largest of these are the Guaranteed Student Loan (GSL; also called the Stafford loan) and the National Defense Student Loan (NDSL; also called the Perkins loan). While originally designed to cater for students from middle and low income families, eligibility restrictions on these schemes have been relaxed somewhat over the years. Numerous other grant and loans schemes exist, making up an extremely complicated American patchwork. The success of the system is suspect as default rates on the Stafford and Perkins schemes are high. The Stafford loan includes various subsidies (such as low interest rates and a guarantee to the lending institution against default); the cost of these subsidies has encouraged the authorities to restrict the availability of these loans to those from low and middle income groups. Nevertheless, a very high proportion of young Americans go to college, and this fact alone suggests that a simplified version of the American system might have substantial advantages.

The Swedish system of grants and loans has attracted considerable interest for a number of reasons. It is unusual in that it covers all students over the age of 16 years so that senior secondary school pupils are covered, as well as students in further and higher education. Claiming a grant and loan package is therefore part of a natural progression: when the pupil reaches the age at which family allowances (child benefits) are no longer paid to her parents, she becomes entitled to the grant and loan package (if she remains in education). Local committees make decisions about the eligibility of applicants for grant and loan packages, but these committees are guided by rules laid down at central level by the State Study Assistance Committee. Student maintenance is available for secondary, tertiary and (under certain conditions) adult education. The loan is repaid over a long period, and the terms are favourable in relation to commercial rates of interest. After completing their course of study, students may take advantage of a six-month grace period before they start to repay their loan. Repayments are income-related, so that borrowers repay an amount equal to 4 per cent of their (gross) income (two years previously) until the debt is repaid.

Japan is an unusual case in that its system of student support involves no grant component. The extent of subsidy provided by the Japanese loans system is considerable, however. Students from poor families receive interest-free loans (Woodhall, 1989). Tuition fees in Japan are also partly paid by students, though in this case the Current Cost Subsidy scheme to some extent shifts the burden from students and their parents on to the general taxpayer.

In the UK, student grants are provided by government and administered by local authorities. These grants have, since 1990, been supplemented by loans which are financed by central government. The nominal value of the grant has been frozen at its 1989 level, so that in real terms it is being eroded by inflation. Meanwhile, the government – operating through the Student Loans Company – guarantees each student a loan, the value of which equals that of the grant times the ratio of current prices to 1989 prices minus one. The proportion of student maintenance financed by loans will continue to rise until one half of the total is funded in this way.

Repayment of student loans in the UK follows a broadly similar pattern to that observed in other countries. Repayments begin in April following completion of the course, or when the borrower's salary reaches 85 per cent of the national average. Five years are allowed for the repayment of debt in most cases, but students whose courses last for more than three years are allowed a repayment period of up to seven years. In accordance with Section 2 of the 1990 Education (Student Loans) Act, the *real* rate of interest payable on the loans will be zero per cent; in order to satisfy this requirement, the Secretary of State for Education must make periodic adjustments to the nominal rate of interest due. The Secretary of State has discretion to alter both the size of the maximum annual loan and the length of the repayment period; he also has the discretion to defer or cancel loans in particular cases.

Proposals for a graduate tax scheme have, in recent years, been introduced in Australia and New Zealand (Woodhall, 1989). These proposals emanated from the Wran Committee and the Hawke Group respectively. Both schemes are geared towards the payment of tuition fees, and do not address the issue of maintenance. In Australia the tax is payable by all those who receive higher education, thus providing a disincentive to drop out of courses.

Ex-students on low incomes do not pay the tax, but once income rises above a predetermined threshold they are liable to tax payments of up to 3 per cent of their income. They must continue to pay the tax until, for each year of study, they have paid an amount roughly equal to 20 per cent of the average cost of tuition.

Having described some of the programmes in existence, we are now almost ready to consider the merits and demerits of grants, loans and the graduate tax. One important point needs to be made first, though. *All* systems of student maintenance can accommodate government subsidy. This affects the manner in which the following arguments should be interpreted. For example, it is not sufficient, as a defence of grants, to argue that there are externalities to education which justify public expenditure on student maintenance; such expenditure could be fed into a loans system by way of interest relief, or into a graduate tax by way of tax relief. Let us now consider the arguments.

First, it is sometimes asserted that grants (or systems involving a large subsidy) are preferable to other forms of student support because they impose a lower burden of debt repayment after graduation than do the other systems. While this is certainly true, *ceteris paribus*, it is true only because under the grants system a relatively heavy burden of tax is paid by workers who have *not* received the benefit of higher education. Any scheme which involves a reduction of subsidy to the recipients of education would probably reduce the demand for higher education, because it would reduce the private rate of return. Whether or not a subsidy from the uneducated to the educated is justifiable depends on whether or not higher education confers beneficial externalities on the rest of the economy. For the moment we assume that such externalities do indeed exist. The question of how the subsidy from the uneducated to the educated should be provided – by a grant or by a loan system with favourable interest rates (or by a combination of both) – is less important than the determination of the appropriate level of the subsidy.

Second, advocates of grants argue that potential students are less likely to be discouraged from entering higher education under a high subsidy scheme (like grants) than under the alternative systems. In particular, young people whose parents are on low incomes may be especially eager to receive grants since they may be reluctant to go heavily into debt. This can conveniently be labelled the equity case against loans. There may be substance in this argument, but there is little empirical evidence either to support or refute the claim. We know that some low income families do borrow to buy consumer durables (Maynard, 1975). The 1989 Family Expenditure Survey indicates that, on average, only about 0.2 per cent of family income is spent on the repayment of debts; however, this proportion was about twice as high for families whose gross income was above the median as it was for those in the lower half of the income distribution. It may be the case, therefore, that students from poorer families are less willing than others to borrow in order to pay for their maintenance while engaged in higher education. On the other hand, Halsey (1992) finds that the class distribution of students in the UK has changed little since the introduction of maintenance grants. Nevertheless, much more empirical work needs to be done before reaching a firm conclusion on the validity of the equity argument against loans.

Third, some commentators argue that the adoption of a loans scheme involving a low degree of subsidy will encourage students to opt for courses for whose graduates there is high labour market demand. This is because the students seek to optimise their expected capacity to pay off their loans. Students are therefore in some cases discouraged from following the courses which most interest them. This may be so, but whether this is an advantage or disadvantage of the loans system is open to question.

Fourth, loans schemes pose a problem if the graduate emigrates before the debt is repaid. Collection of the debt then becomes difficult. Some commentators have argued in favour of international agreements for the recovery of the debt through the host country's tax system. Another possibility would be to raise an exit tax on emigrating graduates. It should be noted, however, that the emigration problem applies equally when a grant or graduate tax system is in operation; in all cases the emigrant has an opportunity to escape payment for her higher education. For instance, a graduate who studies in a country which awards grants and who then migrates to one which has a system of loans escapes the relatively high income tax rates in the former country, *ceteris paribus*. The migration problem therefore affects *all* student maintenance programmes, and a solution (tax treaties or an exit tax) should be sought regardless of the system in operation.

Fifth, concern has been expressed that a system of loans could be biased against women. Female graduates who wish to marry and raise a family may be deterred from doing so by their debt. This has often been referred to as the 'negative dowry' argument. Indeed, the graduate tax proposal was devised largely as a response to this criticism of loans. Proponents of loans have generally been acutely aware of this problem, and have suggested that the payment of the loan should either be deferred or should be made by the government for a given number of years after childbirth.

The three schemes – grants, loans and graduate tax – are not as different from one another as might at first sight be supposed. For instance, it would be easy to assume that loans and grants differ substantially from one another because, apparently, the former has to be paid back while the latter does not. Loan repayments are (like the graduate tax proposal) a type of post-study tax. Likewise, graduates who, as students, received a study grant also pay a sort of post-study tax; in this case the post-study tax takes the form of the higher income tax payments which graduates typically incur (relative to non-graduates) on account of their higher earnings.

This might suggest that the differences between the alternative systems of student maintenance have been somewhat exaggerated by some observers. Nevertheless, the systems *are* different in two crucial respects. First, they carry different implications for the progressivity of the tax system. A loan repayment plan, coming on top of progressive income tax bands, redistributes income more in favour of the poor than does a system of student grants, other things being equal. The redistributive implications of the graduate tax, meanwhile, are unclear; while those graduates whose incomes are low (relative to other graduates) may be favoured by the scheme, the extent of this bias is an empirical issue on which there is, so far, little evidence. Second, exclusive reliance on grants – using the progressive income tax as a means of repaying the costs of maintenance – discriminates against those who achieve high income (and so have high tax dues) without having enjoyed the benefit of higher education. It is for these reasons that all countries with an interest in student maintenance now operate some sort of loans or graduate tax scheme (and in most cases combine this with a limited grant component).

## Conclusion

Several radical proposals for the funding of education have emerged over the last few years. These have been designed to free the market for education, enhance the opportunity for choice, and provide a more efficient education industry. Over the same period, financial and other pressures on the education system have, in many countries, been particularly severe. An unfortunate consequence is that some observers have erroneously perceived an inevitable link between the new ideas and the curtailment of funding.

Auctions aimed at allocating government support for students to the least costly institutions can, if properly designed, encourage institutions to become more efficient. As has been demonstrated in this chapter, though, the outcome of an auction can be sensitive to the rules of the bidding process, so the auctions must be carefully designed. Vouchers which enable students to attend the school of their own (or their parents') choice likewise impose the disciplines of competition on the suppliers of education services. Voucher schemes tend to impose a heavy administrative burden, however, and this detracts somewhat from their appeal. Schemes like these can be useful in identifying and removing sources of allocative and x-inefficiencies. If, however, cost savings can be made only by reducing standards, these schemes will not succeed in making efficiency gains.

The maintenance of students is a further issue which bears on efficiency and the education system. Choosing the degree of subsidy provided to students through the grants, loans or graduate tax scheme is a matter of achieving the desired balance between efficiency and equity. In the interest of efficiency, students should be compensated for any positive externalities which their education confers on society in general. Equity considerations require that the government should compensate for any disadvantage faced by students from poor families in securing a given level of support while in full-time study. As ever, the goals of efficiency and equity may conflict. Choosing the 'right' balance then involves making value judgements (a job which the impartial economist would willingly leave to the politicians).

# 8 Universities as Multi-Product Firms

## Introduction

Most of our attention hitherto has been devoted to the teaching function of educational institutions. This is natural enough, since most of the education system is devoted primarily to the dissemination of knowledge, understanding and skills. In this chapter we consider the special case of the universities: institutions of tertiary education where the dissemination of knowledge occurs side by side with the creation of knowledge. At the tertiary level, the expertise of staff is typically concentrated in very narrow areas. In general this precludes the possibility of allowing staff to double up as teachers of, say, history and religious studies. Indeed, it is usual for the focus of interest of an academic to be much narrower than her discipline: for example, a member of an economics department may consider herself to be a labour economist, or a development economist, or an econometrician. While primary and secondary schools produce educated individuals, only in the case of the tertiary sector is that education so narrowly focused as to enable distinct teaching outputs – graduates of economics, physics, history, and so on – to be separately identified. Yet universities in general provide a wide curriculum.

As producers of both teaching and research in a wide variety of subject areas, universities are best regarded as multi-product firms. The theory of multi-product firms has developed rapidly over the last 20 years, and will occupy much of the remainder of this chapter. In later sections we shall also consider the issue of the balance between teaching and research activity, and we shall investigate the determinants of the optimal mix of subjects taught at a given university.

## Teaching and Research

Bear (1974) has listed three broad brush types of output of the typical university. The first two are common to all educational institutions, while the third is unique to institutions at tertiary level. The categories of output are:

(a) the accumulation of the human capital stock of students;
(b) the present consumption by students of utility directly derived from an interest in their specialism;
(c) the growth of the stock of knowledge possessed by the human race.

This third category represents the fruits of research. It makes universities fundamentally different from institutions at the primary and secondary levels of the education system, since it raises questions of the optimal allocation of inputs between the functions of teaching and research.

Before proceeding further it is necessary to emphasise a few points concerning the nature of research activity within a university. First, academic staff typically devote a considerable proportion of their working time to research. The Robbins report indicates that the average British academic in the 1960s spent, *in term-time alone*, 89 per cent as much time on research as they did on teaching, course preparation, and marking; during students' vacations, of course, considerably more time is available for research. Moreover, since 1963 the pressures to publish have increased, so that the proportion of time now devoted to research is likely to be higher than before. Research is the means whereby individual academics and their institutions gain reputations in the national and international sphere. This being so, it is crucial for academics to have a good record of research in order either to gain promotion or to transfer to a more prestigious institution. So the incentive to devote time to research is strong.

Second, research is a very time-consuming exercise. Publication of research results represents only the final stage, and what we see when reading the published oeuvre is only the finished product. There is, not surprisingly, a tendency for published work to report only successful results. But it is the nature of research that – like a maze – many unsuccessful efforts have to be made at solving a problem before a successful one is found. Since original research at the frontiers of knowledge is intrinsically difficult, each of these failed attempts can absorb a considerable amount of time. To write an article for an academic journal, therefore, normally requires many months of intensive effort.

Third, competition is intense for space in the prestigious academic journals. In addition to the editor, articles submitted for publication are read by independent referees (usually two) who are experts in the relevant topic. Their critical evaluations of the paper inform the editor as to whether the paper should be published or not. The most prestigious journals in economics publish only 10–12 per cent of articles submitted (see, for example, the annual editor's report of the *American Economic Review*, published at the back of the May issue of each year). This generally ensures a high quality of output in those journals. Even in cases where articles are accepted, referees almost invariably require certain revisions before the paper is published. Obviously this adds to the time taken to complete the research. The publication process for books is not dissimilar, though considerations such as the size of the market for the book are more to the fore in this instance.

The above should convince the reader that research is far from being a peripheral activity. After all, the vast bulk of the knowledge acquired by students over their courses of secondary and higher education represents just some of the fruits of academic research. Academics write not only the textbooks used by students, but also the original research articles upon which those texts are founded. The fraction of research which is considered to be of sufficiently general interest to be reported in the textbooks is itself small, so the position of research as one of the two key functions of higher education is beyond question.

Suppose that the utility, $U$, derived by a university can be expressed as a function of research output, $R$, teaching output, $T$, and the inputs of faculty, $F$, and students, $S$. To maintain the analogy with the model of the multi-product firm, it is supposed that the utility function resembles a profits function so that

$$U = p_R R + p_T T - c_F F - c_S S \qquad (8.1)$$

where $p_i$, $i = R, T$, represents respectively the contribution made to the institution's utility by each unit of research and teaching produced, and where $c_i$, $i = F$, $S$, denotes respectively the unit cost of inputs of faculty and students. The production function imposes a constraint upon utility, in that the costs attached to each student or faculty member have to be incurred in order to produce outputs of research and teaching. The production function may be written as

$$F^{\alpha} S^{1-\alpha} = R^{\beta} T^{1-\beta} \tag{8.2}$$

The problem is simply to choose the values of $R$, $T$, $F$ and $S$ which maximise (8.1) subject to the constraint given by (8.2). This is easily done using the usual Lagrangian method. The solution implies the following results

$$\alpha K/(1-\alpha)L = c_F/c_S \tag{8.3}$$

$$\beta T/(1-\beta)R = p_R/p_T \tag{8.4}$$

$$-p_i \frac{\partial Y/\partial j}{\partial Y/\partial i} = c_j;\ i = R, T;\ j = F, S \tag{8.5}$$

where

$$Y = F^{\alpha} S^{1-\alpha} - R^{\beta} T^{1-\beta} \tag{8.6}$$

Equation (8.3) says that, given outputs, the isoquant should be tangential to the isocost line. Likewise, given inputs, equation (8.4) says that the isorevenue line should be tangential to the production possibility curve. Finally, equation (8.5) says that the marginal value product of any input, defined in terms of any output, must equal the unit price of the input concerned (Bear, 1974). This is a standard set of results borrowed from the field of industrial economics (see, for example, Schneider, 1952), and represents merely the extension of simple profit maximisation methods to the case of multiple outputs and inputs.

The above analysis does beg some important questions, though. For instance, why should the institution simultaneously produce both teaching and research? Why, rather than universities, do we not have research institutes and teaching colleges which are quite separate one from the other? What benefits, if any, attach to the simultaneous provision of both outputs? To answer these questions we need to investigtate more modern theories of multi-product firms and the economies of scope (Bailey and Friedlander, 1982).

Economies of scope are said to exist if the costs of producing two outputs jointly is less than the summed costs of producing them separately. This might occur in certain situations where inputs are shared between the two production processes. In the case of universities, the library facilities needed for teaching are needed also for research. Moreover, the labour of the academic staff is shared between teaching and research. Time which labour dedicates to one activity may, as a costless by-product, increase its output in the other. To be specific, research activity ensures that the teacher keeps fully up to date with the latest developments, and that she has a depth of knowledge and expertise which go well beyond the standard taught curriculum; meanwhile, teaching activity keeps researchers familiar with the basic principles of a discipline which is typically much broader than their own specific field of interest. Some empirical evidence on this comes from the work of Knight (1987), whose study suggests that there is a positive correlation between good teaching performance and productive research activity on the part of individual academics. The sample used in this study is, however, small, and much more work needs to be done in order to establish the nature of the interactions between teaching and research.

A particular problem which emerges once organisations are allowed to produce multiple outputs concerns the identification of returns to scale. Marginal costs can be identified much as in the single product case; that is, they are the change in total cost associated with a marginal change in the output of a given product. But since fixed costs are shared between the various outputs being produced, defining average costs in a multi-product context is not so straightforward. A useful starting point is to define the average incremental cost of the *i*th product as

$$AIC_i = \frac{C(Y_i, Y_j) - C(O, Y_j)}{Y_i} \tag{8.7}$$

where $C(Y_i, Y_j)$ represents the total costs of producing $Y_i$ units of product $i$ and $Y_j$ units of product $j$. The returns to scale of a single product firm are conventionally measured by the ratio of average to marginal costs. By extension we may define the product-specific returns to scale associated with the *i*th product as

$$S_i = \frac{AIC_i}{\partial C/\partial Y_i} \tag{8.8}$$

where $MC_i$ represents the marginal cost associated with the *i*th product (Panzar and Willig, 1981).

A measure of the economies of scope obtainable by an organisation which produces both *i* and *j* is given by the ratio of cost savings due to joint production to the total cost. This may be expressed as

$$S_c = \frac{C(Y_i, 0) + C(0, Y_j) - C(Y_i, Y_j)}{C(Y_i, Y_j)} \tag{8.9}$$

If no economies of scope exist, then $S_c = 0$.

The product-specific returns to scale for an organisation operating in a multi-product context were defined above in equation (8.8). A further useful concept, due to Baumol (1977), is that of ray economies of scale. Define a bundle of goods, $Y = (Y_i^*, Y_j^*)$, and let the quantity of such bundles produced by the organisation be represented by a straight line sloping up from the origin in $(Y_i, Y_j)$ space. This straight line is known as the ray. Ray economies of scale are said to exist if, as the number of bundles produced rises, the unit cost of producing the bundles falls. A natural measure of ray economies of scale, $S$, is the ratio of ray average costs to the weighted sum of marginal costs of the individual products. Hence

$$S_{i,j} = \frac{C(Y_i, Y_j)}{Y_i \partial C/\partial Y_i + Y_j \partial C/\partial Y_j} \tag{8.10}$$

Simple substitution of equations (8.7) to (8.9) into (8.10) yields, after some routine manipulation,

$$S_{i,j} = \frac{\alpha S_i + (1 - \alpha) S_j}{1 - S_c} \tag{8.11}$$

where

$$\alpha = \frac{Y_i \partial C / \partial Y_i}{Y_i \partial C / \partial Y_i + Y_j \partial C / \partial Y_j} \tag{8.12}$$

So the multi-product economies of scale, $S_{i,j}$, are defined by a weighted average of the product-specific scale economies, divided by (one minus) a measure of economies of scope. The presence of $S_c$ in equation (8.11) has an important implication: even if no economies of scale exist in the production of the separate products, it is possible that overall scale economies exist. This is so because a high value of $S_c$ can lead to a value of $S_{i,j}$ in excess of one even if $S_i$ and $S_j$ are both less than unity. Essentially this happens because the returns to scale concept used for the joint product case allows for fixed costs, whereas that used for single products does not.

The idea of scope economies can be illustrated by plotting total costs against the output of two products. This leads to a three-dimensional diagram; while impossible to draw on a two-dimensional sheet of paper, some idea of what this would look like is given in Figure 8.1. As can be seen from this diagram, unit costs vary both with scale (distance from the origin) and scope (distance from the 'horizontal' axes).

In the context of higher education institutions, teaching and research form easily defined and distinguishable output types. Moreover, it is straightforward to distinguish between undergraduate tuition and postgraduate supervision. A study by Cohn, Rhine and Santos (1989) has attempted to apply the above theory of the multi-product organisation to the case of universities and colleges producing these three outputs. The results of the study are instructive and have a number of important policy implications.

The data used in this study are drawn from the American Higher Education General Information Survey (HEGIS) of 1981–2, and cover some 1887 institutions. The figures include total education expenditures, and three measures of 'output': undergraduate numbers, postgraduate numbers and the value of research grants received. (All three measures more truly reflect inputs than outputs, but data constraints preclude the use of more reasonable variables.) These data are used to estimate a three-output flexible fixed-cost quadratic cost function, using standard least squares regression methods. Separate functions are estimated for public and private sector institutions, since there is evidence to suggest that there exist substantial differences between the cost structures in

**FIGURE 8.1**
**Cost Function for a Two-Product Firm**

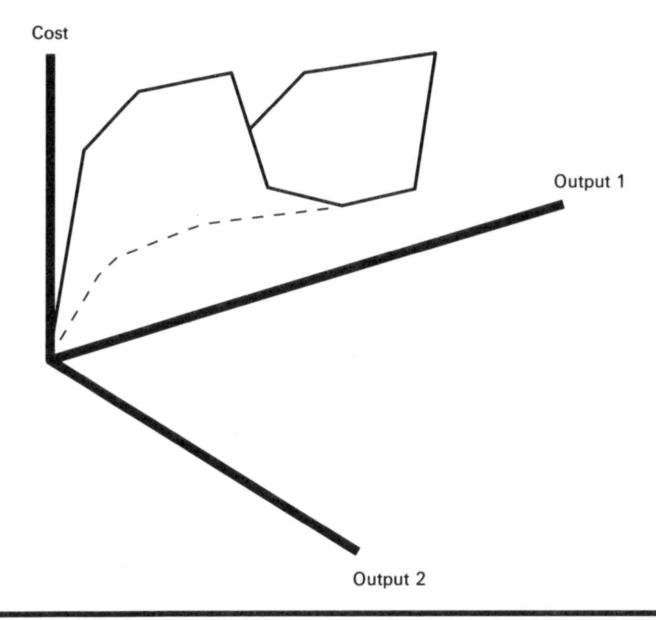


the two sectors. These regression results are then used in conjunction with equations (8.8)–(8.10) to produce estimates of product-specific economies of scale, ray economies of scale, and economies of scope. The extent of scale and scope returns is measured in this way at the mean values of the three 'output' variables, and also at 50 per cent and 200 per cent of the mean output levels. The results are shown in Table 8.1.

A number of interesting features emerge from a careful study of this table. First, ray economies of scale exist throughout the private sector, where institutions are typically relatively small. In the case of public sector institutions, the ray economies of scale are exhausted close to the mean size of institution (around 4500 undergraduates, 360 postgraduates, and $3 million per annum research income). These results are consistent with the existence of high fixed costs in higher education.

Second, product-specific economies of scale are extensively observed only in the public sector. Recall that fixed costs do not

**TABLE 8.1**
**Economies of Scale and Scope in Higher Education**

| Percentage of output means | *Product-specific economies* Under graduate | Post graduate | Research | Ray economies | Scope economies |
|---|---|---|---|---|---|
| | | | *Public sector* | | |
| 50 | 1.40 | 2.63 | 1.61 | 1.24 | −0.18 |
| 100 | 0.94 | 1.69 | 1.27 | 1.05 | −0.06 |
| 200 | 0.67 | 1.27 | 1.00 | 0.91 | 0.03 |
| | | | *Private sector* | | |
| 50 | 0.91 | 0.71 | 0.77 | 1.36 | 0.20 |
| 100 | 0.95 | 0.67 | 0.69 | 1.21 | 0.18 |
| 200 | 0.98 | 0.53 | 0.47 | 1.18 | 0.24 |

Source: Cohn, Rhine and Santos (1989).

appear in the calculation of product-specific scale economies, so that ray economies may exist even where product-specific economies do not. It seems, therefore, that it is largely due to economies of scope that universities and colleges have grown to their present scale. Nevertheless, product-specific scale economies in undergraduate teaching appear to dry up very rapidly as the scale of operations increases; indeed, it is only in public sector schools of below average size that such economies can be realised.

Finally, economies of scope exist in all universities and colleges except for relatively small public sector institutions. This is an interesting result, because it confirms the view that teaching and research are complementary activities. It contrasts, however, with the results obtained by Verry and Davies (1975, pp.56–8).

Economies of scope which might be available to universities take a variety of forms other than those obtainable by performing both research and teaching functions within the same organisation. The subject mix of a university also involves issues of scope economies. For instance, economies of scope can be achieved by teaching economics, education, mathematics, management, politics, sociology, and numerous other disciplines all in one place, because students of these subjects share a need to refer to a common set of books and articles. The optimal subject mix of a university is discussed in the next section.

## Optimal Subject Mix

The means whereby the needs of the labour market influence the demand for higher education courses in various subject areas were discussed in Chapter 4. In order to meet demand and respond to the needs of industry, the higher education system as a whole must supply student places according to a subject pattern which may be in a state of flux. This does not, however, necessarily mean that each institution should respond in identical fashion to the whims of the market.

While it is intuitively obvious that economies can be achieved by concentrating the provision of certain groups of subjects in certain institutions, it is not at all clear that all universities should aim to provide tuition in all subjects. It may be efficient for some to specialise in science, while others concentrate on the arts. In the remainder of this section we extend the above observations to investigate the determinants of the optimal subject mix, first of the system as a whole, and second of the individual institutions.

An early study of the mix of subjects taught in the UK university system is that of Taylor (1990). This study implicitly concerns the determination of subject mix at the level of the system, not of the individual institutions. Several indicators are constructed, each of which is designed to measure the labour market performance of graduates of each degree subject over the six years after their graduation. The indicators measure, separately for each of 25 subject areas, the unemployment rate of graduates, their average salary, the rate of increase of their average salary, and the proportion of graduates who work abroad. The unemployment data refer to graduates' experience both six months and six years after graduation; all other variables are measured at the later of these two dates, so that there are five indicators in total. The first two indicators are standard measures of labour market achievement. The rate of growth of salary and the propensity of graduates to work overseas are measures of dynamic disequilibrium in the subject-specific labour market; increases in these variables indicate, respectively, shortages and surpluses of qualified labour.

In order to arrive at a single measure of labour market performance, the 'z-scores' of the five indicators are derived. The z-score is simply the de-meaned value of the original indicator, adjusted so that the variance defined across all subject areas is unity; put simply, the z-score is the standardised value of the original indicator. The signs on the z-scores calculated for the unemployment and emigration variables are then reversed, so that a high z-score, thus adjusted, indicates a favourable outcome. The mean value of the five adjusted z-scores is then calculated for each of the 25 subject areas. These are shown, separately for males and females, in Table 8.2.

In addition to the labour market indicators discussed above, the National Survey of Graduates and Diplomates (NSGD) allows a number of indicators to be constructed based upon the subjective response of graduates to the value of their course. These responses indicate whether or not each graduate considers that her degree helped her to (a) get an interesting job, (b) secure a good income, and (c) become a widely educated person. These responses can be amalgamated in a fashion similar to that described above for the labour market indicators in order to obtain a single measure of graduate feedback. Table 8.2 reports the mean values of the z-scores on graduate feedback for the 25 subject areas as shown, separately for males and females.

It is clear from Table 8.2 that there is a strong correlation between labour market outcomes and graduate feedback, especially in the case of women. Indeed, the correlation coefficients between these two composite measures are 0.35 and 0.51 for males and females respectively. The following subject areas perform well according to both criteria: law, business, economics, accountancy, mathematics, computing, electrical engineering and health-related subjects. The availability of student places in these subjects should therefore be expanded, possibly at the expense of those subjects which perform relatively badly on both counts. As we saw in Chapter 4, there is an invisible hand which guides institutions to alter their provision over time in such a way as to reflect the needs of the labour market.

The above analysis is not entirely without problems, however. The equal weight attached to each indicator is essentially arbitrary, and the results may be sensitive to this choice of weighting scheme. Moreover it is not altogether clear that a high emigration rate always represents poor performance; the high rate of emigration amongst graduates of modern languages is surely a measure of success, not

**TABLE 8.2**
**Labour Market Performance and Graduate Feedback on Higher Education Courses, by Subject, Mean z-scores**

| Subject | *Labour market performance* | | *Graduate feedback* | |
|---|---|---|---|---|
| | Males | Females | Males | Females |
| Education | −0.27 | −0.23 | −0.45 | −0.19 |
| Pharmacy, health | 0.42 | 0.34 | 0.83 | 0.80 |
| Chemical engineering | −0.21 | 0.11 | 0.32 | 1.86 |
| Civil engineering | −0.28 | 0.38 | −0.82 | −0.95 |
| Electrical engineering | 0.56 | 0.12 | 0.84 | 1.53 |
| Mechanical engineering | 0.07 | −0.27 | −0.01 | −0.23 |
| Other engineering | 0.11 | −0.10 | 0.19 | −0.46 |
| Agriculture, etc. | −0.06 | 0.10 | 0.07 | −0.35 |
| Biology, botany | −0.58 | −0.45 | −0.66 | −0.21 |
| Zoology, physiology | −0.60 | −1.17 | −0.14 | −0.93 |
| Biochemistry | −0.65 | −0.13 | 0.12 | 0.18 |
| Mathematics, computing | 1.04 | 1.08 | 0.28 | 0.29 |
| Physics, maths/physics | −0.31 | −0.38 | 0.19 | −0.08 |
| Chemistry | 0.15 | 0.36 | −0.29 | −0.07 |
| Geology, environmental sciences | −1.17 | −0.98 | 0.53 | −0.40 |
| Other sciences | −0.01 | 0.01 | −0.16 | −0.19 |
| Business, economics | 1.42 | 1.19 | −0.07 | 0.44 |
| Geography | 0.03 | 0.17 | −0.54 | −0.19 |
| Law | 1.96 | 2.12 | 0.66 | 0.96 |
| Other social sciences | 0.11 | −0.10 | −0.47 | −0.33 |
| Architecture, planning | 0.05 | −0.08 | 0.05 | 0.18 |
| English | −0.30 | −0.54 | 0.04 | −0.48 |
| Languages | −0.56 | −0.85 | −0.03 | −0.49 |
| History | −0.18 | 0.00 | −0.20 | −0.28 |
| Other arts | −0.75 | −0.71 | −0.29 | −0.41 |

Source: Taylor (1990).

failure. The z-scores are unlikely to remain stable over time, since the education and labour markets will tend to interact (as seen in Chapter 4) in order to clear disequilibria. Finally, the analysis is based entirely upon teaching output, and makes no allowance for the influence of research.

It was argued earlier that the efficiency of the higher education system might best be served by allowing some institutions to specialise in certain broad fields. Evidence to support this assertion comes from the private sector American universities which operate in a competitive environment, and which might be expected to foster the prosperity only of the fittest. In that sector many institutions have prospered by offering relatively narrow curricula and filling niches; thus there exist a plethora of institutes of technology, business schools and liberal arts colleges. In the remainder of this section we consider why this should be so, and identify the factors which might determine the optimal structure of provision across the various types of university.

Suppose, for simplicity, that attention is focused exclusively on the teaching function of universities, that two universities exist, and that four courses of study ($x_1, x_2, x_3$ and $x_4$) are available. Assume that there are $N$ students in the system. The demand for each course is assumed perfectly inelastic and equals $N/4$. Assume further that the subject-specific returns to scale are declining up to a provision of $N/4$, but thereafter are constant within each institution and for every subject. Suppose that economies of scope arise from the joint production of $x_1$ and $x_2$, and also from the joint production of $x_3$ and $x_4$, but are not available from the joint production of any other pairs of outputs.

Full advantage of economies of scope could be obtained if both universities taught all four courses. This is because in both institutions the complementarity of pairing $x_1$ with $x_2$ and of pairing $x_3$ with $x_4$ would be exploited. Such a situation would not, however, fully exploit the subject-specific returns to scale. This is because the returns to scale could be increased (without affecting the returns to scope) by concentrating the output of $x_1$ and $x_2$ in one university, while $x_3$ and $x_4$ are catered for exclusively by the second institution. Only thus could the full (ray) scale economies be realised.

There is relatively little empirical evidence on which to assess the optimal pattern of provision of subjects across universities. The work of Dolton and Makepeace (1982) in the UK certainly suggests that five very distinct groups of universities exist. These clusters of institutions are characterised as follows: (a) universities specializing in engineering and technology, (b) the 'civic' universities, (c) universities specialising in arts and social sciences, (d) Oxford and Cambridge, and (e) London. If we focus our attention on the first and third groups, it is clear that fluctuations in the demand for student places on certain courses would have dramatic adjustment consequences for some institutions but none for others. The concentration of certain subjects in certain institutions has largely been determined by historical quirk or chance. Formal responsibility for the coordination of the curriculum across institutions lies with the HEFCE, but in this role the Council is inevitably bound by the constraints of historical legacy.

In the USA, almost all states have coordinating agencies or boards which aim to streamline the provision of higher education courses at public institutions within the state (McConnell, 1975). The role of such agencies in the coordination of curricula across universities has mainly been one of minimising unnecessary and inefficient duplication. In the American system, credit transfers allow students to complete different units of their degree at different institutions. The coordinating agencies can enhance efficiency by concentrating the provision of units for which demand will probably be low at just a few universities, rather than allowing all universities to teach all things to classes of sub-optimal size (Berdahl, 1971, Ch. 7). This allows students to take units of their choice even if they are not offered by the institution at which they are based; this they can do by attending summer sessions or by commuting to evening classes at another institution.

These coordination attempts by and large predate the modern theory of multi-product firms, and the extent to which they throw light on scope economies and diseconomies is accordingly limited. Where individual institutions are allowed to determine their own curricula it is important to assess the extent to which the outcome matches the requirements of global efficiency. If the match is not good, then a structure of incentives needs to be devised which will encourage independently operated institutions to develop in the manner which is socially optimal. The optimal pattern of provision in higher education is therefore a field of study where further research is urgently needed.

## Optimal Research Portfolios

Earlier in this chapter the importance of research as an activity efficiently carried out in universities was emphasised. In the present section we consider further the nature of research and, in particular, we address the question of how research activity is organised and coordinated across institutions.

Much research activity is funded by grants from public or private sector bodies rather than directly by the university itself. Individuals or groups of academics apply to a research council or similar body for a grant which is used to cover travel expenses and to hire secretarial and research assistance or time on scientific equipment owned by organisations other than the university. Such grants do not normally supplement the academics' own incomes but, by providing a budget which may be spent at the researchers' discretion, they considerably facilitate research activity. (An exception to this general rule occurs in the USA, where universities typically pay salaries to their faculty only for nine months of the year; in such cases grants may be awarded which compensate researchers for the remaining three months.) There is therefore an incentive for academics to direct their research activity towards areas likely to receive grant finance. In this way, the main grant-awarding bodies can exert some degree of influence on the coordination of research effort.

This influence is not very strong, though. The principle of 'academic freedom' has ensured that one of the few perquisites attached to the job of a university lecturer is that she can choose her own area of research activity. Furthermore, the multiplicity of grant-giving bodies and the relatively feeble nature of the incentive to apply for grants suggests that the degree of coordination of research effort is rather weak. Many academics seek to maximise their fame, and this is done by tackling in their research the burning issues of the day. Since there are fewer burning issues than there are academics, some duplication of effort is likely to occur. In the remainder of this section, we consider whether or not this implies that the national and international coordination of research effort is inefficient.

It is not uncommon for new facts (or inventions) to be discovered (or devised) simultaneously but independently by separate researchers or research groups. Commonly cited examples in economics are the kinked demand curve (Sweezy, 1939; Hall and Hitch, 1939), and the natural rate of unemployment (Friedman, 1968, Phelps, 1967). Instances such as these have been investigated in detail by Robert Merton (1961), and have come to be known as Merton multiples. Researchers who solve a given problem after its solution has been found by another team typically find it difficult to publish their results; it is likely therefore that the reported incidence of Merton multiples greatly understates the extent to which research effort is duplicated.

At first glance, it might seem as though the existence of Merton multiples betrays an inefficiency in the manner in which research is conducted, since it confirms that effort is duplicated. The fact that such multiples occur is not, however, of itself sufficient to demonstrate inefficiency. This is because research is inherently a risky activity, and consequently it may be optimal at the outset of a research programme to allow more than one group to investigate the problem. Thus if one group fails, another might still succeed. If more than one group succeeds it may appear, *ex post*, as though resources have been wasted; but *ex ante* the arrangement may have been efficient in that it may have maximised the *expected* surplus.

Although Merton multiples do not necessarily imply a waste of resources, it is nonetheless important to ascertain whether the research portfolios of various groups are, in terms of economic efficiency, too similar to one another. The remainder of this section tackles this question by reference to the theoretical work by Dasgupta and Maskin (1987). This work refers to the effect which imperfections in competition between research groups can have on the similarity or otherwise of the research projects which they undertake. To keep matters as simple as possible, we consider here a particularly simple variant of the Dasgupta and Maskin model; this recalls the much earlier work on industrial location pioneered by Hotelling (1929), and see also the textbook treatment by Smith (1981).

Consider a research programme in which two institutions, $i$ and $j$, are involved. Both institutions are seeking an answer to a specific problem and, in so doing, they may adopt approaches which are either very similar to one another or very different. Suppose that the degree of similarity of their approaches can be measured along a continuum; to be more precise, suppose that the continuum runs from $-1$ to $+1$, and that if an institution is midway along the continuum it adopts a very conventional approach to the problem. An institution located close to $-1$ takes a very unconventional approach, as does an institution located close to $+1$; but the ways in which these two institutions differ from convention are different from one another. For instance, the norm may be to take a consensus approach to solving economic problems; some institutions may be unconventional in that they adopt extreme Keynesian stances ($-1$), while others may adopt extreme monetarist positions ($+1$). For simplicity, suppose that the two institutions under examination lie on opposite sides of the mid-point, so that $i$ lies at a location whose address is positive, while $j$ lies at a location whose address is negative. Let $Q_i$ denote the research approach adopted by institution i, and let $Q_j$ represent the approach of institution $j$.

We assume that there exists a solution to the research problem under consideration; this solution will henceforth be referred to as 'truth'. Truth is certain to be found as a consequence of the research programme, though we do not know which research group will succeed in finding it. Moreover, truth has a known and given economic value. We assume also that past experience suggests that truth is equally likely to be found at any point along the continuum of possible research approaches. Thus for any specific problem we know that truth lies somewhere along this continuum, but we do not know where; what we do know is that it is as likely to be located at one point as at any other.

Suppose further that the costs to each institution of finding truth rise as the distance of truth from the institution's address increases, so that $C_i = |Q_i - A|$ and $C_j = |Q_j - A|$, where $A$ represents the (unknown) location of truth along the continuum. When truth is discovered, it is the institution which can reach truth with the lowest cost that makes the find. Society wishes to minimise the total cost of finding truth. To show how this can be done, it is useful to inspect Figure 8.2. Since truth is uniformly distributed across the interval from $-1$ to $+1$, and since the return to truth is given, the expected social surplus due to research activity is maximised by minimising costs – that is, by minimising the shaded area – with respect to choice of $Q_i$ and $Q_j$. Using the formula for the area of a triangle, this problem amounts to minimising, with respect to $Q_i$ and $Q_j$, the area

$$J = \{(1 + Q_j)^2 + (1 - Q_i)^2 + (Q_i - Q_j)^2/2\}/2 \qquad (8.13)$$

Differentiating with respect to $Q_i$ and setting the result to zero yields the condition

$$Q_j = 3Q_i - 2 \qquad (8.14)$$

while differentiating with respect to $Q_j$ and setting the result to zero gives

$$Q_i = 3Q_j + 2 \qquad (8.15)$$

Simultaneous solution of this pair of first order conditions gives the result $Q_i = 1/2$ and $Q_j = -1/2$. This makes good intuitive sense: optimisation of social welfare requires that the research groups are symmetrically located around the central point (zero), and they are placed at the points which guarantee the most even spread of costs across the continuum (see Figure 8.3).

**FIGURE 8.2**
**Leapfrogging to the Market Solution**

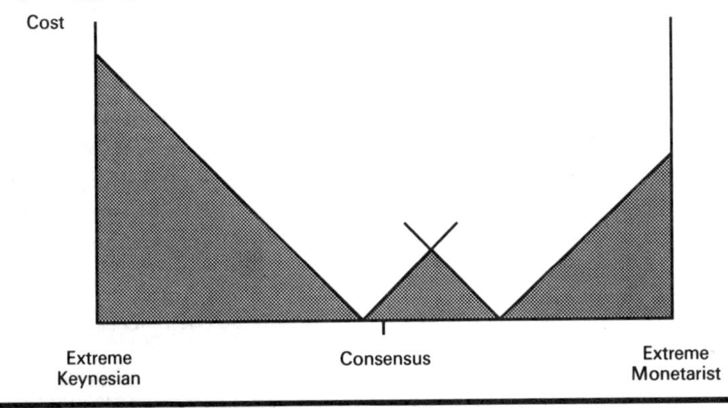


**FIGURE 8.3**
**The Social Optimum**

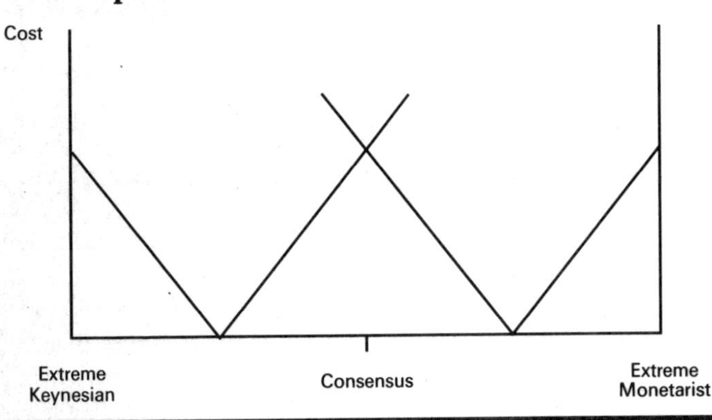

The incentive for individual research groups to behave in a manner consistent with social welfare optimisation is, in many circumstances, strong. If, for example, the returns to successful research were evenly spread across all research groups, the private benefit from research would reflect the social benefit, so the research groups would organise themselves in such a way as to maximise the social return to the research programme. However, this is not the way of the world. Typically the returns to successful research are enjoyed only by the research group which (first) discovers truth. This is so, for example, in the case of the drug company which first discovers a cure for AIDS: it will make large profits which are not shared with the unsuccessful losers in the research race. Likewise it is also true for the first research group to develop a new theory of wage or price rigidity: the credit for developing and publishing a new theory can belong only to one research group.

In such a winner-takes-all scenario, the incentive for individual research groups to behave in a socially optimal manner is absent. There is an incentive, instead, for each research group to 'cheat' by trying to 'steal' some of the province of the other group. For example, suppose that group $i$ remains located at the point $+1/2$ along the

**FIGURE 8.4**
**The Market Solution**

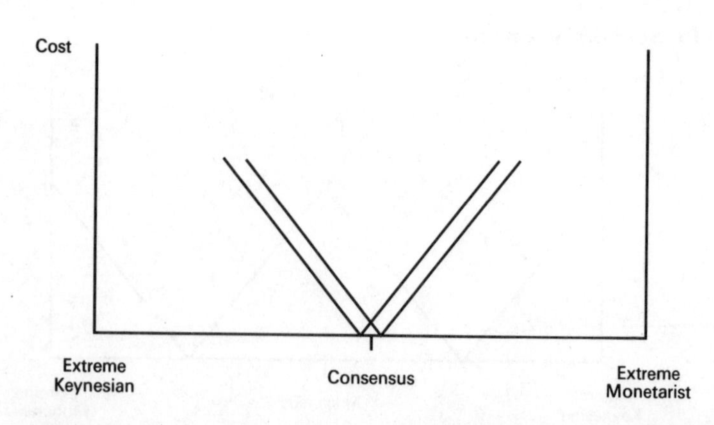

research continuum; then group *j* can increase its chances of winning the research race by moving in towards the centre. By moving from $-1/2$ to $-1/4$, say, group *j* raises its chance of winning from $1/2$ to $9/16$. Once group *i* realises what group *j* has done, it will retaliate by moving in towards the centre itself. This process continues until, in the extreme, both groups are located at the centre of the research continuum (see Figure 8.4). The Cournot adjustment process, typical of situations where competition is imperfect, here results in research groups conducting their work using methods which are, from society's point of view, too similar to one another.

The above model can vividly be illustrated by considering a pair of policemen searching for clues in a field. They start at one end of the field and walk straight across to the other end, using binoculars to search the territory. Suppose initially that the policemen share a reward if one of them finds a clue. Their best chance of finding a clue is realised when one policeman is located a quarter of the way along the width of the field, while the other is located three-quarters of the way along (cf. Figure 8.3). Now suppose that the entire reward goes to the policeman who finds the clue. Starting from a position where the two policemen are evenly spaced across the width of the field, each policeman will try to 'steal' some of the other's territory by moving into the middle. They will gradually edge towards each other until both are located at the centre. The behaviour which is (in a non-cooperative Cournot setting) privately optimal for the policemen thus differs substantially, in the winner-takes-all scenario, from the socially optimal approach.

While society is indifferent about which policeman (or institution) first achieves success in search (or research), each of the individual policemen (or institutions) has an unusually strong interest in its own success so long as a winner-takes-all reward scheme is in place. Each therefore chooses its 'address' along the field (or research continuum) according to its own (not society's) preferences. In the case of research groups, society would prefer that the two institutions should adopt very different approaches, since it does not want to place all its eggs in one basket. Equally clearly, there is an incentive for each institution to adopt an approach similar to that of its competitor. The result is that 'academics are not lone wolves trying . . . to differentiate themselves from their rivals; they work on projects which are far too similar!' (Dasgupta and Maskin, 1987, p.594).

# Conclusion

Tertiary education has much in common with primary and secondary schooling: all three sectors exist in large part to augment human capital stocks; they respond to the needs of the labour market; and they are the subject of choices made by the public. To be sure, there are differences; universities are usually larger than schools – a result of the cost factors studied in Chapter 6 – and consequently many students must live away from their parental home while studying. This is in itself, of course, an educational experience. The most important difference between universities and schools in the primary and secondary sectors, though, is that the former exist not only to impart knowledge and understanding. They also create it.

This multiproduct aspect of a university's operation – the need to provide teaching (of various kinds) and research – makes the tertiary sector distinctive. The university sector must therefore face and answer questions about the relative support which should be afforded to its various activities. In particular, what is the appropriate balance between teaching and research? And should some institutions be encouraged to specialise more in either research or teaching activity than others? These are questions which cannot be answered in the absence of a great deal of management information. Rational decision making requires the use of a variety of measures of university performance. These – along with analogous measures designed for use in the primary and secondary sectors – form the subject of the next two chapters.

# Performance Indicators

## Introduction

To measure the performance of any organisation, it is first necessary to know the goals which it seeks to achieve. A firm is said to perform well if it seeks to maximise its profits and succeeds in this aim. A charity performs well if it tries to minimise the impact of famine and indeed does so. It would not be appropriate, however, to measure the charity's performance by reference to its profit and loss account; neither would it make sense to assess the performance of a car manufacturer by the league position of the soccer team whose players bear the firm's logo on their shirts.

For the organisations described above, the measurement of performance is fairly straightforward; there is a 'bottom line' – such as profits, or numbers of lives saved, or some other measure – which alone can serve as the objective function to be maximised. In education (as in many public services), however, things are not so simple.

Educational institutions are multi-product firms. Their output consists of the development of the individual student, and (in the case of universities) the advancement of knowledge. The development of the individual involves the acquisition of a peculiar mix of many different skills: literacy, numeracy, manual dexterity, physical strength, mental agility, facility with languages, cultural appreciation, scientific understanding, and so on. Typically a given individual, upon leaving an institution, will have acquired only some of these skills during her course of study; the institution therefore produces many different types of graduate, and in this sense produces multiple products.

The market for education is not a perfect one since there are externalities attached to the production of literate and numerate individuals as communication becomes easier; likewise there are externalities associated with passing on cultural values; and, in the case of the universities, basic research has the properties of non-rivalness and non-excludability characteristic of public goods. So market prices do not exist for the output of educational institutions. In this respect, schools and colleges are very different from other types of multi-product firm. The absence of market prices means that it is not possible to calculate an unambiguous 'bottom line' measure of overall performance; this is because no guidance is available from the market on what weights should be attached to each type of output in calculating a summary measure of performance.

There are several aspects of the performance of educational institutions which the authorities might wish to monitor. One is the achievement of students as measured by examination results. Another is the rate of truancy or dropping-out. A third is the employability and labour market performance of school leavers or graduates. All these indicators concern the teaching aspect of the educational system. In the case of the universities, where research is also a primary objective, measures of research performance might also be required. Indicators have been developed which attempt to measure all of these aspects of institutional performance (see, for example, J. Johnes and Taylor, 1990; Cave, Hanney and Kogan, 1991; G. Johnes, 1992).

Since there are several dimensions to the performance of educational institutions (and since each dimension needs a separate measure), it is very likely that no institution will perform uniformly well or uniformly badly across all dimensions. For example, a school which concentrates its resources on the most able and highly motivated pupils may send a high proportion of its pupils on to higher education, but it may simultaneously have a high truancy rate amongst the less able pupils. Likewise a university department may achieve a good research record by devoting little time to teaching. It is this type of complexity which has spawned a vast literature on performance indicators.

It is clear from the above discussion that the evaluation of performance in educational institutions is by no means an easy matter. Two problems in particular may be identified. The first concerns the relationship between the output of the education system and the inputs used in production. In constructing measures of school performance it is clearly not sufficient simply to measure the output of a group of schools; allowance needs to be made for inter-school differences in the quantity and quality of inputs used in the production process. Thus it should be no surprise to find that examination results are better in a school which benefits from the voluntary contributions of predominantly professional parents than in a poorly resourced inner city school. Such a finding would not, of itself, provide much information about the relative effectiveness of the two schools. This problem – identifying the relationship between inputs and outputs – has been addressed in the literature by the use of regression analyses and multi-level modelling.

The second problem which is addressed in this chapter concerns the means by which weights can be assigned to the various outputs of the education system. Market prices cannot be used because of the severe imperfections in the market for education. A possible solution to this predicament is to use data envelopment analysis (DEA). This method uses the tools of linear programming to provide measures of technical efficiency in multi-product organisations, and was designed specifically for use in contexts where market prices are absent.

The remainder of this chapter discusses these two problems in greater depth, and provides examples of the use of regression analysis, multi-level modelling and DEA in the study of educational institutions' performance. The examples concern a number of possible indicators of performance, including truancy rates, drop-out rates, examination results, and the production of published research results.

## The Relationship between Inputs and Outputs

In evaluating the competence with which an institution carries out its tasks, it is necessary first to establish the difficulty of those tasks. So performance evaluation is rendered more difficult where institutions have a multiplicity of goals, especially where different institutions do not attach the same degree of importance to each goal. Furthermore, if institutions do not all enjoy the same resources, the task of realising a given set of targets is harder for some institutions than for others. For instance, it is harder for a comprehensive state school located in a socially deprived area to achieve given levels of pupil performance at national examinations than is the case for a selective private school. Because of this, considerable interest has developed in the concept of value-added performance indicators (Gallagher, 1991).

The basic idea underlying value added performance indicators is that institutions should be judged according to the change in their students' performance during their time at that institution. Thus the degree results awarded by two universities could be compared directly against each other if the entry examination (or General Certificate of Education – Advanced level) grades of their intakes are similar. Where data are available on students' performance before entry to high school, value-added performance indicators can be constructed for secondary institutions too.

Clearly the problem becomes more complicated if the quality of intake differs across institutions. This complication can, to some extent, be bypassed by measuring comparative value added. This is done as follows: the actual distribution of examination or degree results achieved by students at a given institution is compared with the distribution which might have been expected on the basis of the entrance qualifications of the students and the performance of similar students in all institutions nationally. Thus, in a given university, more students than expected might graduate with first-class honours while fewer than expected graduate with third-class honours. It is tempting to conclude that such an institution is performing well relative to the national average. But what if the same institution has fewer numbers graduating with upper second-class honours and more with lower second-class honours than would be expected on the basis of the quality of intake? Unambiguous conclusions cannot be drawn in this case. A scalar measure of comparative value added can, of course, be derived, but only by assigning essentially arbitrary values to degrees of different classes and entry qualifications of different types (McGeevor *et al.*, 1990).

The problems inherent in the use of such naive value added performance indicators can, at least partially, be alleviated by the use of regression analysis. Where only one type of output is produced using many inputs, statistical methods designed to estimate the functional form which best fits the observed scatter of data points enable the full impact on output of marginal increments of each input to be assessed. Moreover, multi-variate regression allows a much richer variety of inputs to be considered than do the naive value-added models discussed above. In the remainder of this section three examples of the use of regression analysis in the study of school or university performance are considered; these concern drop-outs from university, school truancy and school examination results.

The rate at which students prematurely drop out of higher education courses has been proposed as an indicator of institutional performance. The social rate of return on drop-outs, though positive, is lower than that achieved on graduates who stay the course. Consequently high rates of student drop-out are indicative of wasted investment. For this reason the problem is frequently referred to as that of student 'wastage', or attrition. Since universities experiencing high wastage rates presumably generate a lower surplus to society than do other institutions, rates of student attrition might provide an indicator of one aspect of institutional performance. The extent of inter-university differences in rates of student attrition in Britain is quite remarkable: for those who entered university in 1980, for example, the drop-out rate (calculated as the percentage of entrants who failed to complete their degree successfully within six years of entry on to their course) varied from 3.4 per cent (Cambridge) to 23.6 per cent (Aberdeen).

Great care needs to be taken in interpreting these figures, though. In the UK, student characteristics such as ability, gender, family background and labour market experience are known to be powerful determinants of the probability of dropping out (J. Johnes, 1990). Similar results have been obtained for the USA by Astin (1975), Peng and Fetters (1978) and Tinto (1982); work on data for individual students suggests further that psychological variables are of considerable importance in determining attrition propensities. Choice of degree subject also influences student wastage, possibly because failure rates are higher for some subjects than for others.

At university level, then, it is likely that wastage is determined by factors such as the quality of the student intake and the mix of subjects in which tuition is supplied. J. Johnes and Taylor (1989) study the determinants of student attrition in a weighted regression analysis run over a cross-section of 45 UK universities. The dependent variable, *WASTAGE*, is the percentage of entrants in 1980 who had not graduated six years later. This is explained as a function of four variables: the quality of student intake, *QUAL*, measured by the institution-specific average A-level score of entrants (assigning 5 points to grade A, 4 to grade B and so on); subject mix, *SUBJECT*, measured by the percentage of entrants at each institution enrolling for degree schemes in language, adminstrative, business, or social studies; a residence variable, *RESIDE*, which measures the percentage of full-time undergraduates at each university who live in halls of residence; and a binary variable which has unit value for the Scottish universities, *SCOT*. University entrants in Scotland are, on average, younger than their counterparts elsewhere in Britain; furthermore, university courses in Scotland are typically longer than are corresponding courses south of the border, thus giving students an extra year in which to drop out.

Typical of the results obtained in this study is the following equation:

$$\underset{}{WASTAGE} = \underset{(18.3)}{36.46} - \underset{(9.0)}{1.59}\, QUAL - \underset{(5.1)}{0.14\, SUBJECT}$$

$$\underset{(3.1)}{-0.06\, RESIDE} + \underset{(4.7)}{4.05\, SCOT}$$

Figures in parentheses are *t* ratios. The coefficient of determination, at 0.83, indicates that the equation provides a good fit to the scatter of data points. Indeed, it suggests that after controlling for variations in the four explanatory variables the inter-university differences in attrition rates are very modest.

These results confirm that the quality of intake negatively influences attrition. More able students are less likely to drop out than are others because they are less likely to fail examinations; they may also be more highly motivated. Improving the average A-level score of entrants by three points (from CCC to BBB, say) would improve a university's wastage rate by almost five percentage points. The wastage rate is relatively low in universities which specialise in language, business and social studies, possibly because the spread of examination performance in these subjects is generally relatively narrow (Winters, Ulph and Taylor, 1989; Mar Molinero and Portilla, 1993). Finally, universities which are able to offer rooms in residence to a large proportion of their students are likely to benefit from a lower wastage rate than other (otherwise similar) institutions; this may be due to the proximity of students in these universities to computing and library facilities and to the fostering of an academic culture. The impact on wastage of accommodation arrangements is, however, quite small.

The personal characteristics of the individual student – especially ability – are the main factors which influence the probability of not completing a degree course. That being so, the scope for using student attrition as an indicator of university performance is limited.

Regression methods have also been used to investigate truancy rates in secondary schools (Galloway, Martin and Wilcox, 1985). In this study, weighted logit analysis is used to investigate the determinants of persistent absenteeism across 33 schools in the Sheffield area. The dependent variable is a measure (specifically, the logged odds) of the proportion of a school's pupils who miss most of their schooling at the time of three annual surveys held over the period 1974–6. Despite testing for the significance of over 50 potential determinants of absenteeism, the authors find support for a very simple model. Absenteeism thus depends on just a handful of explanatory variables: these are the percentage of the school's pupils who are entitled to receive free school meals owing to low parental income, and the percentages of households in the school's catchment area living in (a) shared dwellings and (b) furnished tenancies. A quadratic term in the free school meals variable is also included. This last variable enables the tendency for the absenteeism rate to rise, but to do so at a decreasing rate, as the proportion of pupils entitled to free school meals increases. It should be noted that each of these variables is a measure of social disadvantage, and each positively influences the rate of persistent absenteeism. Together they explain some 92.4 per cent of the variance observed in the absenteeism rate across schools (this being measured by the reduction in the deviance).

All the determinants of absenteeism reported above concern characteristics of the school's catchment area. Despite testing for the significance of more than 30 variables which may be under the school's control – the presence of banding by ability, remedial teaching, pastoral care, careers guidance, teacher turnover and so on – none of these proved to be statistically significant. Thus it would be inappropriate to use truancy rates as a measure of school effectiveness, since absenteeism depends almost entirely upon social factors related to the location of the school; the way in which the school is run appears to have little impact.

Typically educational performance indicators must be developed on the basis of information collected at the level of the school, college or department. Large-scale surveys yielding detailed information about individual students at many different institutions are rare. Where such information is available, however, regression analyses can be used to provide far richer conclusions than are available from studies employing less informative data sources. Variations in performance due both to differences across institutions and to differences across the students attending each of those institutions can be distinguished. Moreover, inter-institutional variation in the effects of student characteristics on performance can be identified. Since the data used in studies of this type refer to two levels – namely the educational institution and the individual student – the method of analysis is often referred to as multi-level modelling (Schagen, 1991).

A particularly interesting application of multi-level modelling in the field of education concerns the relative performance of a 25 per cent random sample of pupils drawn from 18 secondary schools in a single Local Education Authority in Britain (Aitkin and Longford, 1986). This builds on the pioneering work of Rutter *et al.* (1979). The aspect of performance considered in the former study is a measure of the number of passes obtained in external examinations typically taken at the age of 16 (the General Certificate of Education or Ordinary Level, and Certificate of Secondary Education examinations). Following the scoring system used by the Inner London Education Authority (ILEA), O-level grades of A, B, C, D and E are awarded 7, 6, 5, 4 and 3 points respectively, while CSE grades 1, 2, 3, 4 and 5 are counted as 5, 4, 3, 2 and 1 points respectively. Thus a pupil who achieves four grade B passes at O-level plus three grade 1 passes at CSE has an ILEA score of 39 points. The mean ILEA score varies considerably across the comprehensive schools in the study from 11.8 to 26.9; the two single-sex grammar schools achieved mean ILEA scores of 37.6 and 52.0.

The input variable used in this study is pupils' average Verbal Reasoning Quotient (VRQ) – a measure of intellectual ability – on entry to the school. Mean VRQ in the comprehensive schools ranged from 89.0 to 104.5; not surprisingly, the grammar schools enjoyed considerably higher mean VRQs, at 120.4 and 121.9.

The analysis proceeds by first using data collected at the level of the individual pupil to regress the ILEA score against the VRQ and a set of binary variables, each of which captures the effect of one of the schools in the sample. This yields

$$ILEA = 0.82\ VRQ + 18\ school\ dummies \tag{9.1}$$

The coefficient on VRQ is highly significant and the overall fit of the regression is good. It should be noted, though, that the fit is also good if the 18 school dummies are replaced by a single constant intercept term; this suggests that most of the variation in ILEA score is the consequence of differences in pupils' innate ability, and cannot be attributed to differences in school effectiveness. Nevertheless it is tempting to use equation (9.1) to produce a ranking of the institutions by reference to the coefficients on the dummy variables. Other methods of ranking institutions are also available, but are not discussed here (see Aitkin and Longford, 1986).

School rankings of this kind always assume that the slope of the relationship between inputs (VRQ) and outputs (ILEA) is constant across institutions; it is only the intercept term which is allowed systematically to vary, and it is the variation of this intercept term that provides the analyst with a performance indicator. However, the constant slopes assumption might be a strong one. It would, for example, be reasonable to suppose that the marginal effect on ILEA score of increased VRQ is greater for comprehensives than for grammar schools; this is simply because the scope for improved pupil performance is, in the former case, more substantial. This hypothesis can be tested by running 18 separate regressions of pupils' ILEA scores on VRQ, one regression for each school in the sample. F tests can then be conducted to establish whether the coefficients on VRQ differ significantly across schools. In the study under consideration the slope coefficients do indeed differ across schools.

This result suggests an intriguing possibility. Consider two schools, *A* and *B*. Suppose that the coefficient on VRQ is substantially higher for school *A* than for school *B*. It may then be the case that school *B* outperforms school *A* where the mean VRQ of the intake is low, but that the reverse is true where mean VRQ is high; that is, there is a crossover point at a plausible value of mean VRQ. This is illustrated in Figure 9.1. The data used in the study considered here provide an interesting example. Where the pupil intake of schools has a mean

**FIGURE 9.1**
**Multi-Level Modelling**

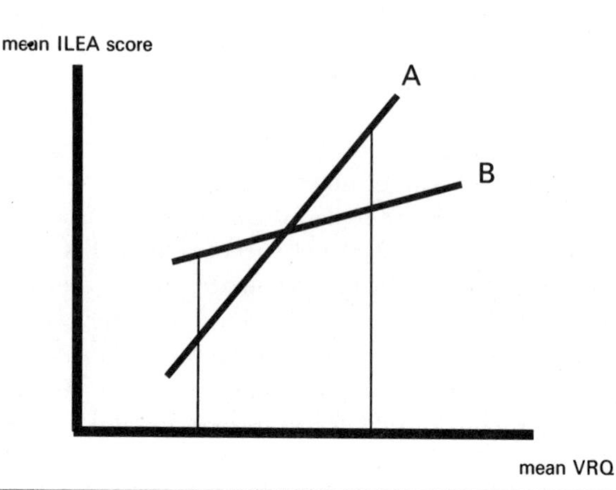


VRQ of 95 or less, the grammar schools are the two highest-ranking institutions: that is, these are the schools which (given mean VRQ) promise the highest return in terms of mean ILEA score. If, however, mean VRQ rises to 110, the girls' grammar school falls to eighth place in the rankings. This implies that many of that school's pupils would be better served by attending one of the local comprehensives, while some pupils currently at comprehensive schools would benefit by attending the girls' grammar! So assessing the relative performance of the schools in the sample is no easy matter; both the absolute performance of a school and its performance relative to other institutions depend crucially upon the average quality of its intake. The conclusions that schools (and teachers) differ considerably in their effectiveness has been replicated in studies conducted in many different countries (see, for example, Hanushek, 1971, 1986; Scheerens, 1992).

A second example of multi-level modelling is the influential study of 50 London primary schools conducted by Mortimore *et al.* (1988). Their analysis controls for pupils' characteristics such as gender, ethnicity, social class, family composition, health and experience of nursery education. They control also for measures of the pupils' ability and behaviour on entry into primary schooling. Despite such an impressive battery of control variables, they find statistically significant differences across schools in pupil performance. For instance, some 9 per cent of the variation in reading attainment observed across the 2000 pupils in the sample is due to membership of different schools. The remaining 91 per cent, however, is due either to pupil characteristics or to purely random variation. Table 9.1 shows corresponding data for the percentage variation in a number of further measures of performance due to school effects. These figures are not high but neither are they negligible; they are in general statistically significant, and this suggests that schools do indeed vary in the quality of educational services provided. It should be noted that schools which perform well according to one measure do not necessarily do so according to others. Although there is a positive correlation between school rankings defined by the various measures in Table 9.1, this correlation is generally weak. Different schools have different strengths.

Multi-level modelling therefore suggests that the ranking of institutions is a far more complicated exercise than would at first appear. There are horses for courses; some schools serve some kinds of pupil well but not others. Unfortunately, multi-level modelling is expensive in terms of data requirements, and this has limited its use so far to a handful of exercises which are best viewed as pilot studies.

Overall, the regression approach to performance indicators provides an opportunity fully to allow for the role of input variations

**TABLE 9.1**
**Percentage of the Variation in Performance Attributable to Primary School Effects, Pupil Characteristics Controlled**

| Performance measure | School effect (%) |
|---|---|
| Reading | 9 |
| Writing | 13 |
| Speaking skills | 27 |
| Mathematics | 11 |
| Behaviour | 10 |
| Attendance | 6 |
| Self-esteem | 8 |
| Attitude towards school | 8–12 |

Source: Mortimore *et al.* (1988), Ch. 9.

in determining inter-institutional differences in output. It provides information about the resource mix which is best suited to effective production in the education sector. It has become the dominant methodology in the field of performance indicators. In addition to the studies of truancy, dropping out and secondary school examination results referred to above, a considerable body of research uses regression methods to study aspects of performance such as graduate employability (G. Johnes, Taylor and Ferguson, 1987; J. Johnes and Taylor, 1990), degree results (Bee and Dolton, 1985; J. Johnes and Taylor, 1987) and research productivity (G. Johnes, 1988a; J. Johnes and Taylor, 1990; J. Johnes, Taylor and Francis, 1993).

The conclusion of this section is clear. Attempts to measure the performance of educational institutions should carefully allow for inter-institutional differences in inputs, otherwise measures designed to test the effectiveness of schools would instead reflect only their output. Far from rewarding lean and fit institutions, such efforts might encourage obesity.

## Measuring Efficiency in Non-Market Multi-Product Organisations

Educational institutions are typically multi-product organisations. For example, secondary schools produce at least two types of school leaver: those with a vocational orientation and those with an academic orientation. Universities produce graduates with many different skills, and moreover also produce research in a variety of subject areas. By no means all of these outputs are supplied to perfect markets, and consequently there are no market prices available to provide an objective evaluation of the relative worth of the various outputs. Because no such prices exist, particular problems attach to the measurement of efficiency in non-market multi-product organisations.

Fortunately, recent developments in the field of linear programming allow some progress to be made in evaluating the relative efficiency of educational institutions. In particular, the method of DEA allows an assessment to be made of the technical and managerial efficiency of each decision-making unit (DMU) in the sample. DEA does not allow questions of allocative efficiency to be addressed, since it has been designed for use in situations where returns to scale are constant and where no market prices exist. For this reason, it is most commonly used to determine the efficiency of public sector organisations, such as local authorities, hospitals or schools. The method of DEA is explained in detail by Sexton (1986) and Boussofiane, Dyson and Thanassoulis (1991), and the interested reader is referred to these sources for further information; here only a brief and intuitive outline is provided.

Each DMU (say a local education authority, a school or a university department) produces a number of distinct outputs using several inputs. To simplify as far as possible the exposition, it is henceforth assumed that only one input is used (the labour input of teachers, say), and only two outputs are produced (say, vocationally oriented school leavers and academically oriented school leavers). This simplification has the advantage of allowing the DEA problem conveniently to be represented on a graph. (More complicated and realistic examples need to be solved by computer using linear programming techniques such as the simplex algorithm.)

To proceed, suppose that there are just four DMUs, and that these are labelled *A*, *B*, *C* and *D*. The inputs used and outputs produced by these four DMUs are shown in Table 9.2. It is helpful to think of these DMUs as schools producing different types of school leaver. Clearly the priorities of the four schools differ considerably. School *B* concentrates substantially on vocational education, while *C* has a much more academic orientation, and *A* fills the middle ground. Any

**TABLE 9.2**
**Inputs and Outputs of Four Decision-Making Units**

| DMU | Labour input | Output of vocationally oriented graduates | Output of academically oriented graduates | Per capitum output of vocationally oriented graduates | Per capitum output of academically oriented graduates |
|---|---|---|---|---|---|
| A | 45 | 135 | 135 | 3 | 3 |
| B | 60 | 240 | 60 | 4 | 1 |
| C | 75 | 75 | 300 | 1 | 4 |
| D | 90 | 270 | 180 | 3 | 2 |

weighting scheme which attaches relatively great value to an academic education would therefore favour *C*, while a scheme which puts a relatively high weight on vocational education best serves the interests of *B*.

One thing that is clear from Table 9.2, though, is that there is no weighting scheme that can make school *D* appear more efficient than school *A*. Each staff member at school *D* produces two academically oriented graduates per year, but each staff member at school *A* produces three, and there is no difference between these two schools in terms of per capitum output of vocationally oriented leavers. So *D* must be a technically inefficient DMU.

The above argument can be made clearer by appealing to a graphical analysis. The piecewise linear concave production possibility frontier implied by the data in Table 9.2 is illustrated in Figure 9.2. The axes measure the per capitum output of academically and

**FIGURE 9.2**
**Data Envelopment Analysis**

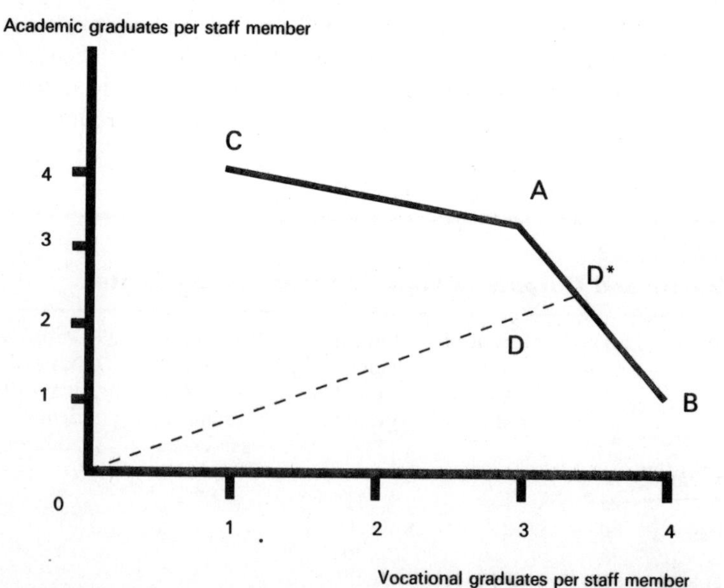

vocationally oriented school leavers. Schools *A*, *B* and *C* all lie on the production possibility frontier. The input–output combinations used by these schools are known to be feasible because they occur in life; the combinations observed on the lines joining the three points representing these schools must also be feasible given the standard concavity assumption. Since the input–output combination used by school *D* lies entirely within the frontier, this school must be technically inefficient. This is so no matter what weights are assigned to the two per capitum output measures in the problem.

Suppose now that weights are assigned to the two outputs produced by the schools in the sample, so that a weighted total of per capitum output can be calculated for each school. The vector of weights most favourable to school *D* (that is, the set of weights which would bring the school closest to the efficiency frontier) in this case assigns exactly twice as much weight to vocationally oriented as to academically oriented school leavers. It is for this reason that Figure 9.2 is drawn with different scales on the two axes. It is now clear that a useful measure of *D*'s technical efficiency is the ratio OD/OD* on this diagram. In this example, then, *D*'s *efficiency score*, OD/OD*, equals 8/9. This means that, even if the weighting scheme most favourable to *D* is assumed, school *D* is only 88.9 per cent as efficient as it could be.

As observed earlier, school *D* is the only DMU in the current example which lies below the efficiency frontier. The other schools must therefore all have efficiency scores of unity. It should be noted that this does not imply that school *C*, say, is pursuing objectives which are in any sense socially optimal; it merely implies that each school on the efficiency frontier is unsurpassed in the efficiency with which it pursues the particular set of goals for which it has chosen to aim. Thus a criticism of DEA is that it deems some DMUs efficient simply because they are different from the norm. By allowing each DMU to choose the weights vector most favourable to itself, DEA is generous in what it terms efficient. However, if (even under such favourable assumptions) a DMU falls short of technical efficiency, then there is scope for efficiency gains. No value judgements are necessary in order to reach this conclusion so, even though DEA does not provide complete answers to impossible questions, it nevertheless can usefully highlight cases of technical inefficiency.

The first useful property of DEA, then, is that it can identify technically inefficient DMUs, and can provide an indication of the extent of inefficiency. A second advantage of the technique concerns the managerial information yielded by the analysis. In particular, a glance at Figure 9.2 shows that school *D* is strictly dominated by schools *A* and *B*. That is, *A* and *B* lie on a concave frontier which passes both above and to the right of school *D* on the diagram. That is, *A* and *B* are the efficient schools which most closely resemble school *D* in terms of their input–output technologies. So it is by emulating schools *A* and *B* that *D* can aspire to reach the efficiency frontier in future. For this reason, *A* and *B* are referred to as the *efficient reference set* of school *D*.

Having outlined the principles of the method of DEA, it is now appropriate to consider examples of its use in the evaluation of the performance of educational suppliers. Two examples will be considered in the remainder of this section. The first concerns secondary school examination results; the second concerns the research output of university departments of economics.

Jesson, Mayston and Smith (1987) and Mayston and Jesson (1988) use DEA to study the effectiveness of the 96 English Local Education Authorities (LEAs). Four inputs are assumed to influence the output of schools within each LEA. The first of these is educational expenditure. The remaining three inputs represent the percentage of pupils within each LEA whose head of household is respectively of high socio-economic status, a single parent, and unemployed. The output variables used in the study concern two different levels of student achievement; the percentage of school leavers respectively passing (at least) five and (at least) three standard public examinations at the age of 16 (O-levels or their equivalent). These output measures are designed to capture the success of each LEA in catering for academic high-flyers and the general body of pupils respectively.

In these studies exactly one-third of all LEAs lie on the efficiency frontier estimated using DEA, so most LEAs suffer from x-inefficiency. The least technically efficient authorities (Barking and Norfolk) achieve efficiency scores of 0.88. This is encouraging in that it suggests that losses due to technical inefficiency in LEAs are not very considerable.

The second example of the use of DEA in the construction of education performance indicators concerns the research output of university departments. Three broad approaches to the analysis of research performance can be identified (Irvine and Martin, 1983; G.

Johnes, 1988b). The first is *peer review*. This involves identifying a group of eminent researchers in the field concerned, which then forms a collective subjective assessment of the research performance of each department. The periodic research assessment exercises of the British UFC are conducted by means of a peer review informed by quantitative data.

The second method which is used to assess research performance is to count, over a given period, the number of times research publications authored by members of the department are referred to elsewhere in the literature. This method is known as *citations analysis*. To tot up citations in this way sounds a formidable task, but data are available from the Institute of Scientific Information (ISI) in Philadelphia which greatly facilitate the task. The ISI produces the Social Science Citations Index (SSCI) as a tool to help researchers locate publications relevant to their field of interest. The SSCI is available in machine readable form, and can be used to establish the number of references made in the literature to the work of individual researchers over a given time period. Frequency of citation is likely to provide a good measure of the impact of a department's work on the scientific community. However, it is not necessarily the case that impact goes hand-in-hand with quality: some publications are cited because they provide views which conflict with those of the author (Moravcsik and Murugesan, 1975). An example of citations analysis applied to the field of economics is the work of Liebowitz and Palmer (1988).

The third measure of research performance involves a *publications count*. In this case, a weighted sum of all publications produced by members of a department over a given period is obtained. Different weights are assigned to different types of publication. For instance, a book may be deemed to be worth four times as much as a journal article (or twice as much, or ten times as much). In more refined publications counts, extra weight might be attached to articles published in the 'core' journals of the field: in economics, for example, such journals might include (amongst others) the *American Economic Review*, the *European Economic Review*, and the *Economic Journal*. It is in these journals (whose contents are often cited elsewhere in the literature) that the most influential work tends to be published. A publications count approach has been used by numerous researchers, including Harris (1988, 1990) and Graves, Marchand and Thompson (1982).

Numerous problems are associated with all three of the above methods (G. Johnes, 1988b). For this reason Irvine and Martin (1983) have argued that the results of research assessment exercises should be taken seriously only to the extent that the three methods produce similar rankings of departments. However, in the remainder of this section, we shall focus on just one of the difficulties faced by analysts wishing to conduct a publications count. To be specific, where the ranking of departments is sensitive to the choice of weights associated with various types of publication, how can the relative efficiency of different departments be assessed?

A number of studies have used DEA to assess research performance in university departments. Beasley (1990) has studied departments of physics and chemistry, while Tomkins and Green (1988) have considered departments of accounting. G. Johnes and J. Johnes (1992) use DEA to tackle this issue in their evaluation of the research performance of 36 British university departments of economics over the period 1984–8. Their analysis makes use of data collected by the Royal Economic Society as part of a study running alongside the UFC's research selectivity exercise (G. Johnes, 1990). A typical example of the results achieved by applying DEA to this data set is shown in Table 9.3. This table shows the efficiency scores derived from an analysis where two inputs and three outputs are taken into account. The first input is the total number of faculty members in the economics department; the second is the number of faculty members in the department employed on research only contracts (that is, they have no teaching responsibilities). The first type of output considered is articles in academic journals (articles in top journals are separately identified so that they can be assigned extra weight); the final output is chapters in edited books.

The efficiency scores estimated by this method are instructive. York and Birkbeck appear to be technically efficient, though both departments are known to be unusual: the former employs a large number on research-only contracts, while the latter has an extremely light undergraduate teaching load. Both these departments received the top rank in the UFC peer review which covered the same time period. Another department which performed well in the UFC peer review is Warwick, and this department also scores highly in the DEA. Overall, the correlation between the DEA rankings and the results of the peer review is fairly high, at 0.58.

**TABLE 9.3**
**Efficiency Scores of UK University Economics Departments, based on Publications Analysis**

| Department | Efficiency score |
|---|---|
| Aberdeen | 0.88 |
| Aberystwyth | 0.55 |
| Bangor | 0.74 |
| Bath | 0.76 |
| Belfast | 0.43 |
| Birmingham | 0.40 |
| Bristol | 0.68 |
| Cambridge | 0.64 |
| Cardiff | 0.29 |
| City | 0.28 |
| Dundee | 0.70 |
| Durham | 0.70 |
| Edinburgh | 0.40 |
| Exeter | 0.30 |
| Glasgow | 0.44 |
| Heriot-Watt | 0.38 |
| Hull | 0.56 |
| Keele | 0.66 |
| Kent | 0.48 |
| Lancaster | 0.63 |
| Liverpool | 0.65 |
| London (Birkbeck) | 1.00 |
| London (QMC) | 0.59 |
| London (UCL) | 0.71 |
| Loughborough | 0.80 |
| Nottingham | 0.61 |
| Reading | 0.55 |
| Salford | 0.37 |
| Sheffield | 0.37 |
| St Andrews | 0.69 |
| Stirling | 0.48 |
| Strathclyde | 0.24 |
| Surrey | 0.73 |
| Sussex | 0.48 |
| Warwick | 0.79 |
| York | 1.00 |

Source: G. Johnes and J. Johnes (1993).

A word of caution is needed at this stage. The results of DEA can be extremely sensitive to the choice of inputs and outputs. This is well illustrated by the example of research performance of university departments. The correlation between the rankings in Table 9.3 and the UFC peer review results lends a degree of plausibility to this particular set of DEA results. However, if a third input is introduced into the analysis, the picture can change quite substantially. Suppose that the third input is the per capitum level of grants obtained by the faculty over the period. Greater financial resources ought to make it easier to produce research. The efficiency scores resulting from this new application of DEA are quite different from those which were discussed earlier and reported in Table 9.3. The correlation coefficient between the two sets of results, at 0.61, indicates that the addition of the extra input leads to a non-negligible change in the efficiency rankings. Moreover, the correlation between the new set of efficiency scores and the UFC peer review is weak, with a coefficient of 0.35. These results provide a strong reminder that great care should be taken in choosing the appropriate inputs and outputs for inclusion in DEA. All relevant inputs and outputs which have a strong impact on the outcome of the exercise should be included. The results obtained here also imply – somewhat disturbingly – that the UFC peer group took little account of financial resources when forming their judgement of departmental research performance.

Finally, it should be noted that DEA is not a statistical technique. It is not based upon probabilistic distributions of random variables; the frontier is identified by reference only to the DMUs which are deemed technically efficient. This means that the usual battery of statistical diagnostic tests is not available. It is not therefore possible to establish whether the efficiency of a given DMU is significantly below unity (in the statistical sense). While the degree of confidence which can be attached to the results of statistical exercises is known, the same is not the case for DEA.

DEA cannot determine a socially optimal set of input and output weights; even the market is unable to do that. Nevertheless, DEA clearly offers a way forward. In the context of multi-product organisations where market prices are absent it enables a value-free judgement to be made about the technical and managerial efficiency of the DMUs in the sample; meanwhile it makes no judgement about the relative contribution to society made by any pair of DMUs located at different points along the efficiency frontier.

# Conclusion

Once a league table has been constructed, it has considerable visual impact. If teaching performance indicators are published, then schools which are seen to perform well will enjoy an increase in the demand for their services. So long as fees are paid on a per student basis, this ensures that 'good' schools are rewarded by an increase in financial resources. Thus it is assumed that the marginal benefit associated with a change in educational expenditure is greater if the marginal resources are spent at a school which does well in the league tables than if they are spent at one which does badly.

This is a strong assumption. According to conventional economic theory, given a concave production function, the gains to marginal investments would be greatest from the institutions whose production of educational services is lowest; that is, improvements are more easily realised when starting from a low base. This implies that resources should be diverted towards schools which (seem to) perform badly, not those which (seem to) perform well! However, if poor performers were seen to be rewarded, the incentive effects of the performance evaluation exercise would be perverse. Schools would compete with each other to come bottom of the league table, so that they might be better resourced in future. So the only sensible resource allocation rule to adopt is to reward good performers at the expense of poor performers. This might make economic sense if the weaker units are unusually x-inefficient, since the reward structure would then encourage poorer institutions to become more x-efficient.

The above argument can be succinctly summarised as follows: inter-institutional differences in measured performance may be due to differences in allocative efficiency or to differences in x-efficiency. In order to provide the right incentives, the resource implications of the performance evaluation exercise must be geared to the reduction of x-inefficiency. Consequently the programme of tying funding to performance indicators has both benefits and costs: it is beneficial to the extent that it reduces x-inefficiency, but it is harmful to the extent that it exacerbates allocative inefficiency.

Public expenditure on education is considerable, and it is desirable that the resources spent in this way are efficiently managed. Since the market for education is imperfect, the market cannot itself be relied upon to ensure the survival of the fittest (or the most efficient) producers. Instead attempts must be made at comparing the efficiency of institutions so that the appropriate allocation of public resources can be made. Ideally the marginal benefit resulting from the evaluation of institutions' performance should equal the marginal cost in terms of increased bureaucracy.

The benefit of introducing performance indicators as a harbinger of selectivity in the allocation of resources may be limited if the institutions subject to monitoring can adjust their behaviour in response. For example, if a school is to be judged by its truancy rate, it might expel persistent non-attenders in order to massage its truancy figures downwards. Likewise, if the research performance of university departments is to be assessed by counting the number of books published, staff might be encouraged to write many short, journalistic books rather than a few thoroughly researched and more lengthy tomes; thus the introduction of the performance indicator could have an effect which the authorities deem undesirable. Put simply, performance indicators are subject to cynical manipulation by the institutions which are being assessed. This is an interesting application of Goodhart's law (Goodhart, 1975): once a variable is chosen by the authorities to be a performance indicator which exerts pressure on economic agents, those same agents quickly seek and find means of circumventing the new rules of the game.

Attempts at measuring the performance of non-market organisations inevitably face the further handicap that the relative value of the various outputs must (more or less) arbitrarily be assigned. (Even advanced methods such as DEA can offer only a partial solution to this dilemma.) This contrasts with the situation of a multi-product firm operating in a perfect market; in the latter case the market can non-arbitrarily be allowed to determine the relative value of the various outputs. But performance indicators are not constructed for firms which operate in perfect markets, since the competitive conditions which such firms face are sufficient to force firms to be efficient. This leads us to a subtle irony: the paradox of (ideal) performance indicators is that they can be constructed only when they are not needed.

The above should not be taken to imply that the performance indicators hitherto used in education are entirely without value. Indeed there is no need for performance indicators to measure performance with complete accuracy in order to provide an incentive for institutions to improve their technical efficiency. So long as institutions which are perceived to perform relatively well are favourably treated in the allocation of resources, all that is required is that there should be a positive correlation between measured and actual performance. This being so, the incentive effects of performance indicators may well serve to improve the efficiency of the educational system as a whole.

# The Graduate Labour Market 10

## Introduction

The performance indicators discussed in the last chapter concerned various aspects of the work of institutions of higher education. Degree results reflect academic achievement. The quantity and nature of research output mirrors the institution's contribution to the development of knowledge. Student attrition – while arguably lying largely outside the control of the institutions – may measure a wastage of resources. In this chapter we focus more narrowly on the human capital approach to education. Specifically, we shall consider performance indicators which attempt to measure the addition to an individual's human capital which results from attendance at an institution. This entails an analysis of the graduate labour market.

Performance indicators based upon the labour market performance of graduates over the years after their graduation have appealed to many observers since they address directly what many perceive to be the *raison d'être* of the education system. Data on many aspects of the graduate labour market are readily available, and have been the subject of much study. In this chapter we shall examine in detail two aspects of the graduate labour market. The first will concern the employability of graduates, and the second will focus on their earnings.

# The Employability of Graduates

Since the acquisition of human capital is a major aim of higher education, and since the object of acquiring human capital is to obtain a return for it, we would expect that graduates of successful institutions would secure employment quickly after their graduation. It is, at first sight, therefore surprising to find that the employment rates of graduates, measured six months after graduation, exhibit very substantial differences between universities. In the UK this has led to the construction, on an annual basis, of 'league tables' of universities. Institutions whose graduates have a high employment rate are perceived to be more successful than those with a lower graduate employment rate. The 'league tables' have been published in a series of articles by Michael Dixon in the *Financial Times* (see, for example, *Financial Times*, 17 October 1990).

The crude data on graduate employability conceal a number of subtleties, however, and it would be very dangerous to regard 'league tables' of institutions based upon these data as satisfactory indicators of performance.

A major determinant of a student's success in the labour market is the subject which she studied. Human capital acquisition is not the only reason for studying for a degree; as we have seen, there is likely to be a significant consumption element in education too. Consequently graduates of degree schemes where the consumption element is high may find their skills relatively difficult to sell in the labour market. Moreover, labour market signals inevitably work with a lag. To illustrate this, suppose that an oil shock occurs which causes the oil companies to concentrate more of their activity on domestic production. The demand for linguists will fall while the demand for engineers rises. Given the lags necessitated by long training periods, and given also the short-run inflexibility of wages, this will make job hunting relatively more difficult for linguists and easier for engineers. Associated with some disciplines, therefore, will be high rates of graduate employment, while other disciplines will be relatively less successful in this respect.

It follows that differences in the mix of subjects taught can have a substantial impact on the pattern of graduate employability across institutions. A college which concentrates heavily on teaching subjects whose graduates are much in demand in the labour market will fare much better in the crude 'league tables' than will another institution which concentrates on other disciplines, other things being equal. The importance of structural considerations – in particular inter-institution differences in subject mix – in determining the graduate employability rate of an institution has been the subject of a considerable amount of research in recent years (Gregson and Taylor, 1987; G. Johnes, Taylor and Ferguson, 1987; J. Johnes and Taylor, 1989). The methodology of these studies is discussed below.

To allow for structural differences in the study of graduate employability, it is usual to construct for each institution a measure of the graduate employment rate which it could be expected to achieve, standardised according to its subject mix. This standardised employment rate may be defined as

$$n_j^* = \sum_i [G_{ij}(\sum_j N_{ij} / \sum_j G_{ij})] / \sum_i G_{ij} \qquad (10.1)$$

where $G_{ij}$ is the number of graduates of subject $i$ from institution $j$ in a given year, and $N_{ij}$ is the number of those graduates which succeed in obtaining employment within a specified time after their graduation. Intuitively, equation (10.1) gives the employment rate which would obtain if, *within each subject area*, the employment rate of graduates were constant and equal to the national average. Thus institutions with a favourable subject mix would have a relatively high $n_j^*$, while those with an adverse structure would have a low $n_j^*$.

For each institution, the actual graduate employment rate can be compared to the standardised graduate employment rate in order to establish the extent to which subject mix affects the out-turn. If $n_j^*$ exceeds the actual rate of graduate employment for a given institution, then that institution's failure to match its graduates with jobs cannot be attributed solely to an adverse structure. Likewise, graduates of another institution may be able to secure employment with a greater propensity than would be expected given their institution's subject mix; this would be evidenced by a value of $n_j^*$ which is below the out-turn employment rate.

Subject structure is not, however, the only determinant of graduate employability. Studies in this area have indicated that the following variables are also important determinants of labour market success. First, performance at high school positively influences a graduate's employment prospects. Other things being equal, good A-level scores raise the probability that a graduate will find work within six months of leaving college. Employers typically recruit new graduates before they complete their degrees, and so high-school performance is the most recent formal screen available to guide them in their hiring decisions. Institutions which succeed in attracting a large proportion of student entrants of high calibre are likely, therefore, to find that a large proportion of their graduates secure employment quickly after their graduation, *ceteris paribus*.

Second, the type of high school attended may affect graduates' employability in the period immediately following their graduation. Those who attended independent or grammar schools are more likely than others to obtain employment at this stage. It is possible that the type of school attended proxies certain socio-economic characteristics of the student which cannot otherwise be measured; equally plausibly, employers use school type as a further screening mechanism in reaching their recruitment decisions. So institutions which attract a large proportion of their students from independent and grammar schools will, *ceteris paribus*, tend to perform well in 'league tables' of graduate employability.

Third, the vigour of the instituion in marketing its graduates to potential employers is likely to be important in this context. In particular, the annual circuit of employer visits to the universities and other colleges – the 'milkround' – is an opportunity for final year students to secure employment. An institution which is able to attract a large number of graduate recruiters on to its milkround programme is likely to achieve a relatively high rate of graduate employment, other things being equal, since there are thus more opportunities available for matching graduates with job vacancies.

Fourth, the age of the institution matters. A large proportion of the graduates of many of the older universities – such as Cambridge, Durham, Oxford and St Andrews – traditionally proceed to further education and training once they have graduated. The employment rates achieved by these institutions is therefore rather low. Far from being a sign of poor performance, this merely indicates that the destinations of graduates of these institutions typically differs from those of other colleges.

Fifth, certain types of institution may use pedagogic methods which enhance the students' chances of obtaining employment rapidly. Those British institutions which were awarded university status during the 1960s and which were previously known as Colleges of Advanced Technology (CATs) provide a good example. Many of the 'ex-CATs' have particularly strong and long-established links with industry, and a high proportion of their students have work experience gained during placements in sandwich courses. This equips these students with an extra advantage at job interviews, and so helps raise the graduate employment rate of these colleges.

Sixth, students at institutions located in geographically peripheral areas are disadvantaged when seeking work. They must travel further to interviews, and may not therefore be able to afford the time or money to engage in such extensive job search as their counterparts elsewhere. Many students at these colleges will prefer to search full time for employment after they have graduated, and may indeed then move to a less remote area in order to carry out their search.

The variables listed above have all been shown to be significant determinants of graduate employability in the UK during the 1980s (J. Johnes and Taylor, 1989). The statistical significance of the coefficients obtained in a regression analysis varies somewhat over time, but their signs and magnitude appear to be reasonably robust. As an example of such an equation, consider the following specification of the model, which is based on a cross-section regression defined across some 43 universities in Great Britain. This uses data for 1983 gathered from the First Destinations Survey (FDS) of the Universities Statistical Record (USR):

$$\begin{aligned} PEMP = -38.57 &+ \underset{(3.64)}{1.00}\, PEMP^* + \underset{(2.11)}{1.21}\, ALEVEL \\ &+ \underset{(2.75)}{0.15}\, SCHOOL + \underset{(2.91)}{0.01}\, AGE + \underset{(4.53)}{6.43}\, EXCAT \end{aligned}$$

$$R^2 = 0.51$$

where *PEMP* represents the proportion of economically active graduates who, within six months of graduation, have entered full-time employment; $PEMP^*$ is the graduate employment rate, standardised in order to allow for subject mix; *ALEVEL* is the average A-level score obtained by the graduating cohort (a student's A-level score is based on her best three subjects on leaving high school); an A grade contributes 5 points to the A level score, a B is worth 4 points, and so on; *SCHOOL* is the percentage of students who attended a grammar or independent school; *AGE* is the foundation year of each university; and *EXCAT* is a binary variable which equals 1 if the institution was once a CAT, and is zero otherwise. The figures in parentheses are *t* statistics; the coefficient on *PEMP** is constrained to equal unity. The signs on the estimated coefficients confirm the hypotheses developed in the discussion above. Other studies have established similar patterns (see, for example, Taylor, 1986; Tarsh, 1987).

A further matter of importance concerns the alternatives to employment which graduates face. New graduates may choose to seek employment, or they may choose to continue their full-time education, or they may become unavailable for employment (because of family commitments, or because they choose to travel the world, for example), or they may become unemployed. An institution which has a poor record of graduate employability (after correcting for subject mix and other pertinent factors), does not therefore of necessity have a high graduate unemployment rate. Many of its graduates may proceed to further education and training. More than one measure is therefore required to evaluate the labour market history of an institution's alumni.

This being so, it is possible to conduct a study of graduate *unemployment* rates, and achieve results which differ from those obtained when determinants of *employment* rates are investigated. Consideration of the influences upon both employment and unemployment rates together therefore provides a substantially richer set of results than does an examination of just one or the other.

In addition to those variables which we have already listed as being important determinants of graduate employment rates, the following are significant determinants of the rate of graduate *unemployment* six months after graduation (G. Johnes, Taylor and Ferguson, 1987). First, institutions which employ a large number of careers staff per student tend to have lower graduate unemployment rates than do others, *ceteris paribus*.

Second, institutions located within large conurbations tend to have relatively low rates of graduate unemployment. This follows from the easy access enjoyed by their students to a large local labour market.

Third, the rate of employment growth in the region surrounding an institution negatively influences its graduate unemployment rate. This suggests that students who attend colleges located in the more prosperous regions of the economy exploit the proximity of a growing local labour market. This finding reinforces the result reported earlier which indicated that graduates of institutions located in the geographical periphery take longer than others to find work.

Finally, students who live at home while at college have a lower propensity to remain unemployed six months after graduation than do others. Such students are able to exploit their familiarity with the local labour market in their job search activity.

Studies of graduate employability typically involve a snapshot view of the employment status of graduates at a single point in time. For example, British data from the FDS of university graduates refer to employment status six months after graduation. This is obviously restrictive. In the UK, two surveys have been conducted in recent years which throw light on the time-path of employment status of graduates. The first of these is the Graduate Employment and Training Survey (GETS) conducted by the Association of Graduate Careers Advisory Services (AGCAS). The second is the NSGD which was carried out as a joint project by the Department of Employment and the Department of Education and Science.

The GETS data were collected at the end of 1985, and consist of a survey of a sample of individuals who graduated in 1984. Evidence from this survey suggests that of those graduates who, six months after graduation, were unemployed, some 70 per cent found permanent employment during the next year. A further 12 per cent entered further education and training (Gregson and Taylor, 1987). A graduate unemployment rate calculated on the basis of the FDS alone is therefore likely to overestimate the true incidence of unemployment amongst graduates. The FDS is better regarded as an indicator of the *speed* with which graduates find jobs than as a means of estimating the propensity with which they find employment.

A particularly interesting aspect of the GETS data concerns information which it provides about the time pattern of graduates' access to jobs. Figure 10.1 shows the cumulative transfers of graduates into permanent employment and into further education and training over the year following the FDS. Economically active graduates who started this period without a permanent job steadily found permanent employment as the year progressed. There is a small positive blip in August, which coincides with the commencement of graduate training programmes in many firms. Towards the end of the year, however, the vast majority of the cohort have found work, so the rate of accession to jobs starts to decline. The pattern of access to further education and training courses is, not surprisingly, completely different. Since most such courses run over a standard academic year, access to these opportunities occurs almost entirely during the months of September and October. Similar results can be obtained from the NSGD over a longer time period after graduation (Dolton and Makepeace, 1992). These are reported in Figures 10.2 and 10.3 for the first 18 months after graduation. Beyond that time, the proportion of both men and women in employment continues to rise, while the proportion in further education and training falls. After six years, only 5 per cent of men are out of work; however, some 15 per cent of women are out of work at this time, this difference being largely due to family commitments.

The data on the employment histories of graduates provided by the NSGD is much more comprehensive than that available elsewhere. Details of up to four jobs held by graduates over the six-year period following their graduation in 1980 are recorded. The duration of any unemployment spell immediately following graduation is recorded, as is information concerning job tenure, occupation, promotion, training and salary. This information is available for the first and (up to three) subsequent jobs held by each individual after graduation. These data have been analysed by Taylor and Johnes (1989) in order to establish whether graduate employment rates (measured six months after graduation) provide a useful indicator of graduates' future employment prospects.

Table 10.1 describes the relationship between employment status of university graduates six months after graduation and their status six years later. The NSGD data clearly support the finding of GETS: the vast majority of those graduates who fail to secure employment quickly eventually succeed in finding permanent jobs. Only one in 400 graduates was unemployed (and had no work arranged) both six months and six years after graduation; still fewer had never worked.

**FIGURE 10.1**
**Cumulative Transfers of Graduates**

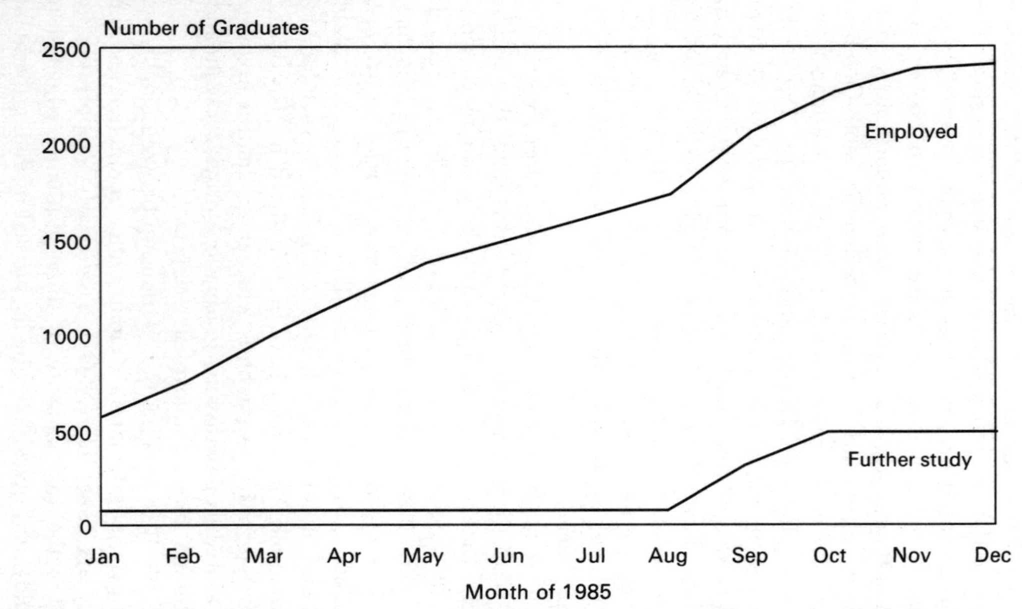


Source: Gregson and Taylor (1987); GETS.

**FIGURE 10.2**
**Cumulative Transfers of Male Graduates**

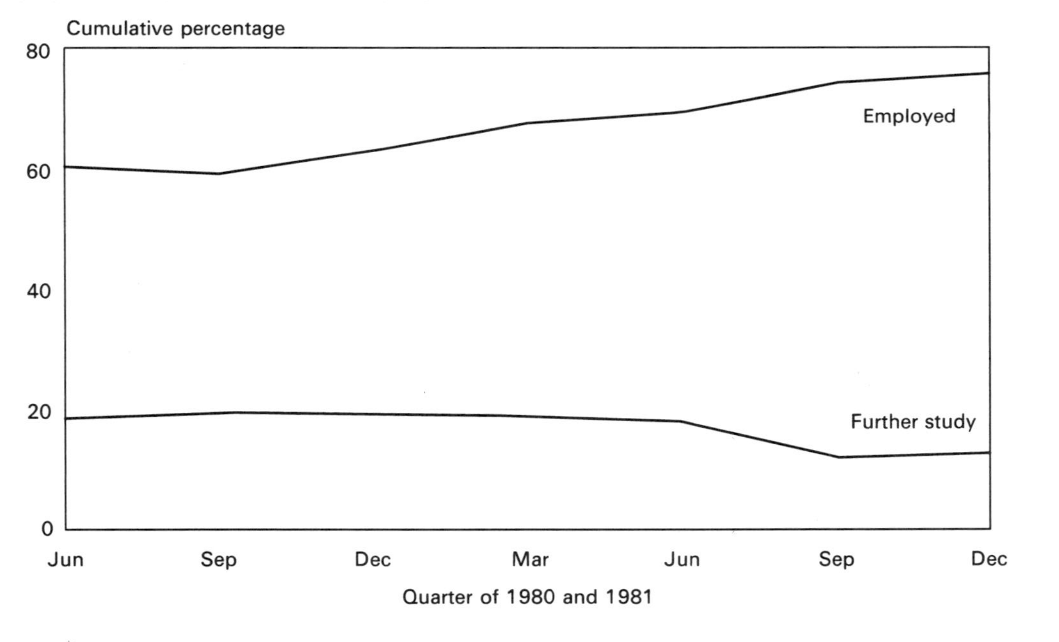

**FIGURE 10.3**
**Cumulative Transfers of Female Graduates**

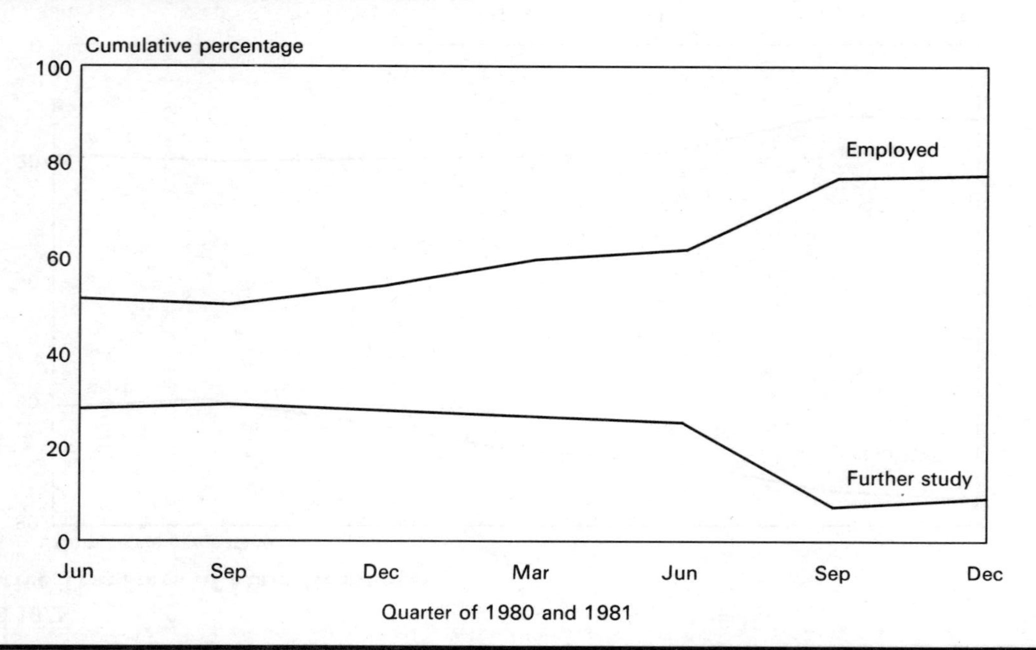

**TABLE 10.1**
**Labour Market Status of UK University Graduates Six Months and Six Years after Graduation, Class of 1980**

| Status at end of 1980 | Status in 1986 (as % of row total) | | | | | | |
|---|---|---|---|---|---|---|---|
| | 1 | 2 | 3 | 4 | 5 | 6 | 7 |
| 1 Permanent employment | 90.8 | 1.0 | 2.2 | 0.6 | 0.2 | 1.2 | 3.9 |
| 2 Short-term employment | 86.2 | 3.3 | 2.7 | 1.1 | 0.9 | 2.9 | 2.9 |
| 3 Further education or training | 88.6 | 1.7 | 2.0 | 0.5 | 0.2 | 2.0 | 5.1 |
| 4 Unemployed (job arranged) | 83.5 | 5.5 | 1.1 | 2.2 | 0.0 | 5.5 | 2.2 |
| 5 Unemployed (training arranged) | 82.8 | 0.0 | 8.6 | 1.7 | 1.7 | 3.4 | 1.7 |
| 6 Unemployed (nothing arranged) | 81.9 | 3.0 | 3.2 | 1.2 | 1.0 | 6.2 | 3.5 |
| 7 Out of the labour force | 59.4 | 12.5 | 3.1 | 3.1 | 0.0 | 0.0 | 21.9 |

Note: Column headings refer to the same categories as the row headings.

Source: J. Johnes and Taylor (1989).

Nevertheless, the rate of graduate unemployment six months after graduation does indicate that those graduates who were jobless six months after graduation remain at a labour market disadvantage (compared with other graduates) over the next few years. Table 10.2 shows that the average number of weeks spent on the jobless register is substantially greater for those who were out of work six months after graduation than for those who at that time were in employment. A particularly interesting figure in this table is the low incidence of unemployment endured by those who, in December 1980, were unemployed but had work arranged. It is possible that some graduates who remain jobless for a while after completing their degrees do so in order more carefully to choose their career.

Unfortunately neither the GETS nor the NSGD data are suited to a comparison across institutions of graduate employment rates. The GETS figures refer to a (non-random) sample of graduates from a sub-set of 24 universities, 5 polytechnics and 4 colleges of higher education. The NSGD data are also of limited usefulness for this purpose; they enable analysts to ascertain detailed information about the labour market status of all respondents only at two points after their graduation: after six months and after six years. It is nevertheless

**TABLE 10.2**
**Number of Weeks Spent Unemployed during 1982–6 of UK University Graduates, Class of 1980**

| Status at end of 1980 | Number of weeks unemployed | | | |
|---|---|---|---|---|
| | Males | | Females | |
| | Mean | Standard deviation | Mean | Standard deviation |
| Permanent employment | 19 | 41 | 20 | 40 |
| Short-term employment | 22 | 50 | 24 | 59 |
| Further education or training | 26 | 46 | 25 | 49 |
| Unemployed (job arranged) | 10 | 25 | 21 | 27 |
| Unemployed (training arranged) | 50 | 67 | 12 | 17 |
| Unemployed (nothing arranged) | 37 | 68 | 38 | 72 |
| Out of the labour force | 39 | 65 | 23 | 30 |
| All graduates in sample | 25 | 50 | 24 | 50 |

Source: J. Johnes and Taylor (1989).

clear that the labour market histories of graduates are far too complicated to be summed up adequately in a single snapshot taken six months (or a year, or five years) after graduation. Snapshot analyses like the FDS certainly provide useful information, but they do not tell the whole story. To interpret them as comprehensive indicators of graduates' labour market performance would therefore be misleading.

Further analysis of the NSGD has been conducted by Dolton and Makepeace (1992). The survey data on graduates' labour market histories allows a useful study to be undertaken which identifies representative career paths and establishes the determinants of job mobility amongst graduates. The information thus acquired enhances our appreciation of the usefulness (or otherwise) of snapshot pictures of graduates' success in the labour market.

Labour market experience after graduation can be classified into a number of career patterns. For example, a graduate may move straight from college to employment and remain in the same job for the next six years. Alternatively, the graduate might enter stable employment only after suffering an initial spell of unemployment. It is convenient to define the following typology of career histories; while the typology is by no means exhaustive, most male graduates fall into one of the the five categories defined below:

(a) in employment throughout the period, one job;
(b) in employment throughout the period, two jobs;
(c) in employment throughout the period, three jobs;
(d) further education or training followed by employment, two jobs;
(e) spell out of work followed by employment, one job.

One or another of these five categories describes the experience over the first six years after graduation of some 53 per cent of males in the NSGD. Almost one in every five male graduates falls into the first of these categories, and a further one in six falls into the second. The proportion of male graduates who experience more complicated labour market histories (such as spells of employment interspersed with periods out of work) is fairly small.

The labour market experience of female graduates is, as might be expected, considerably more complicated than that of their male counterparts. As is the case for men, the above five categories are the most common career paths. However, these paths are followed by only 35 per cent of women. Meanwhile almost 20 per cent of women in the NSGD sample were out of work at the time of the survey. Clearly, then, the job market experience of female graduates is considerably more diverse than that of males, in that the tendency for men to remain in employment once they find jobs is not strongly replicated in the case of women. A plausible explanation for this is that many women temporarily leave employment for family reasons.

The manner in which the proportion of graduates who remain with their first employer falls as time elapses is described by the survivor function. The survivor function is drawn for each sex separately in Figure 10.4. It is easily seen from this diagram that women tend to experience shorter tenure in their first job after graduation than do men. For instance, the median tenure for women is a little under two years, while the median male remains in the job for around three years.

For both men and women, the most commonly offered explanation for quitting the first job after graduation is that a better job has

**FIGURE 10.4**
**Survivor Function for Graduates, by Sex**

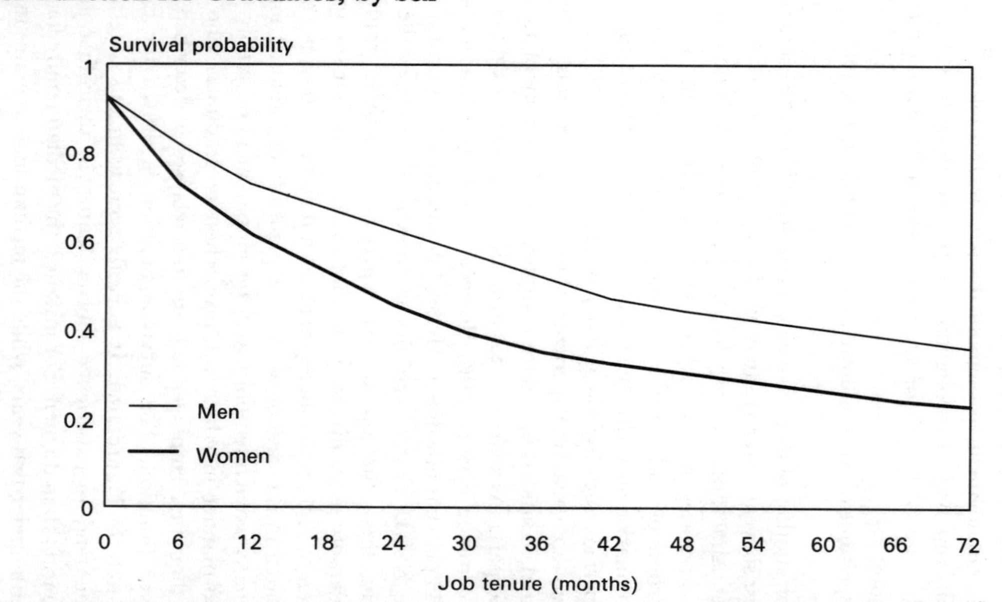


Source: Dolton and Makepeace (1992) Figure 7.5.

been obtained elsewhere. Moreover, women are more likely than men to leave their first jobs for this reason. Five years after graduation, about 43 per cent of men and about 47 per cent of women had quit their first job for this reason alone. In the case of women, the propensity to quit for family reasons rises steadily as time passes. Five years after graduation, some 28 per cent of women had left their first job for this reason.

It is clear from the above discussion that the graduate labour market is considerably more complicated that might at first appear. Workers pass through spells of employment and further education, and – especially in the case of women – may also be economically inactive for quite lengthy periods. Snapshot surveys scratch the surface, but longitudinal studies like the NSGD are needed to acquire richer information about the true costs and benefits of the teaching function of higher education.

## The Earnings of Graduates

The NSGD has been used by a number of researchers to investigate the earnings of graduates over the six-year period immediately following their graduation. Taylor (1988) has classified the data by degree subject, and pays particular attention to graduates of universities, polytechnics and colleges of higher education in the science disciplines. For both males and females, the highest returns are earned by graduates of mathematics and computing. By 1986, male graduates of these subjects who were in full-time employment earned £16 610 per annum on average, while the corresponding group of women enjoyed mean earnings of £13 520. By way of contrast, the corresponding figures for graduates in the disciplines of biology and botany were £11 430 and £9880.

With the exception of mathematics and computing, earnings of science graduates were low in comparison with those who graduated from subjects in the areas of business, economics and law. In the latter areas, mean male full-time earnings were £16 480, while mean female full-time earnings were £13 420 per annum. This strongly supports the conclusion drawn by Weale (1992) that the most acute shortages of graduates in the contemporary British labour market are in the (broadly defined) business disciplines rather than in the sciences and engineering.

The marked gender differential observed in these figures suggests that the graduate labour market is characterised by sex discrimination. This issue has been investigated by Dolton, Makepeace and Inchley (1990), who conclude that the pure discrimination element of the male–female earnings differential amounts to between 6 and 11 per cent. This amounts to about half of the observed difference between male and female earnings. The remaining half is accounted for by gender differences in factors such as work experience, professional training and family characteristics.

Discrimination may also occur between the various ethnic groups in the jobs market for graduates. This question is the subject of a study by G. Johnes and Taylor (1989), the results of which are rather surprising. While graduates of ethnic minorities suffer a somewhat higher incidence of unemployment than do white graduates, those in work typically earn *more* than do their white counterparts. The differential is, however, slight, and is not statistically significant. Moreover, the small number of non-white graduates in the NSGD sample makes statistical inference hazardous.

Further investigation of the earnings of graduates by subject area has been conducted by G. Johnes (1989). This research confirms that inter-subject variations in graduates' salaries are considerable. For instance, male university graduates who were in work at the time of the FDS had salaries which, by 1986 (six years after graduation) ranged from a subject average of £11 342 to £19 359 per annum. Graduates of four subjects (accountancy, management, law and economics) averaged salaries of above £16 000 within each subject, while graduates of four other subjects (history, agriculture, biochemistry and biology) averaged salaries of below £12 000 *per annum*.

Over the long term, these discrepancies might be expected to lead to an increase in the demand by prospective students for places on courses in the subjects which lead to high-paying jobs. At the same time, institutions of higher education might be expected to respond to this rise in demand by increasing the number of places available for students in these subjects (possibly at the expense of other disciplines). Evidence that this has indeed occurred in UK universities is provided by data from the UFC (1990). This indicates that over the period from 1980–1 to 1988–9, the number of full-time undergraduates at UK universities grew by some 4 per cent. Meanwhile, the number of those studying biology declined by 12 per cent and the number studying business and management studies rose by 31 per cent. The institutions concerned have clearly effected a rapid response to the dictates of the market by adjusting the mix of subjects offered at undergraduate level in line with the needs of employers and the derived demand of potential students.

Nevertheless, the continued demand for courses which hold the promise of relatively low remuneration levels in the years following graduation may be regarded as evidence of a consumption demand for education services. Some students are evidently prepared to forgo some of the returns to higher education in order to study subjects in which they have a particular interest.

Dolton, Makepeace and Inchley (1990) have used data from the NSGD in order to estimate human capital earnings functions for a sample of some 3115 males and 1887 females who graduated in 1980 from UK universities, polytechnics and institutes of higher education. Their analysis takes the form of an ordinary least squares regression of (the natural logarithm of) annual earnings achieved six years after graduation (at 1976 prices) against a host of (logged or discrete-limited) explanatory variables. This enables the elasticities of both male and female graduate earnings with respect to a variety of their determinants to be ascertained. A summary of the regression results appears in Table 10.3; some controls included by Dolton *et al.* are not reported in this table for the sake of conciseness. The salient features of the results are discussed below.

The quality of degree obtained influences the earnings which a graduate receives six years after graduation. Controlling for all other influences upon earnings, an improvement of one class in degree performance serves to raise earnings by some 3 per cent. Thus a student who achieves an upper second-class honours degree can (all else being equal) expect to earn 3 per cent more (after six years) than one who receives a lower second-class degree.

Experience of unemployment after graduation reduces the earnings which a graduate can expect to receive six years on. In particular, *each* extra month spent on the unemployment register reduces earnings by 0.7 per cent for men and by 0.5 per cent for women.

Earnings received in the first job secured after graduation has an influence on earnings six years later. Consider two individuals whose first jobs after graduation are different, but who are otherwise identical. Suppose further that graduate *A* receives a salary in his first job which is 10 per cent higher than that of graduate *B*. Six years

**TABLE 10.3**
**Human Capital Earnings Functions for Graduates, by Gender**

| Explanatory variable | Men | Women |
|---|---|---|
| CONSTANT | 5.8402 | 5.2295 |
| | (32.10) | (26.76) |
| MARRIED | 0.0296 | −0.0603 |
| | (2.23) | (4.07) |
| CHILDREN | | −0.0711 |
| | | (2.89) |
| DEGREE | 0.0264 | 0.0303 |
| | (6.29) | (6.18) |
| UNEMPLOYED | −0.0071 | −0.0052 |
| | (5.92) | (3.71) |
| STATUS | 0.0047 | 0.0106 |
| | (5.88) | (11.78) |
| FIRSTWAGE | 0.2271 | 0.1907 |
| | (13.93) | (9.30) |
| UNIVERSITY | 0.0520 | 0.0555 |
| | (3.51) | (3.26) |
| SUBJECT | 0.1057 | 0.1085 |
| | (7.72) | (5.12) |
| PROFQUAL | 0.1113 | 0.1095 |
| | (6.22) | (5.21) |
| MSC | 0.0910 | 0.0655 |
| | (3.60) | (1.98) |
| $R^2$ | 0.3038 | 0.4988 |

Notes: *t* statistics are in parentheses. The dependent variable is the natural logarithm of annual earnings in 1986 (in 1976 prices). The explanatory variables are defined as follows:

MARRIED = 1 if the respondent is married, and 0 otherwise.
CHILDREN = the number of children parented by the respondent.
DEGREE = the quality of degree earned by the respondent (8 for a first, 7 for an upper second, 6 for a lower second, etc.).
UNEMPLOYED = the number of months spent unemployed by the respondent since graduation.
STATUS = status of the respondent's current occupation on the Hope–Goldthorpe scale.
FIRSTWAGE = the natural logarithm of the (indexed) starting salary earned by the respondent in the first job secured after graduation.
UNIVERSITY = 1 if the respondent graduated from a university, and 0 otherwise.

SUBJECT = 1 if the respondent graduated in a 'high growth' subject (see text), and 0 otherwise.
PROFQUAL = 1 if the respondent has a professional qualification, and 0 otherwise.
MSC = 1 if the respondent has a master's degree, and 0 otherwise.

Source: Dolton, Makepeace and Inchley (1990), p.25.

---

later, *A* can expect to earn some 2 per cent more than *B*. Earnings advantages gained early in a graduate's career are therefore likely to persist for a number of years.

Those who, in 1980, graduated with degrees in certain subjects are likely to have found work in occupations where the labour market was expanding rapidly. The first half of the 1980s was a time of extremely rapid structural adjustment in the British economy. Much of the manufacturing sector declined while service industries flourished in the aftermath of the recession. In consequence, graduates with degrees in certain disciplines were well placed to find employment in occupations where average salaries were rising rapidly. These subjects were economics, law, accounting, mathematics, computing, surveying, pharmacy, zoology, aeronautical and electrical engineering, business and management. These may be described as the 'high growth' subject areas of the early and mid-1980s. Graduates with degrees in these subjects earned, on average, 11 per cent more than did other graduates six years after they gained their degrees.

The occupational status of the graduate at the time of the NSGD survey is also a significant determinant of earnings. If, other things being equal, a graduate were to change occupations so that their new occupation had twice the status of their old one, expected earnings would rise by 1 per cent for women, and by half as much for men. The status of each occupation is measured by points along the Hope–Goldthorpe scale (Goldthorpe and Hope, 1974), which divides the workforce into 124 occupational groups. An example of a job change which would represent a doubling of socio-economic status on this scale is given by a worker whose occupation changes from blast furnaceman to primary-school headteacher. According to Goldthorpe and Hope, the lowest status occupations are barrow boys, newspaper vendors and jobbing gardeners (17.52 points), while the highest status attaches to those employed as doctors, lawyers or accountants (82.05 points).

Possession of a master's degree raises the earnings which graduates may expect six years after completing their bachelors degree. The premium attached to a master's degree is about 9 per cent for men and 7 per cent for women. A professional qualification also serves to increase earnings: in this case the premium is about 11 per cent for both men and women at the survey date.

Graduates of universities tend to earn more (at the date of the survey) than do those of polytechnics and institutes of higher education. *Ceteris paribus*, university graduates earn just over 5 per cent more than do graduates of other types of institution.

A common finding of many human capital studies of earnings is that the influence of family composition variables differs between the sexes. The same is true of the study by Dolton, Makepeace and Inchley. In this case, being married raises male earnings by 3 per cent, while it reduces female earnings by 6 per cent. If a female graduate has children (but still works), then typically her earnings are reduced to the tune of 7 per cent for each child. Offspring do not significantly influence male graduates' earnings. The signs on these estimated coefficients all follow patterns which have been well established by the results of other studies. Married men are regarded favourably by employers, since their family obligations provide an incentive to pursue a stable work history. Married women are often disadvantaged in that they are constrained by the geographical location of their husbands' workplace; if their husbands work in peripheral parts of the country, job opportunities may be limited. Moreover, employers may still be reluctant to promote able married women, since their labour force attachment may (rightly or wrongly) be considered weak. Children provide a drain on the time of parents, and women frequently reduce the number of hours which they devote to the labour market as they become mothers.

Further work by Dolton, Makepeace and Inchley – using the Heckman (1979) procedure in order to correct for sample selection biases – implies that the impact of children on female earnings operates via their effect on the labour market participation decision of women. Mothers who choose to drop out of the labour force when they have children experience a 100 per cent fall in their earnings, but those who remain at work may not experience any fall in remuneration at all. While *average* levels of remuneration are reduced by childbearing, therefore, the earnings of those women who remain in work after the birth of their offspring may be unaffected.

Although not reported in Table 10.3, coefficients were estimated by Dolton, Makepeace and Inchley for the Mincerian variables, namely the level and quadratic terms in work experience. These are interesting in that they indicate that, for men, earnings typically peak after some 20 years of work experience. Women's earnings, on the other hand, typically rise throughout their working lives. It is noteworthy that these results obtain despite the fact that the interpersonal variation in work experience in the NSGD data is inevitably not so great as is the case in studies which cover the whole labour force.

The goodness of fit of the earnings function reported in Table 10.3 is impressive for cross-section work of this kind, and the determination coefficient ($R^2$) is in line with that achieved for human capital earnings functions obtained by other researchers. The coefficients obtained are also reasonably robust with respect to changes in specification and estimation methodology.

All the results reported above refer to the United Kingdom. The patterns observed in the UK can also be observed in other economies, however. In particular, a considerable volume of recent research has appeared in the USA, much of which makes use of the National Longitudinal Study (NLS) of the High School Class of 1972. This cohort of students has been surveyed at regular intervals since 1972 in order to gain information about their education and labour market histories, as well as many other personal characteristics. By 1986, five sweeps of the cohort had been conducted. The 1986 sweep yields useful information about more than 2200 baccalaureate graduates; slightly more than half of these were men.

The NLS data have been analysed in detail by Sharp and Weidman (1989) and by James *et al.* (1989). The former study concentrates primarily upon the sub-set of graduates whose major fields of study lay in the humanities, arts and social sciences. The hourly earnings of these graduates in 1979 varied by major subject of study; earnings were highest for those studying business and liberal arts subjects, and were lowest for those majoring in education. The USA clearly shares with the UK a tendency for degree subject to influence remuneration later in life.

The latter study investigates the determination of graduate earnings in the USA in greater detail, and uses more recent earnings data obtained from the 1986 sweep. James *et al.* have grafted on to the NLS data set a wealth of supplementary data about the 519 colleges and universities whose alumni responded to the survey. They are thus able to establish the impact upon graduate earnings of student characteristics, college characteristics and labour market variables. Amongst the college characteristics considered are the institutions' ownership status (public versus private), and the average quality of the student intake. In addition, variables are included which control for individual respondents' choice of major subject, ability, and family background.

The average Scholastic Aptitude Test (SAT) score of an institution's entrants on to baccalaureate degree schemes significantly raises the earnings of its graduates, *ceteris paribus*. Typically a 100 point increase in the average SAT raises graduates' earnings by some 2 per cent; this assumes constant all other variables, including the SAT score achieved by the respondent. In other words, this is a pure reputation effect which reflects the school's quality, not the quality of individual graduates. In the eastern states (but not elsewhere) private institutions produce graduates whose earnings are significantly higher (by around 10 per cent) than those of other colleges. The geographical interaction here is interesting, and probably reflects the elitism of the private schools in the eastern part of the USA.

The grade point average (GPA) obtained by students is another significant determinant of their earnings later in life. A one-point improvement in the student's GPA (say, from a B to an A grade) allows, on average, a 9 per cent improvement in her earnings after graduation. This result tallies well with the finding in the UK that degree class positively influences earnings. The subject mix variables used in the regression analysis confirms the finding of Sharp and Weidman that subject matters: in relation to students whose major subject of study is in a vocational field, students of education earn 10 per cent less, while students of social sciences and engineering earn 8 and 35 per cent more respectively. It is interesting to note that the shortage subjects in the USA during the 1970s were quite different from the 'high growth' subjects in the UK during the 1980s.

Finally, a graduate who has earned a higher degree is rewarded by higher remuneration than others, *ceteris paribus*. In the case of the USA, the premium which attaches to a postgraduate qualification is about 10 per cent. This is very similar to the premium observed in the UK for those possessing masters' degrees.

It is clear from the above that the role of college-specific variables in explaining graduates' earnings is substantially smaller than the impact of subject choice, degree performance, and the students' background. Thus James *et al.* conclude that:

> **while sending your child to Harvard appears to be a good investment, sending him to your local state university to major in Engineering, to take lots of math, and preferably to attain a high GPA, is an even better private investment . . . What matters most is not which college you attend but what you do while you are there.**

As in the UK, then, the opportunities to use measures of graduates' success in the labour market as meaningful performance indicators for American colleges would appear to be limited.

## Conclusion

The results reported in the present chapter should not surprise the informed observer. Graduates' success in the labour market depends on a host of factors, including subject choice and personal characteristics. The available evidence suggests that – controlling for the quality of entrants and for a variety of other variables – some types of institution may be more successful in the production of marketable graduates than are others. The available data and the statistical methodology are not yet sufficiently refined to discriminate between the performance of individual institutions, though. Graduate employability and remuneration do not, at present, promise to be very good indicators of the performance of institutions of higher education.

Nevertheless, the results reported above are likely to be very useful to prospective students and graduates, and also to institutions wishing to maximise the labour market opportunities of their alumni. Students wishing to pursue careers with high financial rewards should study 'high growth' subjects, get a good degree, do postgraduate work, avoid unemployment, apply for jobs of high social standing and obtain a professional qualification. An institution which wishes to produce graduates who follow such advice needs to concentrate on high growth subject areas, attract a high quality intake of entrants, and market its graduates aggressively by employing an active careers service. To the extent that economic welfare is enhanced by such a response, carefully constructed measures of graduate employability and earnings are useful.

# 11 The Labour Market for Educators

## Introduction

In the last chapter attention was focused on the labour market for graduates. In the present chapter the focus is narrowed in order to consider in greater detail a sub-set of those graduates: those who go on to become educators in primary, secondary or tertiary education. Like many other graduates, these workers generally undertake some sort of training at postgraduate level, and this may take the form of teacher training or study for higher degrees.

The market for educators is of necessity highly planned. The authorities control both the demand for teachers and the supply of graduates from teacher training courses. Since both the training and, later, the salaries of many educators are paid for by government, it is appropriate to ask whether the allocation of resources in this area is efficient. This question forms the central part of the next section. In the following two sections, the focus will be on some of the peculiarities of the market for academics. In particular, we shall consider the issues of how academics should be paid, what their terms of employment should be, and the problem of the brain drain (if indeed it is a problem).

# Demand and Supply: School Teachers

The labour market in general is often considered to be less perfect than other markets. This is especially the case if certain sub-groups of the labour force are considered. Teachers are a particularly interesting group of workers, since their stock of human capital is generally very specific and since their training takes a long time. The authorities may, as in Britain, exercise a considerable degree of control over both the demand and supply sides of the market for teachers (through controlling teacher:pupil ratios and admissions into teacher training colleges respectively); nevertheless, fluctuations in either side of the market are notoriously difficult to predict.

The demand for teachers in any one subject area can fluctuate with pupils' tastes (which, as we saw in Chapter 4, are a function, *inter alia*, of labour market conditions). The overall demand for secondary school teachers depends in part on the propensity of pupils to continue their education beyond the compulsory stage. The demand for primary school teachers is inevitably difficult to predict more than five years into the future, simply because the number of births is not easily forecast.

The supply of teachers is harder still to estimate in advance. The main difficulty here involves the construction of estimates of the numbers of teachers who will leave the profession. This is especially difficult because of the concentration of women in the teaching profession, many of whom will interrupt their careers in order to raise a family. The existence and timing of such interruptions are, of course, not accurately predictable. During times of recession, when unemployment is high and overtime opportunities limited, many families might choose to postpone child-rearing so that the relative supply of teachers is high. At other times there may be a shortage of teachers. Neither situation is likely to be easy to predict.

Given the long training period required in order to become a teacher, short-term imbalances between demand and supply cannot be cured overnight. To qualify as a teacher, workers generally need to complete not only a bachelor level degree, but also a course of teacher training. Recent developments aimed at alleviating the shortage of teachers in Britain allow the second of these requirements to be waived if the worker has substantial industrial experience, but this change remains controversial. Planners working in the field of education at national level therefore face much frustration in seeking to iron out shortages and gluts of teachers. The issues of teacher retention and re-entry into the profession after a spell out of the labour force are therefore key areas for research. In the remainder of this section, however, we concentrate on the supply of workers who have recently completed their degree courses to the education industry.

The supply of new graduates into the teaching profession depends not only on the terms of employment offered to starting teachers, but also on the corresponding variables for the other occupations in which graduates are qualified to work. Moreover, the expected time-path of the graduate's salary over her career, and the opportunities for advancement are likely to influence career choice too; these prospects must be assessed both for teaching and for alternative occupations. In a pioneering study, Zabalza (1979) has studied the supply of teachers in a model of occupational choice. The relative supply of new graduates to the teaching profession is determined by the relative wage of teachers, the rate at which teachers' salaries increase over their life cycle (relative to other professions), the state of the labour market and a number of other control variables.

The study uses British graduate employment data from the FDS of the USR, and figures on salaries are obtained from the Department of Education and Science, the New Earnings Survey and the Leeds University Careers Advisory Service. Each series consists of 45 data points, these being the outcome of a pooling of annual time series data from 1963 to 1971 and five subject areas. Estimates of OLS regression parameters are obtained separately for male and female graduates. Although both Zabalza (1979) and Zabalza, Turnbull and Williams (1979) experiment with a large variety of specifications of the supply function for teachers, for conciseness we report here only one (typical) equation. This uses as dependent variable the (natural logarithm of the) supply of female graduates to the teaching profession divided by the supply of female graduates to other jobs; this measure of *relative* supply will henceforth be referred to as $lnS$. Amongst the explanatory variables are binary dummies for science subjects ($SCI$) and for the classics ($CLASS$). In addition, the rate of graduate unemployment ($U$), and the ratio of teachers' wages to graduates' wages in other professions ($W$) appear on the right hand side. The estimated equation is

$$lnS = -2.04 + 0.72\ SCI + 0.85\ CLASS + 3.45\ W_{-1} +$$
$$\qquad\qquad (6.7) \qquad\quad (9.4) \qquad\qquad (3.5)$$

$$0.55\ \dot{W}_{-1} + 0.26\ U_{-1}$$
$$(2.0) \qquad\quad (2.6)$$

where a dot above a variable denotes the annual rate of change of that variable over a typical individual's life cycle. The above equation provides a very satisfactory fit, with an adjusted determination coefficient of 0.75. It says that the supply of graduate teachers is responsive both to the relative wage and to relative long-term prospects (proxied here by the rate of growth of earnings over the life cycle). It says also that there are some interesting variations in the supply of teachers across subject areas. In particular, those who have trained in the classics are significantly more likely to become teachers than are others, *ceteris paribus*; in the case of women (but not men), the same is true of the science subjects. Broadly similar conclusions to these have been obtained recently for the USA by Murnane and Olsen (1989). Finally, a high rate of graduate unemployment increases the relative supply of graduates to the teaching profession. This result carries the rather worrying implication that teaching is seen as a haven of last resort by many graduates.

In general the estimates obtained by Zabalza differ little across the sexes. There is, however, some evidence that women's choice of occupation is more sensitive to the level, but less sensitive to the growth, of relative wages than is that of men. This is consistent with optimising behaviour on the part of women who expect their careers to be interrupted at some future date.

A refinement of the work reported above is to examine the problem of occupational choice at the microeconomic level of the individual decision maker, rather than at the aggregate level. Data from the NSGD allows this to be done (Dolton, 1990). As in the earlier work discussed above, the determinants of the relative supply of teachers include the level and growth of relative wages in teaching, and the supply may vary from subject to subject. By using individual level data, Dolton is able to include also the graduates' individual characteristics as explanatory variables, including data on education, race, gender and social class. He models the problem in a manner which allows individuals' subjective career preferences to be taken into account; to be specific, the choice of occupation six years after graduation is made a function of, *inter alia*, occupational choice immediately after graduation. Simultaneous estimation of the relative supply functions in these two time periods enables these subjective preferences to be incorporated into the analysis. In addition, allowance is made for the fact that wages which a graduate might have earned in an occupation which she chooses not to enter are unobservable; this involves the use of a variant of the Heckman (1979) adaptation of standard probit analysis.

The results of this rigorous analysis confirm the findings of Zabalza: the relative supply of teachers is influenced as predicted by theory by both the level and the growth of the relative wage earned by the representative worker over her life cycle. The use of microeconomic data enable the following results also to be obtained: the propensity to choose teaching as an occupation decreases as the class of degree obtained improves; it declines as social class background rises; and it is relatively low for members of ethnic minorities. There is also some evidence that women are more likely to enter teaching than are men, *ceteris paribus*. Moreover, while university graduates are not less likely than graduates of other higher education institutions to enter teaching as a first career, they are significantly less likely to remain in teaching six years after graduation. Taken together, these findings suggest some bad news and some good news. The bad news is that the education industry struggles to attract and retain graduates of good quality. The good news is that the supply of teachers is not inelastic with respect to remuneration, so it should be possible, if desired, to ameliorate the situation by giving graduates the appropriate price signals.

## Issues in the Job Market for Academics

Many of the problems which occur in the market for teachers at primary and secondary levels also occur in tertiary education. The training required to become an academic is lengthier still, since virtually all academic staff have at least one postgraduate degree, and this is usually a PhD, which takes a norm of three years' full-time research to complete. There are nevertheless substantial differences between the job markets for teachers in primary and secondary schools, on the one hand, and academics, on the other. One obvious difference is that the proportion of women in academe is smaller than in the rest of the education system. Another difference – and one upon which we shall focus in this section – stems from the differences in role played by the two groups of workers.

As we have seen in Chapter 8, the academic has two major roles, teaching and research. The way in which higher education institutions manage their research activity has, in recent years, come under considerable criticism; the main incentive for an academic to do research is a genuine interest in the subject, and some outside observers consider this to be an insufficient motivator. No price system exists for research output, because basic research is characteristically a public good. So it is inevitably difficult to provide a cardinal measure of individuals' research performance. This means that rewarding productive researchers on the basis of their output would be an error-prone activity.

Recent work has, however, suggested that a reform of the system of remuneration for academics might improve the structure of incentives so that a greater quantity of high-quality research is encouraged. This is an exciting possibility, and much of the remainder of this section is devoted to it. To demonstrate the ideas, let us begin by comparing two apparently very different systems of remuneration based upon individual productivity.

Consider first the traditional piece-rate system in which each worker is paid not according to the number of hours worked, but according to her own output. Suppose that the $i$th worker produces $q_i$ units of output per period, and that her productivity is determined partly by her human capital stock, $k_i$, and partly by luck. Hence

$$q_i = k_i + \varepsilon_i \tag{11.1}$$

where $\varepsilon$ is a random variable with zero mean. Suppose further that human capital is costly to acquire, and that the cost, $C$, of acquiring $k$ units of human capital is $k^2$. The utility, $U_i$, enjoyed by the $i$th worker equals her income net of the cost of human capital investment. Income is given by the number of units of output produced multiplied by the wage, $w$, paid by the firm on each unit of output produced. Hence

$$E(U_i) = wq_i - C = wk_i - C \tag{11.2}$$

Each worker seeks to maximise her utility by differentiating (11.2) with respect to human capital and setting the result to zero. This gives the first order condition

$$w = \partial C/\partial k_i = 2k_i \tag{11.3}$$

which implies that workers will invest in their own human capital up to the point at which the marginal benefit equals the marginal cost.

Assuming labour to be the only factor of production, a representative firm paying piece rates makes an expected profit

$$E(\pi) = pq - wq \tag{11.4}$$

where $p$ is the unit price of output in the product market. Under perfectly competitive conditions freedom of entry and exit will guarantee that the price of output will be set by the market so that zero profits are made. Apart from the trivial case where $q=0$, this can happen only when $p=w$. Substituting into (11.3) this implies that

$$p = \partial C/\partial k_i = 2k_i \tag{11.5}$$

Put simply, the social value, $p$, of the product produced as a consequence of a marginal investment in human capital equals the cost of that investment, $\partial C/\partial k$. This means that piece rates are a socially efficient means of encouraging individuals to invest in their own human capital.

Despite this advantage, piece rates are often not used in practice because the productivity of individual workers is difficult to monitor. Certainly universities are unlikely ever to pay each academic on the basis of the social value of her research efforts, since cardinal measures of output would be extremely difficult and costly to produce. It would be relatively easy, however, to produce a rank ordering of the productivity of various workers. This observation leads us to consider the operation of a remuneration system based on rank order tournaments. In a system of this kind, salaries are based neither on the number of hours worked nor on the number of units of output produced; instead, remuneration is a function only of a worker's position (*vis-à-vis* other workers) in a 'league table' of worker-specific productivity. Such a system might appear crude at first glance – for instance, it implies that the link between the wage and the marginal product would be broken – but, as we shall see below, it has some very desirable properties (Lazear and Rosen, 1981; Nalebuff and Stiglitz, 1983).

In a firm employing two risk-neutral workers, the worker with the higher productivity earns $W_1$, while the other worker earns $W_2$, where $W_1 > W_2$. Individual productivities are not measured on a cardinal scale; all the firm needs to know is which of the two workers is the more productive. Equation (11.1) says that, in the piece-rate model, individual productivity may vary because of worker differences in either human capital stock or luck; this is an assumption which we maintain in the construction of the model of rank order tournaments. Hence a worker may improve her chances of 'winning' the tournament and receiving $W_1$ by investing more in her own human capital, $k$. Such investment, as before, involves an outlay of $C$, where $C = k^2$. The presence of the stochastic luck factor means, however, that there can never be a guarantee of winning. Denoting by $\lambda$ the probability of winning, expected utility is given by

$$E(U_i) = \lambda_i(W_1 - k_i^{\,2}) + (1 - \lambda_i)(W_2 - k_i^{\,2}) \tag{11.6}$$

The firm earns revenue equal to the product market price, $p$, times the sum of the outputs of the two workers. Its costs equal the sum of the winnings paid to each worker. Since the luck term has an expected value of zero for each worker, expected profits may be defined as

$$E(\pi) = p(k_j + k_k) - W_1 - W_2 \tag{11.7}$$

So expected profits depend upon the product market price (which is given by market conditions), the winnings $W_1$ and $W_2$ (which are control variables for the firm), and the human capital stocks of the workers themselves. Since the latter variables are determined by the relative magnitudes of $W_1$ and $W_2$, it is clear that it is only by choice of the reward structure that firms can exert influence on their own profitability. Assuming perfect competition allows us to impose the condition that the above equation should equal zero. This means that, while firms have discretion in choosing $W_1$ and $W_2$, they must, in order to survive, choose the reward vector which maximizes their profits.

Noting that in equilibrium the two workers would make the same human capital investment choices (so that $k_j = k_k = k$), equation (11.7) implies

$$pk = (W_1 + W_2)/2 \tag{11.8}$$

Likewise in equilibrium, each worker must have an equal chance of winning the tournament, since the winner is determined by luck alone. This means that $\lambda = 0.5$. Hence, dropping the subscripts and substituting (11.8) into (11.6) yields, after some routine manipulation,

$$E(U) = pk - k^2 \tag{11.9}$$

where $k$ is determined by the reward structure (that is, by the values of $W_1$ and $W_2$). Implicit in (11.9) is the profit maximisation requirement, so the solution of the problem for $W_1$ and $W_2$ may be found by maximising (11.9) with respect to these two choice variables. This implies

$$(p - \partial C/\partial k)\, \partial k/\partial W_x = 0, \; x = 1, 2 \tag{11.10}$$

which is clearly satisfied when

$$p = \partial C/\partial k = 2k \tag{11.11}$$

Comparison of (11.11) with (11.5) indicates that the outcome of the rank order tournament is identical to that of the traditional piece-rate system. Even though the tournament is less demanding than a piece-rate system in terms of information requirements, both systems perform equally well in securing an efficient allocation of resources.

This result has an appealing intuitive interpretation. Although actual rewards to labour do not equal the workers' marginal products, the expected rewards do. Consequently the incentives to invest in human capital before the tournament is conducted are identical to those which apply under a piece-rate system. If remuneration is determined by tournament in each period, the typical worker effectively plays in a sequence of repeated games. Where luck alone determines the outcome of the tournament in each period, and where a career is made up of a large number of periods, the choice between tournament and piece rates has no effect on a risk-neutral worker's long-run earnings.

The implication of the above analysis is that rank order tournaments, like piece rates, are a socially efficient means of remuneration. They generate exactly the same incentive effects as do piece rates and they result in exactly the same allocation of resources. This is so despite the relatively small amount of information required to operate a tournament: only an ordinal measure of individuals' productivity is required, not a cardinal measure. Indeed, given such slack information requirements, tournaments may well be preferred as means of determining workers' pay in situations where individual monitoring of performance is costly. It is remarkable that a tool which, at first sight, seems so blunt-edged should produce an efficient outcome.

In the USA, academics are typically paid a salary by their institutions which covers only nine months of the year; they are not paid by their university for the summer months. During the summer they may work on an unpaid basis on their research, or they may seek research funding. It is the latter option which is of interest here. Research funds are distributed by the grant-awarding bodies on a competitive basis: that is, they resemble rank order tournaments. In the USA (unlike Britain) research grants usually include an element of remuneration for the principal researchers. So, in effect, academics' salaries in America are partly determined by rank order tournament. Given the difficulty of obtaining cardinal measures of academic output at the level of the individual worker, this would appear to be an appropriate form for the remuneration system to take. Amongst others, Hague (1991) has advocated the adoption of such a system in the UK.

A further issue which has generated much controversy in recent years concerns the nature of the employment contract offered by tertiary institutions to their academic staff. In Britain academics, once recruited, received until recently a guarantee that they could remain in their posts until retirement, should they so wish. Exceptions existed only in the cases of proven incompetence or moral misdemeanour. This guarantee was known as tenure. The institution of tenure obviously limits the degree of flexibility which a university can exercise in restructuring its activities, since academic staff working in unfashionable fields of study are protected from redundancy. The aim of tenure is to protect academic freedom: the freedom of academics to choose their own research interests. For example, tenure might prevent the dismissal of an academic at a state university who published the results of scientific research which was critical of public sector practice. Tenure is a sufficient condition, but is unlikely to be a necessary one, for the protection of academic freedom (Vaccaro, 1972). Nevertheless, it continues to be in widespread use in many countries, including the USA, Canada and Australia.

This being so, it may seem surprising that the British Education Reform Act of 1988 denied the offer of tenure to academics signing new contracts (due to either hiring or promotion) after 20 November 1987. Academic freedom continues to be protected by law, though; section 202 of the Act makes provision to 'ensure that academic staff have freedom within the law to question and test received wisdom, and to put forward new ideas and controversial or unpopular opinions, without placing themselves in jeopardy of losing their jobs'. Academics may, however, now be dismissed 'by reason of redundancy' or 'for good cause', where 'good cause' refers to shortcomings in terms of qualifications or 'capability, assessed by reference to skill, aptitude, health or any other physical or mental quality' (s.203). By introducing in law the possibility of redundancy, the 1988 Act overrides the arrangements made earlier by many institutions which gave security of tenure to their staff.

While tenure, like the new provisions of the law, existed to protect academic freedom, its operation was somewhat more blunt. Its application in practice often meant that unproductive academics were protected from dismissal, and this probably explains its fall from favour in the UK. It is not at all clear, though, that the new legislation will improve matters in this regard; the scrapping of tenure should not make it any easier to remove incompetent or idle workers from their posts, since the provision for dismissal on these grounds is not new. The innovation merely makes possible the redundancy of individuals, and this will be difficult to enforce unless entire disciplines become obsolete. Tenure remains an interesting labour market institution, though, and reasons for its continued existence in many countries are the concern of the remainder of this section.

The first economic explanation of tenure relies on differences between firms and workers in their degree of risk aversion. While firms can diversify and spread their risk in the employment market, workers – who usually work only for one employer – cannot. A consequence of this is that workers are generally more risk averse than are their employers. Job security therefore yields utility to the typical worker. Moreover, the utility which a guarantee of job security yields to the average worker exceeds the cost to the firm of providing that guarantee. The increased job security afforded to all risk-averse workers means that they will accept lower remuneration than under a non-tenure system; this gain to the risk-neutral firm under a tenure system offsets the costs which it must, with positive probability, bear of employing an unproductive worker. Tenure can therefore provide the firm with a cheap means of rewarding labour (Freeman, 1977; Kasten, 1984). This explanation is appealing for its simplicity, but it fails to explain why tenure can be observed in academic but not in other labour markets.

A second explanation of tenure relies on moral hazard (Ito and Kahn, 1986). Universities employ academics to do research, but they cannot easily measure how hard these employees work. Moreover, the outputs of research projects are rarely quantifiable with accuracy. In remunerating its research staff, therefore, a university must devise a means of maximising worker productivity, even though it monitors neither effort nor results. Suppose that researchers are risk averse, but that their degree of risk aversion declines as their wealth increases. Then the university can increase research effort (which, in terms of utility costs and gains to the researcher, is inherently risky) by giving its employees a minimum wealth endowment. This it does by means of tenure, which is, in effect a lifetime minimum income guarantee.

The third economic rationale for tenure is due to Carmichael (1988). The academic labour market differs somewhat from many other markets because the hiring decision is – owing to the highly specialised nature of academic expertise – made by the future colleagues of the successful applicant; it is not possible to delegate the responsibility for hiring to members of another department within the university. Consequently, 'tenure is necessary because without it incumbents would never be willing to hire people who might turn out to be better than themselves'. This does not, however, provide justification for awarding tenure to any but the most senior employees within any department. Moreover, in common with the Ito and Kahn model, it misses the point that tenure does *not* prevent the dismissal of the incompetent: it merely protects workers from redundancy.

We have seen above that several arguments may be invoked in order to defend the institution of tenure, but that none of these is wholly satisfactory. However, those who have criticised tenure on the grounds that it protects the idle and incompetent have missed the point: it does not. Methods other than the removal of tenure are necessary in order to remove unproductive workers, and this is a nettle which has yet to be grasped. Apart from the rare instances in which a wholesale restructuring of an institution's offerings is desirable, tenure is at worst a harmless irrelevance.

## The Brain Drain

Much attention has been devoted in recent decades to the issue of the academic 'brain drain' (Johnson, 1967; Grubel and Scott, 1977; Grubel, 1987). This takes the form of human capital migration from countries where remuneration for academics is relatively low, towards countries where salaries are higher. Awareness of the brain drain has increased over the last 30 years or so as the USA relaxed its visa requirements on immigrating scientists during the post-Sputnik era. An indication of the migration to the USA of highly skilled labour is given by the data in Table 11.1.

While the UK loses academic talent to the USA, at the same time it gains from LDCs, especially those, such as India, where English is spoken. Table 11.2 provides some indication of the relative magnitudes of these flows. For most years in the recent past, Britain has been a net gainer in terms of the numbers of brain drainees. Nevertheless, concern has been expressed that the emigrants from the UK universities are typically of exceptionally high repute. The implication is that although Britain is a net gainer from the point of view of a head count, a quality-adjusted measure of the impact of the brain drain on UK tertiary education might conclude otherwise.

This view has been supported by the work of Blanchflower and Oswald (reported in *The Times Higher Education Supplement*, 16 June 1989, p.3). This indicates that those who have migrated from the UK in recent years are typically more widely cited in the academic

**TABLE 11.1**
**Immigration of Professional Workers from LDCs into the USA, post-Sputnik period, 1962–9**

| Country of origin | Physicians, dentists and surgeons | Natural scientists | Social scientists | Engineers |
|---|---|---|---|---|
| Turkey | 562 | 52 | 27 | 429 |
| India | 414 | 1022 | 232 | 4236 |
| China (incl. Taiwan) | 180 | 967 | 220 | 2509 |
| Philippines | 3092 | 726 | 91 | 2372 |
| Other Asia | 2053 | 1436 | 402 | 3887 |
| Central America | 3603 | 1161 | 329 | 2937 |
| South America | 3032 | 875 | 324 | 2522 |
| Africa | 431 | 341 | 76 | 895 |

Source: Bhagwati and Dellafar (1976).

**TABLE 11.2**
**Migration Flows of Academics into and out of the UK, 1980–9**

| Year | Inflow | Outflow | Net outflow |
|---|---|---|---|
| 1980 | 276 | 249 | −27 |
| 1981 | 183 | 203 | 20 |
| 1982 | 118 | 214 | 96 |
| 1983 | 220 | 153 | −67 |
| 1984 | 318 | 138 | −180 |
| 1985 | 292 | 154 | −138 |
| 1986 | 260 | 204 | −56 |
| 1987 | 199 | 191 | −8 |
| 1988 | 244 | 160 | −84 |
| 1989 | 321 | 171 | −150 |

Source: Hansard, 17 February 1989, written answer, pp.413–14; UFC University Statistics, volume 1, Table 32.

literature than are the academics who remain behind. In the remainder of this section we shall consider whether or not this migration represents a problem and, if so, what measures might be taken to recover the cost of any externalities with which it is associated.

Economists generally view the migration decision as an investment, since the present period costs of moving must at least be offset by the discounted value of future net (pecuniary and psychic) returns in order to make the move worthwhile. Migration thus fits neatly into a human capital model. The incentives to migrate between a given pair of countries are therefore a function (amongst other things) of the wage differential between the countries concerned.

If markets were perfect, each worker would receive as remuneration the value of her marginal product. As an initial assumption, suppose that each individual in a world of perfect markets pays for her own education as and when she receives educational services. In this model, the international migration of human capital is not very interesting. Since there are no externalities attached to the employment of a migrant worker in either the country of origin or that of destination, and since there are no fiscal implications, the welfare of non-migrant workers in both societies will remain unaffected. Indeed, the act of migration would increase global welfare since (presumably) the migrant herself must be made better off by the act of migrating, otherwise she would not move.

Of course, life is rarely so simple. Externalities to education do exist, and this means that the country of origin typically loses out when a highly-skilled worker emigrates. Nevertheless, it is important not to overstate the losses. The output of academics is, once published, available internationally. It is not at all clear, therefore, that Britain, say, is worse off as a consequence of the emigration of an economist who specialises in the British labour market. Indeed, given better computing facilities and research support in her new country, that economist could become more productive, and hence produce more work of value to Britain. While it is galling for the poor to pay taxes in order to educate people who then leave the country to earn riches elsewhere (and escape the domestic tax burden), it should be remembered that when such workers emigrate they usually take their children with them, thus reducing the burden on the domestic education system. It may well be that the greatest cost associated with the emigration of academics is the loss of national pride.

In most countries, international migration represents a marginal adjustment, since the number of migrants is small in relation to the total population. There are some important exceptions to this rule. Some Middle Eastern countries, such as Yemen, have experienced large-scale emigration in the direction of their oil-producing neighbours. Even in a country as large as India, the loss of qualified labour can be substantial; some 7 per cent of all Indian doctors were working outside their mother country in 1980 (Balasubramanyam, 1991).

Where migration is non-marginal, it is important to evaluate the skill level of the typical migrant. In a country of origin which loses unskilled workers, migration serves to raise the (sum of human and physical) capital per head, and so leads to an increase in per capitum output. Hence Mexico is rarely heard complaining about the loss of labour to the USA. Conversely, where skilled workers (like academics) are lost through emigration, the country of origin experiences a decline in per capitum output. Since, for equity reasons, most tax systems aim to redistribute income from the rich to the poor, such a decline may significantly lower the welfare of the population which remains. Moreover, the loss of skilled labour can impose upon a country substantial costs of replacement, since unskilled workers must be trained up to do the jobs once undertaken by emigrants.

These concerns led Bhagwati and Dellafar (1976) to propose the introduction of an 'exit tax' for brain drainees. The idea of the exit tax is that emigrants pay a surcharge on their income tax in the destination country, and the yield from this surcharge is then passed on to the country of origin by the tax authorities. Thus the original country can be compensated for the loss to the domestic economy of individuals possessing a high stock of human capital.

There are problems with the exit tax proposal, however (Balasubramanyam, 1991). In particular, it should be noted that the corollary of the argument that the country of origin loses out as a consequence of emigration is that the destination country gains. It would seem, therefore, that the appropriate form of compensation to the original country should be in the form of a transfer from *all* taxpayers in the destination country, not just from the brain drainees themselves. Where, as is often the case, the country of origin is an LDC, this amounts simply to boosting the aid package. Early work by Perkins (1966) suggests that 'the United States . . . has an apparently unlimited demand for precisely those people most desparately needed by the countries we are spending billions of dollars annually to help . . . While we support the idea of foreign development, our domestic needs may be making hash of our best efforts abroad.' This view is confirmed by Grubel (1987), who argues that the value of human capital flows from many LDCs – and especially India – to the USA is large in relation to the value of aid flowing in the other direction; compensation for this net export from India would raise global efficiency by internalising the externalities involved.

# Conclusion

The labour market generates considerable interest and debate amongst economists. This is so because its operation often seems to be imperfect. Spells of skill shortages and of above-trend unemployment are protracted, lasting several years at a stretch. Such phenomena are not easy to reconcile with the usual economic assumptions of a well-oiled and well-behaved market. These observations apply *a fortiori* when the labour market for highly skilled or qualified workers is considered. School teachers form one of the largest groups of such workers in the economy. Educators in higher education are a much smaller group, but they too have a very distinctive labour market.

Although the supply of new graduates to the teaching profession can be predicted reasonably well, it is not so easy to forecast the exit rates of teachers – especially women – from employment. This means that conditions in the market for teachers are very difficult to predict. Even if school pupils have 'rational' expectations about the future time-paths of salaries for teaching and other jobs, and even if they base their educational career and occupational choices on these expectations, there is so much noise in the market that gluts and shortages of teachers are bound to occur. This observation has frequently been used to justify the high degree of government planning in the market for teachers. Such planning may provide a 'second-best' solution given the impossibility of perfect foresight.

Academics working in tertiary education perform roles which differ somewhat from those of primary and secondary school teachers. The labour market in which they operate is international, and is one in which the incentive structure which best secures worker effort is difficult to determine. Recent advances in economic theory suggest ways forward. This is a labour market where things could well change dramatically over the next decade.

# Conclusion 12

Much ground has been covered in the preceding chapters. Moreover, much of the discussion has focused on developments of the last decade or so. The economics of education is certainly a much bigger subject than was the case even a few years ago. In this final chapter we consider a number of directions in which research into this subject might go in the immediate future.

The first of these concerns externalities. Primary education arms the individual with a basic level of literacy and numeracy. This benefits the individual, but is of value also to others, since it facilitates communication. In a free market, externalities of this kind would be a source of market failure; individuals would under-invest in their own education. Externalities are likely to be apparent, albeit to a lesser extent, in secondary and tertiary education too. The presence of such externalities is one of the main justifications given for the state finance of education. However, little empirical work has been conducted which would enable us to evaluate just how strong these externality effects are. This would be a fruitful avenue for future research.

A second justification for state funding is the impact which education can have on equity. We have seen that a non-regressive distribution of outcomes of the education system requires the imposition of progressivity in the allocation of inputs. The market would not therefore converge to an equity of outcomes if left to its own devices. But again, the arguments in the literature have been theoretical, with no serious attempt to evaluate empirically the extent to which current and alternative funding arrangements affect equity. The efficiency–equity trade-off is a serious matter, and warrants quantitative measurement as well as abstract theorising.

Third, the transmission of signals from the labour market via the education system and to prospective consumers of education needs to be investigated. Both empirical and theoretical studies are needed in this area. If the system works well, then HRP can be exercised with a light touch. If, on the other hand, the mechanism is failing, solutions must be sought. Either a more interventionist form of planning must be accepted, or the impediments to the clear perception of labour market signals must be removed.

The evidence of the foregoing chapters suggests that the market for education is not perfect. Expectations by students of their own future labour market performance, even if rational, are often formed with considerable error; lags in the passing of information in this market are considerable; uncertainty abounds. The challenge which students of the economics of education face is first to explain why these imperfections persist, and then to propose remedies.

In an ideal world, this textbook could have given answers to the questions posed above. But economics is not about an ideal world; it concerns a world in which only a finite pool of resources can be devoted to solving these problems. Likewise, education is not about an ideal world; it concerns a world in which some things lie beyond our present understanding. We must hope that, sometime in the future, another book may be written which can throw more light on these matters.

# References

## Chapter 1 Introduction

Blaug, M. (1976) 'The empirical study of human capital theory: a slightly jaundiced survey', *Journal of Economic Literature*, 14, 827–55.
Schultz, T. (1961) 'Investment in human capital', *American Economic Review*, 51, 1-17.
Vaizey, J. (1958) *The Costs of Education* (London: Allen & Unwin).
Wiseman, J. (1959) 'The economics of education', *Scottish Journal of Political Economy*, 6, 48–58.

## Chapter 2 Human Capital

Arrow, K. (1973) 'Higher education as a filter', *Journal of Public Economics*, 2, 193–216.
Becker, G. S. (1964) *Human Capital* (New York: Columbia University Press).
Ben-Porath, Y. (1967) 'The production of human capital and the life cycle of earnings', *Journal of Political Economy*, 75, 352–65.
Blanchflower, D. G. and Oswald, A. J. (1989) 'The wage curve', Centre for Labour Economics Discussion Paper 340, London School of Economics; condensed version published (1990) in the *Scandinavian Journal of Economics*, 92, 215–35.
Blaug, M. (1970) *An Introduction to the Economics of Education* (Harmondsworth: Penguin).
Dixit, A. K. (1990) *Optimization in Economic Theory* (Oxford University Press).
Haley, W. J. (1973) 'Human capital: the choice between investment and income', *American Economic Review*, 63, 929–44.
Heckman, J. J. (1976) 'A life cycle model of earnings, learning and consumption', *Journal of Political Economy*, 84, S11–S44.
Horowitz, S. P. and Sherman, A. (1980) 'A direct measure of the relationship between human capital and productivity', *Journal of Human Resources*, 15, 67–76.
Huffman, W. E. (1981) 'Black–white human capital differences: impact on agricultural productivity in the US south', *American Economic Review*, 71, 94–107.
Lang, K. and Ruud, P. A. (1986) 'Returns to schooling, implicit discount rates and black–white wage differentials', *Review of Economics and Statistics*, 68, 41–7.

Layard, P. R. G. and Psacharopoulos, G. (1974) 'The screening hypothesis and the returns to education', *Journal of Political Economy*, 82, 985–98.
Levin, H. M. (1980) 'Educational vouchers and social policy', in Guthrie, J. W. (ed.), *School Finance Policies and Practices* (Lexington, Mass.: Ballinger).
Meng, R. (1987) 'The earnings of Canadian immigrant and native-born males', *Applied Economics*, 19, 1107–19.
Mincer, J. (1974) *Schooling, Experience and Earnings* (New York: National Bureau for Economic Research).
Murphy, K. M. and Welch, F. R. (1989) 'Wage premiums for college graduates', *Educational Researcher*, 18, 5, 17–26.
Murphy, K. M. and Welch, F. R. (1990) 'Empirical age–earnings profiles', *Journal of Labor Economics*, 8, 202–29.
Pontryagin, L. S., Boltyanskii, V. G., Gamkrelidze, R. V. and Mischenko, E. F. (1962) *The Mathematical Theory of Optimal Processes* (New York: Wiley).
Psacharopoulos, G. (1975) *Earnings and Education in OECD Countries* (Paris: OECD).
Rosen, S. (1976) 'A theory of life earnings', *Journal of Political Economy*, 84, S45–S68.
Spence, M. (1973) 'Job market signalling', *Quarterly Journal of Economics*, 8, 355–74.
Williams, G. and Gordon, A. (1981) 'Perceived earnings functions and ex ante rates of return to post-compulsory education in England, *Higher Education*, 10, 199–227.
Wilson, R. A. (1987) 'The determinants of the earnings of professional engineers in Great Britain in 1981', *Applied Economics*, 19, 983–94.

## Chapter 3 Rates of Return

Blaug, M., Layard, P. R. G. and Woodhall, M. (1969) *The Causes of Graduate Unemployment in India* (Harmondsworth: Penguin).
Dolton, P. J., Makepeace, G. H. and Inchley, G. D. (1990) 'The early careers of 1980 graduates', Department of Employment Research Paper 78.
Duncan, G. J. and Hoffman, S. D. (1981) 'The incidence and wage effects of over-education', *Economics of Education Review*, 1, 75–86.
Freeman, R. B. (1976) *The Over-Educated American* (New York: Academic Press).
King, R. H. (1980) 'Further evidence on the rate of return to schooling and the business cycle', *Journal of Human Resources*, 14, 264–72.
Layard, P.R.G. (1977) 'On measuring the redistribution of lifetime income', in Feldstein, M. S. and Inman, R. P. (eds), *The Economics of Public Services* (London: Macmillan).
Moghadam, R. (1990) 'Wage determination: an assessment of returns to education, occupation, region and industry in Great Britain', Centre for Economic Performance Discussion Paper 8, London School of Economics.
Psacharopoulos, G. (1973) *Returns to Education* (Amsterdam: Elsevier).

Psacharopoulos, G. (1981) 'Returns to education: an updated international comparison', *Comparative Education*, 17, 321–41.
Psacharopoulos, G. (1985) 'Returns to education: a further international update and implications', *Journal of Human Resources*, 20, 583–604.
Psacharopoulos, G. (1987) 'Public versus private schools in developing countries: evidence from Colombia and Tanzania', *International Journal of Educational Development*, 7, 59–67.
Rumberger, R. W. (1981) 'The rising incidence of over-education in the US labor market', *Economics of Education Review*, 1, 293–314.
Sicherman, N. (1991) 'Over-education in the labor market', *Journal of Labor Economics*, 9, 101–22.
Thurow, L. (1975) *Generating Inequality: Mechanisms of Distribution in the US Economy* (New York: Basic Books).
Tsang, M. C. and Levin, H. M. (1985) 'The economics of over-education', *Economics of Education Review*, 4, 93–104.
Willis, R. J. (1986) 'Wage determination: a survey and reinterpretation of human capital earnings', in Ashenfelter, O. and Laylard, P.R.G. (eds), *Handbook of Labour Economics*, volume 1 (Amsterdam: Elsevier).

# Chapter 4 Human Resource Needs

Arrow, K. J. and Capron, W. M. (1959) 'Dynamic shortages and price rises: the engineer-scientist case', *Quarterly Journal of Economics*, 73, 292–308.
Bailey, T. (1991) 'Jobs of the future and the education they will require: evidence from occupational forecasts', *Educational Researcher*, 20, 2, 11–20.
Balasko, Y. and Shell, K. (1980) 'The overlapping generations model I: the case of pure exchange without money', *Journal of Economic Theory*, 23, 281–306.
Borus, M. E. and Carpenter, S. A. (1984) 'Choices in education', in Borus, M. E. (ed.), *Youth and the Labor Market* (Kalamazoo, Mich.: W. E. Upjohn Institute for Employment Research).
Bosworth, D. and Ford, J. (1985a) 'Income expectations and the decision to enter higher education', *Studies in Higher Education*, 10, 21–32.
Bosworth, D. and Ford, J. (1985b) 'Perceptions of higher education by university entrants: an exploratory study', *Studies in Higher Education*, 10, 257–67.
Department of Education and Science (1986) *Projections of Demand for Higher Education in Great Britain, 1986–2000* (London: Department of Education and Science).
Dolphin, A. M. (1981) 'The demand for higher education', *Employment Gazette*, 89, 302–5.
Freeman, R. B. (1975) 'Overinvestment in college training?', *Journal of Human Resources*, 10, 287–311.
Freeman, R. B. (1976) 'A cobweb model of the supply and starting salary of new engineers', *Industrial and Labor Relations Review*, 29, 236–48.
Gleick, J. (1988) *Chaos* (New York: Heinemann).

Glytsos, N. P. (1990a) 'Anticipated graduate job mismatches and higher education capacity inadequacies in Greece', *Higher Education*, 19, 397–418.

Glytsos, N. P. (1990b) 'Modelling future higher education – labor market imbalances: a multi-scenario approach', *Economics of Education Review*, 9, 1–23.

Grandmont, J. M. (1985) 'On endogenous competitive business cycles', *Econometrica*, 53, 995–1046.

Guerney, A. (1987) 'Labour market signals and graduate output: a case study of the university sector', in Thomas, H. and Simkins, T. (eds), *Economics and the Management of Education: Emerging Themes* (Lewes: Falmer Press).

Hinchcliffe, K. (1987) 'Education and the labour market', in Psacharopoulos, G. (ed.), *Economics of Education: Research and Studies* (Oxford: Pergamon).

Levin, H. M. (1987) 'Work and education', in Psacharopoulos, G. (ed.), *Economics of Education: Research and Studies* (Oxford: Pergamon).

Mare, R. D. (1980) 'Social background and school continuation decisions', *Journal of the American Statistical Association*, 75, 295–305.

Mattila, J. P. (1982) 'Determinants of male school enrolments: a time series analysis', *Review of Economics and Statistics*, 64, 242–51.

Micklewright, J., Pearson, M. and Smith, S. (1990) 'Unemployment and early school leaving', *Economic Journal*, 100, S163–S169.

Moser, C. A. and Layard, P. R. G. (1964) 'Planning the scale of higher education in Britain: some statistical problems', *Journal of the Royal Statistical Society, Series A*, 127, 473–513.

Parnes, H. S. (1964) 'Manpower analysis in educational planning', in Parnes, H. S. (ed.), *Planning Education for Economic and Social Development* (Paris: OECD; reprinted in Blaug, M. (ed.) (1968), *Economics of Education*, volume 1 (Harmondsworth: Penguin)).

Pissarides, C. A. (1981) 'Staying on at school in England and Wales', *Economica*, 48, 345–63.

Rice, P. G. (1987) 'The demand for post-compulsory education in the UK and the effects of educational maintenance allowances', *Economica*, 54, 465–75.

Samuelson, P. A. (1958) 'An exact consumption-loan model of interest with or without the social contrivance of money', *Journal of Political Economy*, 66, 467–82.

Tarsh, J. (1987) 'Higher education and the labour market: a view of the debate', in Thomas, H. and Simkins, T. (eds), *Economics and the Management of Education: Emerging Themes* (Lewes: Falmer Press).

Teichler, U., Hartung, D. and Nuthmann, R. (1980) *Higher Education and the Needs of Society* (Windsor: NFER).

Teichler, U. and Sanyal, B. C. (1982) *Higher Education and the Labour Market in the Federal Republic of Germany* (Paris: Unesco Press).

Williams, G. L. and Fulton, O. (1980) 'Higher education and manpower planning', in *The Funding and Organisation of Courses in Higher Education, the Fifth Report from the Education, Science and Arts Committee of the House of Commons*, Session 1979–80, volume 2, Minutes and Evidence, HC 787-II, 443–8.

Wilson, R. A. (1990) 'The changing occupational structure of employment, 1971–95', *International Journal of Manpower*, 11, 2/3, 44–53.

# Chapter 5 Private or Public Sector?


Arrow, K.J. (1971) 'Equality in public expenditure', *Quarterly Journal of Economics*, 85, 409–15.

Bruno, M. (1976) 'Equality, complementarity and the incidence of public expenditures', *Journal of Public Economics*, 6, 395–407.

Bruno, M. (1977) 'Efficiency and equity in public education expenditures', in Feldstein, M.S. and Inman, R.P. (eds), *The Economics of Public Services* (London: Macmillan).

Friedman, M. (1962) 'The role of government in education', in *Capitalism and Freedom* (Chicago University Press), 85–107.

James, E. (1984) 'Benefits and costs of privatized public services: lessons from the Dutch education system', *Comparative Education Review*, 28, 605–24.

James, E. (1991) 'Public policies toward private education: an international comparison', *International Journal of Educational Research*, 15, 359–76.

Kay, J.A. and Silberston, Z.A. (1984) 'The new industrial policy – privatisation and competition', *Midland Bank Review*, Spring, 8–16.

Kay, J.A. and Thompson, D.J. (1986) 'Privatisation: a policy in search of a rationale', *Economic Journal*, 96, 18–32.

Mankiw, N.G. and Summers, L.H. (1986) 'Money demand and the effects of fiscal policy', *Journal of Money Credit and Banking*, 18, 415–29.

McMahon, W.W. (1982) 'Efficiency and equity criteria for educational budgeting and finance', in McMahon, W.W. and Geske, T.G. (eds), *Financing Education: Overcoming Inefficiency and Inequity* (Urbana and Chicago: University of Illinois Press).

Millward, R. (1982) 'The comparative performance of public and private ownership', in Roll, E. (ed.), *The Mixed Economy* (London: Macmillan).

Nicholl, J.P., Thomas, K.J., Williams, B.T. and Knowelden, J. (1984) 'Contribution of the private sector to elective surgery in England and Wales', *The Lancet*, 8394, 14 July, 89–92.

Pring, R. (1988) 'Privatisation', *Educational Management and Administration*, 16, 85–96.

Pryke, R. (1982) 'The comparative performance of public and private enterprise', *Fiscal Studies*, 3, 68–81.

Rees, R. (1985) 'The theory of principal and agent', *Bulletin of Economic Research*, 37, 3–26 and 75–95.

Ross, S. (1973) 'The economic theory of agency: the principal's problem', *American Economic Review, Papers and Proceedings*, 63, 134–9.

Stiglitz, J.E. (1974) 'The demand for education in public and private school systems', *Journal of Public Economics*, 3, 349–85.

Strong, N. and Waterson, M. (1987) 'Principals, agents and information', in Clarke, R. and McGuiness, A. (eds), *The Economics of the Firm* (Oxford: Basil Blackwell).

Ulph, D.T. (1977) 'On the optimal distribution of income and educational expenditure', *Journal of Public Economics*, 8, 341–56.

Vickers, J. and Yarrow, G. (1988) *Privatization: An Economic Analysis* (Cambridge, Mass. and London: MIT Press).

# Chapter 6 The Costs of Provision

Andrew, L. D. and Friedman, B. D. (1976) *A Study of the Causes for the Demise of Certain Small, Private Liberal Arts Colleges in the United States* (Blacksburg: Virginia Polytechnic Institute and State University).

Arrow, K. J. (1951) *Social Choice and Individual Values* (New York: Wiley).

Bowen, H. R. (1980) *The Costs of Higher Education* (San Francisco: Jossey Bass).

Brinkman, P. T. (1981) 'Factors affecting instructional costs at major research universities', *Journal of Higher Education*, 52, 265–79.

Butel, J. H. and Atkinson, G. B. J. (1983) 'Secondary school size and costs', *Educational Studies*, 9, 151–7.

Cave, E. (1990) 'The changing managerial arena', in Cave, E. and Wilkinson, C. (eds), *Local Management of Schools: Some Practical Issues* (London: Routledge).

Coatesworth, D. (1976) 'Is small still beautiful in rural Norfolk?', *Education*, 148, 14.

Cohn, E. (1968) 'Economies of scale in Iowa high school operations', *Journal of Human Resources*, 3, 422–34.

Colman, A. (1982) *Game Theory and Experimental Games* (Oxford: Pergamon).

Condorcet, M.J.A.N. (1785) *Essai sur l'application de l'analise a la probabilité des decisions a la pluralité des voix* (Paris: Imprimerie Royale).

Coombs, P. H. and Hallak, J. (1972) *Managing Educational Costs* (Oxford University Press).

Cumming, C. E. (1971) *Studies in Educational Costs* (Edinburgh: Scottish Academic Press).

Finn, J. D. and Achilles, C. M. (1990) 'Answers and questions about class size: a statewide experiment', *American Educational Research Journal*, 27, 557–77.

Gilmartin, K. J. (1984) 'Measuring the viability of colleges: who is really in distress?', *American Educational Research Journal*, 21, 79–101.

Glennerster, H. (1991) 'Quasi-markets for education?', *Economic Journal*, 101, 1268–76.

Hind, I. W. (1977) 'Estimates of cost functions for primary schools in rural areas', *Australian Journal of Agricultural Economics*, 21, 13–25.

Hough, J. R. (1981) *A Study of School Costs* (Windsor: NFER–Nelson).

James, H. T., Kelly, J. A. and Garms, W. I. (1966) *Determinants of Educational Expenditure in Large Cities of the United States* (Washington, DC: US Office of Education, ERIC report).

Johnes, J. (1990) 'Unit costs: some explanations of differences between UK universities', *Applied Economics*, 22, 853–62.

Kenny, I. W. (1982) 'Economies of scale in school', *Economics of Education Review*, 2, 1–24.

Layard, P. R. G. and Verry, D. W. (1975) 'Cost functions for university teaching and research', *Economic Journal*, 85, 55–74.

Lee, K. (1984) *Further Evidence on Economies of Scale in Higher Education* (Washington, DC: World Bank).

Levin, B., Muller, T. and Sandoval, C. (1973) *The High Cost of Education in Cities* (Washington, DC: Urban Institute).
McAlister, D. and Connolly, M. (1990) 'Local financial management', in Cave, E. and Wilkinson, C. (eds), *Local Management of Schools: Some Practical Issues* (London: Routledge).
Osborne, M.J. (1989) 'On the marginal cost of a student in the public sector of higher education in the UK', *Journal of Further and Higher Education*, 13, 55–65.
Osburn, D. D. (1970) 'Economies of size associated with public high schools', *Review of Economics and Statistics*, 52, 113–15.
Peston, M. (1985) 'Higher education: financial and economic aspects', *Royal Bank of Scotland Review*, 148, 3–17.
Riew, J. (1966) 'Economies of scale in high school operations', *Review of Economics and Statistics*, 48, 280–87.
Spreadbury, D. (1989) 'The logic of devolution', *Education*, 174, 121–2.
Stenner, A. (1987) 'School centered financial management', in Craig, I. (ed.), *Primary School Management in Action* (London: Longman).
Stenner, A. (1988) 'LFM in a primary school', in Downes, P. (ed.), *Local Financial Management in Schools* (Oxford: Basil Blackwell).
Strain, M. (1990) 'Resource management in schools: some conceptual and practical considerations', in Cave, E. and Wilkinson, C. (eds), *Local Management of Schools: Some Practical Issues* (London: Routledge).
Tsang, M. C. (1988) 'Cost analysis for economic policy making: a review of cost studies in education in developing countries', *Review of Educational Research*, 58, 181–230.
Turner, D. A. (1989) 'Local school administration', *Educational Management and Administration*, 17, 199–207.
World Bank (1986) *China: Management and Finance of Higher Education* (Washington, DC: World Bank, report by R. Drysdale, W. Middleton and W. Pierpont).

## Chapter 7 Auctions, Vouchers and Loans

Blaug, M. (1967) 'Economic aspects of vouchers for education', in Beales, A. C. F., Blaug, M., West, E. G. and Veale, D. (1967), *Education: A Framework for Choice* (London: Institute of Economic Affairs).
Clark, P. L. and Round, E. (1991) *Good State Schools Guide* (London: Ebury Press).
Darvish-Lecker, T. and Kahana, N. (1990) 'Study grant schemes and effort: an economic model', *Bulletin of Economic Research*, 42, 229–39.
Friedman, M. (1955) 'The role of government in education', in Solo, R. A. (ed.), *Economics and the Public Interest* (Rutgers University Press, New Jersey; reprinted with revisions as Chapter 6 of Friedman, M. (1962), *Capitalism and Freedom* (University of Chicago Press)).

Friedman, M. (1975) *There's No Such Thing as a Free Lunch* (LaSalle: Open Court).
Glennerster, H., Merrett, S. and Wilson, G. (1968) 'A graduate tax', *Higher Education Review*, 1, 1, 26–36.
Gorman, T. (1986) 'Why vouchers are a good thing', *Education*, 167, 26, 587.
Halsey, A. H. (1992) 'Opening wide the doors to higher education', Briefing Paper 6, National Commission on Education, London.
Hansen, R. (1988) 'Auctions with endogenous quantities', *Rand Journal of Economics*, 19, 44–58.
Howard, M. (1991) 'Training credits', *International Journal of Manpower*, 12, 4, 3–4.
James, E. (1984) 'Benefits and costs of privatized public services: lessons from the Dutch educational system', *Comparative Education Review*, 28, 605–24.
Jencks, C. (1970) *Education Vouchers: A Report on Financing Elementary Education by Grants to Parents* (Cambridge: Centre for the Study of Public Policy).
Johnes, G. (1992) 'Bidding for students in Britain – why the UFC auction "failed"', *Higher Education*, 23, 173–82.
Johnes, G. and Cave, M. (1993) 'The development of competition among higher education institutions in the UK', Lancaster University Discussion Paper.
Johnes, G. and Johnes, J. (1992) 'Education finance in a model of occupational choice', Lancaster University Department of Economics Discussion Paper.
Johnes, J. and Taylor, J. (1990) *Performance Indicators in Higher Education* (Buckingham: Open University Press).
Joseph, K. (1984) 'Education vouchers', Written Reply to Parliamentary Question, *Hansard*, 22 June, 290.
Kelly, A. (1989) 'How will a voucher scheme increase access?', in Sexton, S. (ed.), *Funding and Management of Higher Education* (Warlingham: Institute of Economic Affairs).
Kent County Council (1978) *Education Vouchers in Kent* (Maidstone: Kent County Council).
Lal, D. (1989) *Nationalised Universities: Paradox of the Privatisation Age* (London: Centre for Policy Studies).
Maynard, A. (1975) *Experiment with Choice in Education* (London: Institute of Economic Affairs).
McAfee, R. P. and McMillan, J. (1987) 'Auctions and bidding', *Journal of Economic Literature*, 25, 699–738.
Milgrom, P. (1989) 'Auctions and bidding: a primer', *Journal of Economic Perspectives*, 3, 3–22.
Morse, J. F. (1977) 'How we got here from there – a personal reminiscence of the early days', in Rice, L. D. (ed.), *Student Loans: Problems and Policy Alternatives* (New York: College Entrance Examination Board).
National Union of Teachers (1983) *Our Children, Our Future: A Manifesto for Education* (London: National Union of Teachers).
Paine, T. (1915) *Rights of Man* (London: Everyman).
Peacock, A. T. and Wiseman, J. (1964) *Education for Democrats* (London: Institute for Economic Affairs).

Sugarman, S. D. (1974) 'Family choice: the next step in the quest for equal educational opportunity?', in Levin, B. (ed.), *Future Directions for School Finance Reform* (Lexington, Mass.: Heath).
Tan, N. (1990) *The Cambridge Controlled Choice Program: Improving Educational Equity and Integration* (New York: Manhattan Institute Center for Educational Innovation), Education Policy Paper 4.
Turner, D. and Pratt, J. (1990) 'Bidding for funds in higher education', *Higher Education Review*, 22, 3, 19–33.
UFC (1989) 'Funding and planning: 1991/92 to 1994/95', Circular letter 20/89, London.
Vaizey, J. (1962) *The Economics of Education* (London: Faber & Faber).
Vickrey, W. (1961) 'Counterspeculation, auctions and competitive sealed tenders', *Journal of Finance*, 16, 8–37.
Wagner, L. (1974) 'Vouchers – are they the answer for parental choice?', *Education*, 144, 24, 677–8.
Weiler, D. (1977) 'The first year at Alum Rock', in Baxter, C., O'Leary, P. J. and Westoby, A. (eds), *Economics and Education Policy: A Reader* (London: Longman).
West, E.G. (1967a) 'Dr Blaug and state education: a reply', in Beales, A. C. F., Blaug, M., West, E. G. and Veale, D. (1967), *Education: A Framework for Choice* (London: Institute of Economic Affairs).
West, E. G. (1967b) 'Tom Paine's voucher scheme for public education', *Southern Economic Journal*, 33, 378–82.
Woodhall, M. (1982) *Student Loans: Lessons from International Experience* (London: Policy Studies Institute).
Woodhall, M. (1989) 'International experience of financial support for students: recent trends and developments', in Woodhall, M. (ed.), *Financial Support for Students: Grants, Loans or Graduate Tax?* (London: Kogan Page).

# Chapter 8 Universities as Multi-Product Firms

Bailey, E. E. and Friedlander, A. F. (1982) 'Market structure and multiproduct industries', *Journal of Economic Literature*, 20, 1024–48.
Baumol, W. (1977) 'On the proper cost tests for natural monopoly in a multiproduct industry', *American Economic Review*, 67, 809–22.
Bear, D. V. T. (1974) 'The university as a multiproduct firm', in Lumsden, K. G. (ed.), *Efficiency in Universities: The La Paz papers* (Amsterdam: Elsevier).
Berdahl, R. O. (1971) *Statewide Coordination of Higher Education* (Washington, DC: American Council on Education).
Cohn, E., Rhine, S. L. W. and Santos, M. C. (1989) 'Institutions of higher education as multiproduct firms: economies of scale and scope, *Review of Economics and Statistics*, 71, 284–90.

Dasgupta, P. and Maskin, E. (1987) 'The simple economics of research portfolios', *Economic Journal*, 97, 581–95.
Dolton, P.J. and Makepeace, G.H. (1982) 'University typology: a contemporary analysis', *Higher Education Review*, 14, 33–47.
Friedman, M. (1968) 'The role of monetary policy', *American Economic Review*, 58, 1–17.
Hall, R.L. and Hitch, C.I. (1939) 'Price theory and business behaviour', *Oxford Economic Papers*, Old Series 2, 12–45.
Hotelling, H. (1929) 'Stability in competition', *Economic Journal*, 39, 41–57.
Knight, P. (1987) 'The relationship between teaching and research', *Area*, 19, 350–2.
McConnell, T.R. (1975) 'Coordinating higher education', *Higher Education Review*, 8, 45–58.
Merton, R.K. (1961) 'Singletons and multiples in scientific discovery', *Proceedings of the American Philosophical Society*, 105, 470–86.
Panzar, J.C. and Willig, R.D. (1981) 'Economies of scope', *American Economic Review, Papers and Proceedings*, 71, 268–72.
Phelps, E.S. (1968) 'Money wage dynamics and labor market equilibrium', *Journal of Political Economy*, 76, 678–711.
Schneider, E. (1952) *Pricing and Equilibrium* (London: Allen & Unwin).
Smith, D. (1981) *Industrial Location* (New York: Wiley).
Sweezy, P. (1939) 'Demand under conditions of oligopoly', *Journal of Political Economy*, 47, 568–737.
Taylor, J. (1990) 'Determining the subject balance in higher education: how should this be done?', *Higher Education*, 19, 239–57.
Verry, D.W. and Davies, B. (1975) *University Costs and Outputs* (Amsterdam: North-Holland).

# Chapter 9 Performance Indicators

Aitkin, M. and Longford, N. (1986) 'Statistical modelling issues in school effectiveness studies', *Journal of the Royal Statistical Society, Series A*, 149, 1–43.
Astin, A.W. (1975) *Preventing Students from Dropping out* (San Francisco: Jossey Bass).
Beasley, J.E. (1990) 'Comparing university departments', *Omega*, 18, 171–83.
Bee, M. and Dolton, P.J. (1985) 'Degree class and pass rates: an inter-university comparison', *Higher Education Review*, 17, 45–52.
Boussofiane, A., Dyson, R.E. and Thanassoulis, E. (1991) 'Applied data envelopment analysis', *European Journal of Operational Research*, 52, 1–15.
Cave, M., Hanney, S. and Kogan, M. (1991) *The Use of Performance Indicators in Higher Education* (London: Jessica Kingsley).
Gallagher, A. (1991) 'Comparative value added as a performance indicator', *Higher Education Review*, 23, 3, 19–29.
Galloway, D., Martin, R. and Wilcox, B. (1985) 'Persistent absence from school and exclusion from school: the predictive power of school and community variables', *British Educational Research Journal*, 11, 52–61.

Goodhart, C. A. E. (1975) *Money, Information and Uncertainty* (London: Macmillan).

Graves, P. E., Marchand, J. R. and Thompson, R. (1982) 'Economics department rankings: research incentives, constraints and efficiency', *American Economic Review*, 72, 1131–41.

Hanushek, E. A. (1971) 'Teacher characteristics and gains in student achievement: estimation using micro data', *American Economic Review*, 61, 280–8.

Hanushek, E. A. (1986) 'The economics of schooling: production and efficiency in public schools', *Journal of Economic Literature*, 24, 1141–77.

Harris, G. T. (1988) 'Research output in Australian university economics departments 1974–83', *Australian Economic Papers*, 27, 102–10.

Harris, G. T. (1990) 'Research output in Australian university departments: an update for 1984–88, *Australian Economic Papers*, 29, 249–59.

Irvine, J. and Martin, B. R. (1983) 'Assessing basic research: the case of the Isaac Newton telescope', *Social Studies of Science*, 13, 49–86.

Jesson, D., Mayston, D. and Smith, P. (1987) 'Performance assessment in the education sector: educational and economic perspectives', *Oxford Review of Education*, 13, 249–66.

Johnes, G. (1988a) 'Determinants of research output in economics departments in British universities', *Research Policy*, 17, 171–8.

Johnes, G. (1988b) 'Research performance indicators in the university sector', *Higher Education Quarterly*, 42, 54–71.

Johnes, G. (1990) 'Measures of research output: university departments of economics in the UK, 1984–8', *Economic Journal*, 100, 556–60.

Johnes, G. (1992) 'Performance indicators in higher education: a survey of recent work', *Oxford Review of Economic Policy*, 8, 2, 19–34.

Johnes, G. and Johnes, J. (1993) 'Measuring the research performance of UK economics departments: an application of data envelopment analysis', *Oxford Economic Papers*, forthcoming.

Johnes, G., Taylor, J. and Ferguson, G. (1987) 'The employability of new graduates: a study of differences between UK universities', *Applied Economics*, 19, 695–710.

Johnes, J. (1990) 'Determinants of student wastage in higher education', *Studies in Higher Education*, 15, 87–99.

Johnes, J. and Taylor, J. (1987) 'Degree quality: an investigation into differences between UK universities', *Higher Education*, 16, 581–602.

Johnes, J. and Taylor, J. (1989) 'Undergraduate non-completion rates: differences between UK universities', *Higher Education*, 18, 209–25.

Johnes, J. and Taylor, J. (1990) *Performance Indicators in Higher Education* (Buckingham: Open University Press).

Johnes, J., Taylor, J. and Francis, B. (1993) 'The research performance of UK universities: a statistical analysis of the results of the 1989 research selectivity exercise', *Journal of the Royal Statistical Society, Series A*, 152, 2, forthcoming.

Liebowitz, S. J. and Palmer, J. P. (1988) 'Assessing assessments of economics departments', *Quarterly Review of Economics and Business*, 28, 88–113.

Mar Molinero, C. and Portilla, L. E. (1993) 'Degree results as indicators: an evaluation of a degree classification system', *Education Economics*, forthcoming.

Mayston, D. J. and Jesson, D. (1988) 'Developing models of educational accountability', *Oxford Review of Education*, 14, 321–39.

McGeevor, P., Giles, P., Little, C., Head, B. and Brennan, J. (1990) *The Measurement of Value Added in Higher Education* (London: PCFC and the Council for National Academic Awards).

Moravcsik, M. J. and Murugesan, P. (1975) 'Some results on the function and quality of citations', *Social Studies of Science*, 5, 86–92.

Mortimore, P., Sammons, P., Stoll, L., Lewis, D. and Ecob, R. (1988) *School Matters: The Junior Years* (Wells: Open Books).

Peng, S. S. and Fetters, W. B. (1978) 'Variables involved in withdrawal during the first two years of college', *American Educational Research Journal*, 15, 361–72.

Rutter, M., Maughan, B., Mortimore, P. and Ouston, J. (1979) *Fifteen Thousand Hours* (London: Open Books).

Schagen, I. P (1991) 'Beyond league tables: how modern statistical methods can give a truer picture of the effects of schools', *Educational Research*, 33, 216–22.

Scheerens, J. (1992) *Effective Schooling: Research, Theory and Practice* (London: Cassell).

Sexton, T. R. (1986) 'The methodology of data envelopment analysis', in Silkman, R. H. (ed.), *Measuring Efficiency: An Assessment of Data Envelopment Analysis* (San Francisco: Jossey Bass).

Tinto, V. (1982) 'Limits of theory and practice in student attrition', *Journal of Higher Education*, 53, 687–700.

Tomkins, C. and Green, R. (1988) 'An experiment in the use of data envelopment analysis for evaluating the efficiency of UK university departments of accounting', *Financial Accountability and Management*, 4, 147–64.

Winters, A., Ulph, D. and Taylor, J. (1989) 'Do economists give too few good degrees?', mimeo, Royal Economic Society.

# Chapter 10 The Graduate Labour Market

Dolton, P.J. and Makepeace, G. H. (1992) 'The early careers of 1980 graduates: work histories, job revenue, career mobility and occupational choice', Department of Employment Research Paper.

Dolton, P.J., Makepeace, G.H. and Inchley, G. (1990) 'Early careers of 1980 graduates: earnings, earnings differentials and postgraduate study', Department of Employment Research Paper 78.

Goldthorpe, J. H. and Hope, K. (1974) *The Social Grading of Occupations* (Oxford: Clarendon Press).

Gregson, J. and Taylor, J. (1987) 'Graduates and jobs: the Graduate Employment and Training Survey', *Higher Education Review*, 19, 55–64.
Heckman, J.J. (1979) 'Sample selection bias as a specification error', *Econometrica*, 47, 153–61.
James, E., Alsalam, N., Conaty, J.C. and To, D.-L. (1989) 'College quality and future earnings: where should you send your child to college?', *American Economic Review, Papers and Proceedings*, 79, 247–52.
Johnes, G. (1989) 'Graduate employment: some new evidence', *Higher Education Review*, 21, 2, 63–71.
Johnes, G. and Taylor, J. (1989) 'Ethnic minorities in the graduate labour market', *New Community*, 15, 527–36.
Johnes, G. Taylor, J. and Ferguson, G. (1987) 'The employability of new graduates: a study of differences between UK universities', *Applied Economics*, 19, 695-710.
Johnes, J. and Taylor, J. (1989) 'The first destination of new graduates: comparisons between universities', *Applied Economics*, 21, 357–73.
Sharp, L. M. and Weidman, J. C. (1989) 'Early careers of undergraduate humanities majors', *Journal of Higher Education*, 60, 544–64.
Tarsh, J. (1987) 'What happens to new graduates?', in Harrison, A. and Gretton, J. (eds), *Education and Training UK* (Newbury: Policy Journals).
Taylor, J. (1986) 'The employability of graduates: differences between universities', *Studies in Higher Education*, 11, 17–28.
Taylor, J. (1988) 'Degrees of salary and satisfaction', *Nature*, 334, 393–4.
Taylor, J. and Johnes, J. (1989) 'An evaluation of performance indicators based upon the first destination of university graduates', *Studies in Higher Education*, 14, 201–17.
UFC (1990) *University Statistics*, volume 1 (staff and students) (Norwich: Her Majesty's Stationery Office).
Weale, M. (1992) 'Externalities from education', in Hahn, F. (ed.), *The Market: Practice and Policy* (London: Macmillan).

# Chapter 11 The Labour Market for Educators

Balasubramanyam, V. N. (1991) 'Economics of the brain drain: the case for a tax on brains', in Balasubramanyam, V. N. and Bates, J. (eds), *Case Studies in Development Economics* (London: Macmillan).
Bhagwati, J. N. and Dellafar, W. (1976) 'The brain drain and income taxation: the US', in Bhagwati, J. N. and Partington, M. (eds), *Taxing the Brain Drain: A Proposal* (Amsterdam: North-Holland).
Carmichael, H. L. (1988) 'Incentives in academics: why is there tenure?', *Journal of Political Economy*, 96, 453–572.
Dolton, P. J. (1990) 'The economics of UK teacher supply', *Economic Journal*, 100, S91–S104.

Freeman, S. (1977) 'Wage trends as performance reveals productive potential: a model and application to early retirement', *Bell Journal of Economics*, 8, 419–43.

Grubel, H. G. and Scott, A. (1977) *The Brain Drain: Determinants, Measurement and Welfare Effects* (Waterloo, Canada: Wilfred Laurier University Press).

Grubel, H. G. (1987) 'The economics of the brain drain', in Psacharopoulos, G. (ed.), *Economics of Education: Research and Studies* (Oxford: Pergamon), 201–6.

Hague, D. (1991) *Beyond Universities: A New Republic of the Intellect* (London: Institute of Economic Affairs).

Heckman, J. J. (1979) 'Sample selection bias as a specification error', *Econometrica*, 47, 153–61.

Ito, T. and Kahn, C. M. (1986) 'Why is there tenure?', Stanford University Center for Economic Research Discussion Paper 228.

Johnson, H. G. (1967) 'Some economic aspects of the brain drain', *Pakistan Development Review*, 7, 379–97.

Kasten, K. L. (1984) 'Tenure and merit pay as rewards for research, teaching and service at a research university', *Journal of Higher Education*, 55, 500–14.

Lazear, E. P. and Rosen, S. (1981) 'Rank order tournaments as optimum labor contracts', *Journal of Political Economy*, 89, 841–64.

Murnane, R. J. and Olsen, R. J. (1989) 'Will there be enough teachers?', *American Economic Review, Papers and Proceedings*, 79, 242–6.

Nalebuff, B. J. and Stiglitz, J. E. (1983) 'Prizes and incentives: towards a general theory of compensation and competition', *Bell Journal of Economics*, 14, 21–43.

Perkins, J. A. (1966) 'Foreign aid and the brain drain', *Foreign Affairs*, 44, 608–19.

Vaccaro, L. C. (1972) 'The tenure controversy: some possible alternatives', *Journal of Higher Education*, 43, 35–43.

Zabalza, A. (1979) 'The determinants of teacher supply', *Review of Economic Studies*, 46, 131–47.

Zabalza, A., Turnbull, P. and Williams, G. (1979) *The Economics of Teacher Supply* (Cambridge University Press).

# Index